CRITICAL INCIDENTS IN
TEACHING

EDITORS:

RAYMOND J. CORSINI

Associate Professor
Department of Psychology and Education
Illinois Institute of Technology

DANIEL D. HOWARD

Dean
Pestalozzi-Froebel Teachers College
Chicago, Illinois

CRITICAL INCIDENTS IN
TEACHING

Englewood Cliffs, New Jersey

PRENTICE-HALL, INC.

L. C. CATALOG CARD NO.: 64-11027

Printed in the United States of America

C-19396

PRENTICE-HALL INTERNATIONAL, INC., London
PRENTICE-HALL OF AUSTRALIA, PTY., LTD., Sydney
PRENTICE-HALL OF CANADA, LTD., Toronto
PRENTICE-HALL FRANCE, S.A.R.L., Paris
PRENTICE-HALL OF INDIA (PRIVATE) LTD., New Delhi
PRENTICE-HALL OF JAPAN, INC., Tokyo
PRENTICE-HALL DE MEXICO, S.A., Mexico City

PREFACE

Critical Incidents in Teaching is testimony to the cooperative attitudes of many teachers and professional people engaged in a common endeavor in the field of education.

Our book is based on the theory that teachers can learn general principles of classroom leadership through the case approach and through discussions of cases by people who have special knowledge and special interest in good teaching. The individuals listed in the contributors' and consultants' sections gave freely of their time and energy to this end. Our contributors are all teachers—either active or retired. Our consultants fall into four general groups: teachers, administrators, teachers of teachers, and professional people in the helping disciplines such as social work, psychology, and psychiatry.

In addition to the consultants and contributors listed elsewhere, we wish to thank the following persons for their help and advice.

Roger Holloway and Edgar Thomas of Prentice-Hall were unflagging in their interest and helpfulness during the long period of the book's construction.

Miss Evelyn Anne Corsini served as our research assistant and obtained most of the names of potential contributors through her search of education literature.

Miss Constance Vogt, and later Miss Arlene Lieberman, oversaw the mechanics of the book's construction and kept correspondence in order. Miss Lorraine Minkus and Miss Olivia Prytikin did the typing. Miss Kathryn Anderson managed details of revision of the preliminary manuscript.

Miss Dorothy Sparks and Mrs. Arlene Shelley read the manuscript, rated incidents and comments, and gave us many valuable opinions. Dan Simon, Superintendent of Schools at East Chicago, Indiana, reviewed the entire manuscript and gave us many helpful suggestions. Miss Marilyn McCormick read the manuscript for style. Miss Judy Rubin corrected the text and checked accuracy of references. Irwin Novick helped formulate our thought questions. Mrs. Ann Cornog reorganized and cut the manuscript and completed a comprehensive editing.

It is our hope that our common work will be of value to members of the teaching profession and to all citizens who are concerned with the proper nurture of our nation's most priceless possession—our children.

RAYMOND J. CORSINI
DANIEL D. HOWARD

NOTE

The format and procedures for this book were derived primarily from a companion volume.* The steps taken in developing the book were as follows:

1. A research assistant looked through educational journals to locate names and addresses of teachers who had written articles on educational topics relating to teaching problems. A list of some 500 names was compiled and to each of these people the following materials were sent: (a) a letter explaining the purpose of the book, requesting submission of an incident in teaching; (b) a sample incident demonstrating the desired format for incident; (c) a personal data blank in which the teacher was asked to submit personal information for inclusion in the contributors' section. Teachers were also asked to suggest consultants.

2. We also sent sets of the above materials to people teaching summer courses in graduate schools of education. These educators were asked to distribute this material to their students.

3. From these two sources we received more than 300 incidents, some of them anonymous.

4. Every incident was read by the editors and independently rated in terms of our concepts of suitability. Incidents rated by both of us as "below average" were dropped from further consideration, leaving us with some 200.

5. We classified the incidents and discovered that many were essentially

* S. W. Standal and R. J. Corsini, *Critical Incidents in Psychotherapy* (Englewood Cliffs, N.J.: Prentice-Hall, Inc., 1959).

duplications. We selected what we thought were the best incidents and in this manner reduced our incidents to about 50.

6. These remaining incidents were then given to two classes of experienced teachers taking advanced courses at a teachers' college with the following instructions:

"We shall give each of you some incidents in teaching written by a teacher. The purpose of these incidents is to serve as the basis of a book to be called *Critical Incidents in Teaching*. We would like each of you to read ten incidents and rate them in terms of their suitability for inclusion in this book.

"If the incident reads well, if it discusses what you think is an important problem, if you would feel that a discussion of this incident would be well worthwhile for teachers-in-training, rate the incident as an A. If not too suitable, rate it as a B. If you think the problem is unimportant, rate it as a C."

We received at least ten ratings for each incident. The incidents found in this book are those which received the greatest number of A's.

7. We proceeded to what was the most difficult part of our work—obtaining consultants. From the list of names submitted to us by the original contributors, and from other sources, such as *Who's Who in Education*, publisher's lists of authors of education books, lists of educational psychologists, and personal acquaintances, we selected more than 200 potential contributors and sent the following materials to them: (a) a letter requesting participation in the project; (b) a personal data sheet requesting information about the prospective consultant; (c) a sheet telling how the comments should be prepared; (d) five critical incidents selected at random.

8. When sufficient comments had been submitted, we evaluated each comment, being especially concerned with clarity of communication. In some cases comments were returned for revision. In some cases comments received were not used.

The above description of how *Critical Incidents in Teaching* was constructed should provide assurance that a variety of sources and opinions was solicited, and that the talents and evaluations of many people are represented in the final product.

COMMENTING CONSULTANTS

Dr. Grace T. Altus was formerly a school psychologist with the Santa Barbara County Schools in California, serving as chief of guidance services. Prior to this position she taught school at a junior high school in Redlands, California. She is now temporarily retired, devoting her attentions to her three preschool children. She has a Ph.D. from the University of California in Berkeley and is a Fellow of the American Psychological Association.

Her publications include:

"Some Correlates of the Davis-Eells Tests." *Journal of Consulting Psychology*, 1956, 20, 227-232.

"WISC Profile for Retarded Readers." *Journal of Consulting Psychology*, 1956, 20, 155.

"Measure of Native Intelligence?" *Educational Leadership*, 1954, 11, 377.

Dr. Joseph Andriola has 20 years of social work experience and is chief social worker at the Atascadero State Hospital in California, the only hospital in the United States for the treatment of male sex offenders. He also has a part time practice of marriage counseling. He holds A.B. and M.S.W. degrees from the University of Michigan and a Ph.D. in social work from the University of Minnesota. He was a contributor to *Critical Incidents in Psychotherapy*.

His publications include:

"Success and Failure in the Treatment of Twenty-five Truants at a Child Guidance Clinic." *American Journal of Orthopsychiatry*, 1943, 13, 691.

"Paranoid States and Hospitalized Teachers." *Psychiatric Quarterly Supplement*, 1950, 24, 89.
"A Comparative Study of Non-truant and Truant Children." *Proceedings of the Oklahoma Academy of Science*, 1955.

Dr. George R. Bach is a psychologist in private practice in Beverly Hills, California, where he is the Director of the Institute of Group Psychotherapy. He also is a lecturer in psychology at Pomoma College and Claremont Graduate School and a training consultant in group therapy at Camarillo and Patton Psychiatric Hospitals, California. He received his Ph.D. from the University of Iowa.
His publications include:
"Young Children's Play Fantasies." *Psychological Monographs*, 1945, No. 272.
Intensive Group Psychotherapy. New York: The Ronald Press Company, 1954.

Dr. Kenneth L. Bean is a professor of psychology at Baylor University, Waco, Texas. He is also in part-time private practice in clinical psychology. Formerly an examiner with the Louisiana State Civil Service for eight years, he was also on the staff of the New Orleans Child Guidance Center. He has a Ph.D. from the University of Michigan.
His publications include:
"An Experimental Approach to the Reading of Music." *Psychological Monographs*, 1939.
The Construction of Educational and Personnel Tests. New York: The McGraw-Hill Book Company, Inc., 1953.

Rev. Donald E. Brennan, O.S.A., is at Mendel Catholic High School in Chicago. He serves as a teacher, chaplain, and a counselor of teenagers. His preparation work consisted of four years of theology at the Augustinian College and graduate courses at the Catholic University of America and DePaul University. He received a B.A. in philosophy from Villanova University. He taught for five years at Austin Catholic Preparatory School, Detroit.

Mary Louise Butler is a teacher of world history at the Harding High School in Charlotte, North Carolina. She has served as the chairman (1959-60) of the Junior and Senior High School Social Studies Teachers of Charlotte, is a member of the executive board and scholarship chairman of the Charlotte Music Club and was editor for three years of the Charlotte *NCEA Bulletin*. Formerly she taught at the Fisher Street School,

Burlington, North Carolina, and Lindley Junior High School, Greensboro, North Carolina. She received her A.B. from the East Carolina College and did graduate work at the University of North Carolina.

Dr. Donald G. Ferguson is an associate professor in the Department of Special Education at Kent State University, Kent, Ohio. He is also affiliated with the Ohio State Department of Education as a supervisor of school psychological services for the Division of Special Education. Formerly, Dr. Ferguson taught in the public schools in Canton, Ohio, and for four years was school psychologist for the Lorain, Ohio, schools. Before coming to Kent State in 1955, he was an instructor of educational psychology and student teacher supervisor at Western Reserve University, Cleveland, Ohio. He received his Ed.D. from Western Reserve University.

Dr. William J. Fielder is a staff psychologist of the Child Study and Consultation Service in Phoenix, Arizona. He also has been an instructor at Phoenix College, Arizona State University, and the University of Arizona. Prior to this he was assistant superintendent of schools for special services in Aurora, Illinois, and an area psychologist for the Office of State Superintendent of Public Instruction in Illinois. Dr. Fielder received both his M.A. and his Ph.D. from the University of Chicago.

Malinda Dean Garton is an assistant professor and supervising teacher at the Illinois State Normal University in Normal, Illinois. Formerly, she was an elementary and high school teacher and an elementary school principal in Oklahoma and a special teacher in Peoria, Illinois. She received her M.A. from Colorado State College of Education. She has done additional graduate work at the University of Oklahoma, Pacific University, Bradley University, and the University of Illinois.

Her publications include:

Practical Methods for Teaching the Educable Mentally Retarded. Springfield, Illinois: Charles C. Thomas, Publishers, 1961.

"The Mentally Retarded in School." *Part II—The Educable Mentally Retarded, Guide for Exceptional Children*, 80-83, Bismarck, North Dakota: Superintendent of Public Instruction, State of North Dakota, 1961.

"Emotional Release Through Clay Modeling." *American Childhood*, (three parts), 1954-55, 40, Dec. 16-18: Jan. 16-18; Feb. 11-13, Springfield, Massachusetts.

Leland J. Gritzner is the assistant superintendent of the Osage Community Schools, Osage, Iowa. He is also affiliated with the Nevada Larger Parish Mission Schools in Las Vegas, and the Mopa Indian Reservation,

Mopa, Nevada, during the summer months. He has also taught school in Nashua, Iowa, and Nora Springs, Iowa. At present he is the president of the Iowa Department of Elementary School Principals. Leland Gritzner received his M.A. from the Iowa State Teachers College in Cedar Falls, Iowa.

Dr. Alvin Grossman is a consultant in guidance for the Bureau of Guidance, California State Department of Education, Sacramento, California. He is also chairman of the Integrated Data Processing Committee for the State of California. Formerly he was an assistant professor of education at the University of Georgia, a psychologist with the Seattle public schools, a guidance consultant in Napa County, California, and an assistant chief psychologist at the U.S. Army Hospital, Tacoma, Washington. He received his M.Ed. from the University of Georgia and his Ed.D. from the University of Washington.

His publications include:

The Future and You. Napa, California: Office of the County Superintendent of Schools, 1958.

Co-author with John Barr, *Film and Filmstrips for Career Guidance.* Sacramento: California State Department of Education, 1960.

"Data Processing in California Schools." *California Schools,* 1960, XXXI, (6), 304-306.

Bernice Grunwald is a teacher at the Emerson School of the Gary, Indiana, public school system. She is also a staff member of the Alfred Adler Institute in Chicago. Formerly she was a special teacher at the Ffoulkes School, a private school in Chicago. Her M.E. degree was received from Roosevelt University in Chicago, Illinois.

Her publications include:

"A Teacher Helps Children with Emotional Problems." *Orim.,* 1959, 6, 376-380.

"The Application of Adlerian Principles in a Classroom." *The American Journal of Individual Psychology,* 1955, 11, 131-141.

"The Basic Needs of Children." *Individual Psychology Bulletin,* 1950, 8, 62-64.

Dr. Frances R. Harper is a home-school counselor with elementary and junior high schools in Arlington, Virginia. She formerly taught in Pennsylvania; was a curriculum and teaching assistant at Teachers College, Columbia University, where she received her Ed.D.; was director of parent and family life education with the Great Neck, Long Island, Board of Education; and was a staff member of the Merrill-Palmer Institute of Human Development and Family Life.

Her publications include:

"An Evaluative Study of a Large Class in the Psychology of Family Relations." *Journal of Family Welfare*, 1957, 3, 42-52.

"Are Educators Afraid of Sex?" *Journal of Marriage and Family Living*, 1957, 19, 240-244.

"The Guidance-oriented Elementary Teacher." *NEA Journal*, 1960, 49, 17-19.

Brother Philip Harris, O.S.F., is a counseling psychologist and director of student personnel services at St. Francis College, Brooklyn, New York. During the summer months he is a lecturer at numerous Catholic colleges throughout the country. He produced "Insight for Youth" a 37-week television series on NBC based on his book, *It's Your Life*. He received his teaching certificate from the Brooklyn Diocesan Normal School and his Ph.D. from Fordham University.

His publications include:

It's Your Life. New York: Harcourt, Brace & World, Inc., 1957.

It's Your Education. New York: Harcourt, Brace & World, Inc., 1959.

It's Your Personality. New York: Harcourt, Brace & World, Inc., 1960.

Dr. Eloise DeLay Hayes is an assistant professor of education at the University of Hawaii in Honolulu. In former years she was director of elementary education at Cedar Crest College, Allentown, Pennsylvania, and earlier an elementary teacher in Durham, North Carolina; Berlin, Germany; Fairbanks, Alaska; and St. Cloud, Minnesota. She received both her M.A. and her Ph.D. from the University of North Carolina.

Richard W. Hinds is an elementary school principal in the public school system in Eugene, Oregon. He is affiliated with the teacher training program at the University of Oregon. Formerly he was a teacher and a principal at the Central Elementary School, Los Alamos, New Mexico, and an administrative assistant with the U.S. Armed Forces Institute in Madison, Wisconsin, and a tutor in Neenah, Wisconsin. His M.Ed. degree was obtained from the University of Colorado.

His publications include:

"Guidance Is Part of Administrative Responsibility." *Elementary Principal's Yearbook*, Chapter II, Washington, D.C.: National Education Association, 1954.

Dr. Chester W. Holmes, presently superintendent of schools in Malden, Massachusetts, was formerly a teacher at the Ringe Technical School, Cambridge, Massachusetts; principal of junior high schools in Holyoke,

Massachusetts, and Washington, D.C.; and associate superintendent of schools, Washington, D.C. He received B.S. and Ed.M. degrees from Harvard University and the Ed.D. degree from George Washington University.

His publications include:

"Activities in Curriculum Improvement in the District of Columbia." *Curriculum Journal*, 1941, 12, 123-125.

"Demonstration Classes for the In-service Training of Junior High School Teachers." *Elementary School Journal*, 1939, 39, 407-408.

Willis B. Inman is guidance director of East High School, Aurora, Illinois. He has held the position of high school counselor at Thomas A. Edison School, Gary, Indiana, and that of head teacher at Acorn High School, Mena, Arkansas. He holds a Master of Arts degree from Teachers College, Columbia University, and an A.B. from the University of Illinois.

John A. Jackson, an elementary school principal in the Amarillo, Texas, public school system, was formerly vice-principal of Booker T. Washington High School, Wichita Falls, Texas, and has also taught American history, American government, and world history. His Masters of Education thesis, done at the University of Colorado, concerned attitudes and interests of Texas secondary school students.

His publications include:

"Administration Techniques for Reducing Teacher-tension." *Texas Standard*, 1956, 30, 8-25.

Dr. Elizabeth Z. Johnson is a clinical psychologist at the Veterans Administration Hospital, Lexington, Kentucky, and in part-time private practice in the same city. She is associated with the Psychiatric Clinic, Kentucky Village, and the Children's Bureau, and is a lecturer at the Episcopal Theological Seminary. Dr. Johnson formerly taught remedial reading and psychology at Mills College in Oakland, California. She was research psychologist (child psychotherapy) at Wayne County Training School, and also Assistant Research Professor of Psychiatry at the University of Utah Medical School. She obtained her Ed.M. and Ed.D. from Harvard University.

Her publications include:

"The Clinical Use of Raven's Progressive Matrices to Appraise Potential for Progress in Play Therapy." in Chalmer L. Stacey and M. F. DeMartino (Eds.), *Counseling and Psychotherapy with the Mentally Retarded.* New York: The Free Press of Glencoe, Inc., 1957, Chapter 24, 263-269.

"Sex Differences and Variability in the Performance of Retarded Children on Raven, Binet & Arthur Tests." *Journal of Clinical Psychology*, 1952, 8, 298-301.

"Individual Patterns of Emotional Functioning in Children of Comparable I.Q.'s—Implications for Education." *American Journal of Mental Deficiency*, 1953, 57, 681-686.

Dr. Orval G. Johnson is presently director of special education and psychological services of the Lewis County Schools in Washington. He was formerly the senior psychologist at the Wisconsin State Reformatory and later was affiliated with Michigan State University, the Michigan State Department of Public Instruction, Office of Vocational Rehabilitation, and later with the public schools of Jackson, Michigan, as school psychologist. He has a Ph.D. from the University of Wisconsin.

His publications include:

"Teacher and the Withdrawn Child." *Education Digest*, 1957, 22, 19-22.

"Teacher's Role in Providing a Climate to Grow in." *NEA Journal*, 1957, 46, 233-236.

"A Comparison of H-T-P Responses of Handicapped and Nonhandicapped Children." *Journal of Clinical Psychology*, 1958, 14, 160-162.

Dr. Leslie W. Kindred is Professor of Educational Administration at the College of Education, Temple University, Philadelphia. He is also a private consultant in education, and has formerly served as teacher, supervisor, and administrator. He has the Ph.D. degree from the University of Michigan.

His publications include:

School Public Relations. Englewood Cliffs, N.J.: Prentice-Hall, Inc., 1957.

How to Tell the School Story. Englewood Cliffs, N.J.: Prentice-Hall, Inc., 1960.

The Teacher and School Organization. Englewood Cliffs, N.J.: Prentice-Hall, Inc., 1958.

Dr. Charles Kram is a psychologist affiliated with the National Childrens Rehabilitation Center in Leesburg, Virginia, where he serves as director. He is also the executive director of the Epilepsy Foundation in Washington, D.C. and is on the faculty in the psychiatry department at Georgetown University. Formerly, he was the chief psychologist in the mental health division of the Texas State Health Department in Austin. He received his Ph.D. from Washington University.

Dr. Nicholas J. Long is assistant professor of educational psychology at Indiana University, Bloomington, Indiana. He was formerly a teacher in the poliomyelitis ward at the University of Michigan Hospital and principal of the Childrens Psychiatric Hospital School, University of Michigan. He was chief of the Childrens Treatment Residence at the National Institute of Mental Health, Bethesda, Maryland. He holds the Ph.D. from the University of Michigan.

His publications include:

Co-author with Mildred H. Walton, "Going to School in a Respirator Center." *Nervous Child*, 1956, 11, 53-60.

Co-author with Victor Stoeffler, Kenneth Krause, and Charles Jung, "Life-space Management of Behavioral Crises." *Social Work*, 1961, 36-45.

Dr. R. N. Lowe is the coordinator of school psychological services at the School of Education, University of Oregon, and is director of the Community Parent-Teacher Education Centers in Eugene, Oregon. His experiences in education include teaching in elementary, junior, and senior high schools in Massachusetts; officer in charge of a Navy school, Great Lakes, Illinois; and assistant to the president, Eastern Montana College of Education, Billings, Montana. He received an Ed.D. from Northwestern University. He has written articles in the area of behavioral science as it relates to the teaching and learning process.

His publications include:

Co-editor, *Adlerian Family Counseling*. Eugene, Oregon: University of Oregon Press, 1959.

Sister M. Loyola (Engelman), I.H.M., is principal of St. Patrick Grade School and Girls Catholic Central High School of Detroit, Michigan. Formerly, she was a teacher in public and parochial grade and high schools in Michigan and Ohio. She is also the community coordinator for sodality work for the Sisters of the Immaculate Heart of Mary. She is interested in sodality training and in leadership training of pupils in social, moral, political, and religious spheres. She received her M.A. from the University of Detroit.

Her publications include:

"Meditation in Religion Class." *Catholic School Journal*, 1944, 44, 140-142.

"Toward a Christian Recreation Program." *America*, 1950, 83, 441-443.

Dr. Frederick L. Marcuse is a psychology professor at Washington State University, Pullman, Washington. Formerly, he was an assistant professor at Cornell University. He received his Ph.D. from Cornell.

His publications include:

Hypnosis: Facts and Fiction. Baltimore: Penguin Books, Inc., 1959.

"Methods of Teaching Elementary Psychology." *Journal of Educational Psychology*, 1951, 42, 326-340.

Dr. Joseph Mersand is the chairman of the English Department of Jamaica High School in Jamaica, New York. He has been a high school teacher since 1931. Prior to that time he taught for one year at University Heights College of New York University. He holds a Ph.D. from New York University. He is past president of the New York State English Council (1952-53), and past president of the National Council of Teachers of English (1958-59). At present he is editor of *Studies in the Mass Media.* Dr. Mersand has written over a dozen books and has published over 100 educational articles.

His publications include:

"Discovering the Individual in Large Classes." *English Journal,* 1957, 46, 406-409.

"Teaching Listening in High School." *National Association Secondary School Principals Bulletin,* 1958, 42, 123-130.

"Homogeneous Grouping." *English Journal,* 1951, 41, 141-147.

Roberta Morgan Moltmann, Dean of Girls at Highland View Junior High School, Corvallis, Oregon, has had varied teaching experience from first through ninth grade, including two years in an eight-grade rural school. She did her undergraduate work at Iowa State College and received her M.A. from New Mexico Highlands University. Prior to her assuming her present position, she served as critic teacher in conjunction with the schools of education both of New Mexico Highlands University and Oregon State University.

Ann Taylor Moore is a psychotherapist in a private guidance center in Brooklyn, New York. She was formerly in the field of psychiatric social work. She received her M.A. from the School of Social Service Administration, University of Chicago.

Her publications include:

"Medical Care in Britain." *The New Republic,* 1959, 140, 10.

Dr. Paul Richard Neureiter is a teacher at State University of New York College of Education, Geneseo, New York. He is an occasional lecturer for Redpath Bureau (Eastern Management) and editor of the *New York State Mathematics Teachers Journal.* He was a Fulbright exchange teacher in the Netherlands, 1952-1953. Formerly he was on the faculty of Western Illinois State Teachers College, Macomb, Illinois; University of Kansas City, Mo., and Michigan State University, East Lansing. He received his Ph.D. from the University of Vienna, Austria.

His publications include:

"Hitlerism and the German Universities." *Journal of Higher Education,* 1934, 5, 264-270.

"Watch the German Universities." *Journal of Higher Education,* 1946, 17, 171-179

"Een Noord-Amerikans oordeel over het onderwijs in Nederland en de U.S.A." *Paedagogische Studien,* 1954, 27, 46-56.

Dr. Warren Winters Nixon is a junior high school principal at the Washington Irving School, in the Des Moines, Iowa, independent community school district. He teaches summer school at Drake University. Formerly, he was teacher-principal, Riceville (Iowa) High School; teacher, Minburn (Iowa) High School; veterans department director, and vice-principal of schools in Des Moines. He received his Ed.D. from Colorado State Teachers College.

Don H. Otto is an English teacher at Western High School, Anaheim, California. He is also a part-time English instructor at Cerritos College, Norwalk, California. Formerly he was a secondary English teacher in Des Moines, Iowa, and Pillsbury Academy, Owatonna, Minnesota. He received his M.A. from Drake University.

His publications include:

"Supervisory Counseling and Teacher Morale." *Teachers College Journal,* 1957, 29, 42-43.

"Checklist for Salary Committees." *Midland Schools,* 1957, 72, 13.

Robert E. Price is a social studies teacher at Liberty Junior High School, Tillamook, Oregon. He was formerly principal of the Garibaldi (Oregon) Grade School; sixth grade teacher in Florence, Oregon; principal, Siuslaw Junior High School, Florence; and superintendent, District 14, Tillamook County, Oregon. He received his M.S. degree from Oregon College of Education.

His publications include:

"Your Philosophy Is Showing." *The Clearing House,* 1958, 12, 241-242.

"How to Teach the Meanings of Communism." *The Clearing House,* 1955, 10, 73-75.

"Valentine Gift from Plaster." *The Instructor,* 1955, 2, 49.

Douglas C. Rigg is warden at Minnesota State Prison, Stillwater, Minnesota. He has served as a consultant in correctional administration. He was formerly associate warden for care and treatment, supervising the educational department at San Quentin, with the California Department of Corrections. He received his A.B. from the University of California.

His publications include:

"Penalty Worse than Death." *Saturday Evening Post,* 1957, 230, 13-15.

"The Socially Handicapped." In Esther Pike, *Who is My Neighbor?* Greenwich, Connecticut: Seabury Press, 1960.

Dr. Jordan M. Scher is a psychiatrist in private practice in Chicago. He is assistant professor with the Department of Neurology and Psychiatry, Northwestern University, and consultant to the Sheriff's Office and Cook County Jail in Illinois. He is the editor of the *Journal of Existential Psychiatry* and secretary, American Ontoanalytic Association. Formerly, he was research psychiatrist with the National Institute of Mental Health, Bethesda, Maryland. He is a diplomate from the American Board of Psychiatry. He received his M.D. from the University of Maryland.

His publications include:

Co-author with L. Appleby and J. Cumming, *Chronic Schizophrenia.* New York: The Free Press of Glencoe, Inc., 1960.

"Flicker Fusion Frequency and Hypertension." A.M.A. *Archives of Neurology and Psychiatry,* November, 1957.

"Schizophrenia and Task Orientation: the Structured Ward Setting." A.M.A. *Archives of Neurology and Psychiatry,* November, 1957, 78, 531-538.

Paul W. Schmidtchen is superintendent of schools for the Cape May City Board of Education and Lower Cape May Regional High School Board of Education in Cape May, New Jersey. He is on the editorial board of *The Clearing House;* book page editor of *Hobbies Magazines,* and a member of Phi Delta Kappa. He was formerly a teacher, coach, and high school principal at Metuchen, New Jersey, and on the history staff of University College, Rutgers University. He received his M.Ed. from Rutgers University.

His publications include:

"Education Toward What?" *Clearing House,* 1957, 32, 235-236.

"Vox Academiae." *The School Executive,* 1958, 78, 59.

R. Clinton Schulze is a science teacher in and also serves as fiscal agent (business manager) for the Mason Independent School District, a county-wide system in Mason, Texas. He began his public school career in the same system 19 years ago as principal of Mason High School. He has a B.S. from Southwestern University and a M.A. fom the University of Texas. He is active in state organizations concerned with the teaching of science and administration.

Regine Seidler is a senior psychologist with the Des Moines, Iowa, Child Guidance Center. In former years she had been a school teacher in Vienna, Austria; head of the Alfred Adler Child Guidance Center in Vienna; a lecturer in individual psychology and education at the "People's University," also in Vienna; and director of settlement work in a neighborhood house in Auburn, New York. She holds a M.A. from Syracuse University.

Her publications include:

"Understanding the Pupil's Personality." *International Journal of Individual Psychology*, 1935, 1, 71-78.

"Escape into Delinquency." *Individual Psychology Bulletin*, Vol. 3.

"School Guidance Clinics in Vienna." *Individual Psychology Bulletin*, 1935, 13, 217-220.

Dr. Harold G. Shane is Dean of the School of Education and professor of education at Indiana University, Bloomington, Indiana. Dr. Shane has been an elementary school teacher and principal in Ohio. He also was connected with the State Department of Education for Ohio as state supervisor of elementary education, served as superintendent of schools in Winnetka, Illinois, and was professor of education at Northwestern University for ten years. He has been on the editorial board of Childhood Education, and was chairman of the publications committee of the Association for Supervision and Curriculum Development. He holds the Ph.D. degree from Ohio State University. Dr. Shane has written over 180 publications of which 40 were books, with a combined circulation of 25,000,000.

His publications include:

Co-author with E. T. McSwain, *Evaluation and the Elementary Curriculum*, New York: Holt, Rinehart & Winston, Inc., 1958.

Editor, *The American Elementary School*, XIIIth Yearbook of the John Dewey Society, New York: Harper & Row, Publishers, 1953.

Willye B. Shanks is a fourth grade elementary teacher at Myrtle Hall School, Clarksdale, Mississippi. She is active in the Clarksdale Teachers Association, the Mississippi Teachers Association in Jackson, Mississippi, and the American Teachers Association in Montgomery, Alabama. She received her B.S. from Jackson State College.

Louise S. Sinderson is an instructor with the department of special education at the Joliet Township High School in Illinois. She is also a visiting instructor at Pestalozzi-Froebel Teachers College in Chicago. She has been a teacher of multiple-handicapped children with the Chicago Public Schools and a teacher of brain injured children with the Joliet Public Schools. She holds a M.Ed. from the University of Illinois in Urbana.

Dr. Robert W. Smail is a professor of education and chairman, Division of Education, Clarion State College, Clarion, Pennsylvania. He is also a visiting lecturer in elementary education at the State University of South

Dakota. Formerly, he was a high school English teacher in Andover, South Dakota, and principal-teacher at the Iron Lightning Day School, Cheyenne Agency, in South Dakota. He received his Ed.D. from the State University of South Dakota.

His publications include:

"Building Geographical Skills." *The School and Your Child*, 1959, 11, 2-3.

Manford A. Sonstegard is a professor of teaching and a director of guidance and counseling at Malcolm Price Laboratory School, Iowa State Teachers College, Cedar Falls, Iowa. He is also a psychological consultant for Beaman-Conrad Community Schools in Conrad, Iowa. Formerly he was an elementary and high school teacher and then an elementary and high school principal in public schools located in Minnesota and Iowa. He also was a consultant in teacher education at the Ethiopian Ministry of Education and Director, Teacher Training School in Harar, Ethiopia. He received his Ph.D. from Northwestern University.

His publications include:

Co-author with Edward L. Ruman, *Helping Teachers Understand and Utilize Consultant Services*. The Association for Student Teaching, 1959, 10.

Co-editor, *Adlerian Family Counseling*. Eugene, Oregon: Oregon University Press, 1959.

Co-author with Herbert Graeber, In-service Teacher Education in Counseling. *Midland Schools*, 1960, 75, 10-12.

Clarence H. Spain is principal of Binford Junior High School, Richmond, Virginia, and is also affiliated with the Richmond City School Board. He is a member of the National Education Association; Virginia Education Association; and the National Association of Secondary School Principals. He also is on the editorial board of the *Clearing House*. Formerly, he was the Virginia State Supervisor of the Adult Education Executive Committee, NASSP, and president of the Richmond Principals Association. He holds a M.A. from the college of William and Mary.

His publications include:

Co-author, "The High School in a Changing World." *36th Yearbook*, *AASA*, 1959.

Dorothy E. Sparks is a high school English teacher with the Roosevelt Public High School in Chicago, Illinois. Formerly, she has been a free-lance writer and coach, book reviewer for the *Chicago Sun Times*, and book-page editor with the *American Family Magazine*. She has a Ph.B. from the University of Chicago, and a M.A. from DePaul University in Chicago.

Her publications include:

Strong is the Current: a History of the Illinois Congress of Parents and Teachers. Illinois Congress of Parents and Teachers, 1948.
Nothing as Before. New York: Harper & Row, Publishers, 1944.

Violet Strimbu is a primary teacher attached to the Eugene Field School, East Chicago, Indiana. She has also taught school in Rensselaer, Indiana. She holds a B.S. from Purdue University.

Leo E. Tarutz, Ed.D., is chairman of the Social Studies Department at East Boston High School, Boston, Massachusetts. He has lectured on guidance, audio-visual aids, and methods of teaching.

His publications include:

"Curriculum Guide in Hebrew for Senior High Schools." *Boston Public Schools Publication*, 1949, revised 1957.

"Roxbury's Plan for A-V in Social Studies." *The Clearing House*, 1955, Vol. 29.

CONTRIBUTORS
OF CRITICAL INCIDENTS

The incidents in this book were selected from contributions generously supplied by teachers and former teachers from all parts of the country. A partial list of these contributors and their locations is given below.

Mary B. Blackburn	Tuscaloosa, Alabama
Walter Bowlby	Coral Gables, Florida
Robert Brandner	Aberdeen, South Dakota
E. M. Bridges	Griffith, Indiana
R. P. Brimm	Cedar Falls, Iowa
Paul Brodsky	Hollywood, California
Douglas Broun	Tallahassee, Florida
Marguerite Burkholder	Elkhart, Indiana
Floyd Camp	Roswell, New Mexico
Robert W. Clark	Philadelphia, Pennsylvania
Russ Crossman	Honolulu, Hawaii
Elizabeth Crumrine	Dayton, Ohio
Elmer Danuser	Hermann, Missouri
John D. Davis	Exeter, New Hampshire
William Duffy	Detroit, Michigan
Virginia Durham	Kirkwood, Missouri
Charles A. Eck	Detroit, Michigan
Philip Eisman	Brooklyn, New York
Margaret Engelhardt	Detroit, Michigan
P. M. Falls	Center Line, Michigan
Robert L. Gantert	Seattle, Washington
Maurie George	Vermillion, South Dakota

Contributors of Critical Incidents

Robert Gies	Detroit, Michigan
A. S. Green	Chicago, Illinois
M. M. Gunkle	Harvey, Illinois
Millard Harmon	Auburndale, Massachusetts
Edgar W. Hebert	San Diego, California
Viola Johnson	Norman, Oklahoma
Phyllis Kaup	Eugene, Oregon
Kathryn D. Lunt	Huntington Woods, Michigan
Ella F. McDaniel	Columbus, Georgia
Shirlee G. McGreer	Springfield, Oregon
Eva C. Macklin	Sioux City, Iowa
Harold W. Meagher	Detroit, Michigan
Ethel M. Middleton	Coburg, Oregon
Clete L. Miller	Mesa, Arizona
Mary Ely Moffat	Santa Barbara, California
Willie Catherine Murphy	Trenton, Texas
Pauline Nicholson	Detroit, Michigan
Dorothy O'Mara	Roseville, Michigan
Charles W. Owens, Jr.	Dallas, Texas
Helen K. Painter	Mansfield, Ohio
Lillian Pennington	New York, New York
Orval L. Petersen	Montclair, California
Allan Pitkanen	Los Angeles, California
David Powell	East Detroit, Michigan
Elizabeth Renggli	Chehalis, Washington
June Richards	Detroit, Michigan
Donald W. Robinson	Belmont, California
Melvin L. Rogers	Yonkers, New York
Willie H. Scarborough	Chicago, Illinois
Arthur R. Schiffer	Lithonia, Georgia
Mattie M. Scholin	Royal Oak, Michigan
Edward J. Shoben	New York, New York
Marguerite A. Shuman	Chehalis, Washington
Joseph M. Stefanko	West Allis, Wisconsin
Julius A. Stratton	Gary, Indiana
Ronald R. Tonks	St. Clair Shores, Michigan
William L. Triplett	Vicksburg, Mississippi
William O. Tuominen	Chicago, Illinois
Sandyan Turrou	Granda Hills, California
Gene Udell	Philadelphia, Pennsylvania
Sister Catharine Virginia	Philadelphia, Pennsylvania
Sister M. Irenaea Winkeljohn	Norwood, Ohio
E. Joseph Zaccardelli	Berkley, Michigan

CONTENTS

I

The Dilemmas of Discipline

II

Problems of Social Adjustment

III

Academic Adjustment

IV

Extra-Classroom Relationships

Contents

INTRODUCTION

If elementary school teaching were simply a matter of imparting information to uniformly receptive children, how relatively simple, but how dull, the profession would be.

In reality, the profession presents a far more stimulating challenge. The teacher is involved in dynamic interpersonal relationships with heterogeneous classes of vital, growing children—parents, school administrators, and others interested in the education of youth. As might be expected, the tensions underlying these normally smooth relationships sometimes erupt dramatically in the form of *critical incidents*. Experienced teachers are familiar with such classroom crises as those that arise when a boy refuses to respond to directions; a girl wishes the teacher to become a surrogate for a recently deceased mother; or an irate father demands to have a failing grade raised.

In a sense, a critical incident confronts the teacher much as an iceberg appears before a ship's captain. What appears above the surface is a sign of a larger problem below. In order to plot an effective course of action, the teacher must be able to recognize the full dimensions of the crises and resolve them in terms of a well-integrated frame of reference.

Critical Incidents in Teaching is a case-history approach to the study of classroom crises. It is the outgrowth of the editors' awareness that neither traditional courses in education nor preteaching experiences prepare the new teacher for dealing with critical incidents. Even experienced teachers, school administrators, and parents may be uncertain as to the most effective course of action in some difficult interpersonal classroom situations.

Recognizing that there are no simple mechanical precepts for the solution of human problems, we ask the reader—whether a college student using this volume as a textbook, a teacher, a school administrator, a member of a school board, or a parent—to join with us in actively exploring and analyzing a number of classroom crises taken from real life.

As editors, we have utilized the time-tested case-history technique of telescoping experience onto the printed page. Seventeen critical incidents are presented in this volume. They have been selected, from hundreds of incidents submitted to us by teachers throughout the nation, as being characteristic of problems an elementary school teacher can expect to encounter.

Each incident is presented as written by the teacher. As a result, the reader will discover how a teacher's understanding of an interpersonal problem and his solution to it is affected by his conception of his role as a teacher and his philosophical and psychological frame of reference.

Each incident is followed by a number of comments from consultants whose training and experience enable them to contribute illuminating insights. These comments will heighten the reader's awareness that there is no single point of view, either with respect to what occurs during a critical incident or as to how it should be resolved. The consultants discussing a particular incident may disagree with the reporting teacher on his definition of the problem, and they may find his interpretation and action unsatisfactory. Furthermore, the consultants often disagree with one another.

Thus, we are confronted with a state of affairs basic to the serious study of all the social sciences. Just as no expert or group of experts can obtain universal acceptance of the validity of a particular theory of sociology, economics, history, or psychology, no consultant represented in this book has reached complete unamity with his colleagues.

As as result, the reader is required to make his own personal synthesis, as do serious students in allied disciplines. We recommend that the following systematic approach will be of value in this effort.

HOW TO USE THIS BOOK

Whether using this book as a class text or reading it as an individual project, we suggest the following study sequences:

I. Read the critical incident, but not the comments that follow it. Then attempt to answer the following questions:

Using your own definitions and perceptions, describe the problem presented by the reporting teacher.

How would you react to this problem in terms of your knowledge?

How does the reporting teacher see the problem?

Compare your analysis with that of the reporting teacher. What does your analysis reveal about your conception of the role of the teacher and your psychological and philosophical orientation? How do these differ, if at all, from those of the reporting teacher?

II. This careful evaluation will prepare you to read the consultants' comments with greater understanding. Read all the comments of a particular incident before answering the following questions:

How does each consultant see the problem?

What is the frame of reference of each consultant, (consider in terms of his vocation as a teacher, administrator, psychologist, etc.; his implicit psychological orientation and philosophical position, and his conception of the role of the teacher and the goals of the school)?

What philosophical and psychological assumptions are shared by two or more consultants?

What differences of philosophy and psychology are implicit in the consultants' comments?

III. At this point, your understanding will have broadened sufficiently to motivate you to re-evaluate the analyses you made before reading the consultants' comments. Review your original analyses made in Part I above.

IV. Having clarified your point of view regarding the specific critical incident under consideration, you will probably want to relate what you have learned to such basic educational issues as the meaning of effective discipline; grading, or otherwise evaluating student progress; students' emotional adjustment; determining readiness for school; determining bases for promotion; the use of counseling and other special services; and the relationship of these specifics to teaching and professional ethics.

These relationships are brought into focus by the questions at the end of each chapter and the discussion questions at the end of each section. As you proceed from one chapter to the next, review your answers. You will probably want to modify them.

If you are reading this book as a class text, your answers to the questions that apply to all critical incidents as well as the specific questions at the end of each chapter will probably be modified as the result of class discussions.

We would recommend a round-table format for class discussions. Let students be assigned to read various consultants' comments, and then present these special points of view to the class, permitting cross discussion by the panel members. The class as a whole can participate in asking further questions. This procedure not only enlivens the class discussion but creates a desirable atmosphere of free inquiry.

We recognize that these recommended study techniques require the reader to keep questioning and revising conclusions on the basis of growing understanding of the problems being considered. No reader attuned to the methodology of this book should ever feel his understanding of critical incidents in teaching is complete. Instead, he will utilize his broadened perspective as the basis for continuing growth in the understanding of interpersonal problems in the classroom.

RAYMOND J. CORSINI
DANIEL D. HOWARD

CRITICAL INCIDENTS IN
TEACHING

I

THE DILEMMAS OF DISCIPLINE

1

"THE FEAR OF GOD"

CRITICAL INCIDENT

Background

Chuck Moss was a repeater in my eighth-grade English class during my first year of teaching. He was seventeen, 5′ 10″ in height, and of medium build; he had a haircut with long sideburns. He had previously spent two years each in the sixth and seventh grades and was now starting his second year in the eighth grade.

Of the twenty-eight students in the class, twenty-two were boys and six were girls. Thirteen were repeaters. Two boys other than Chuck were about seventeen years of age. Grouping was arranged alphabetically, and all thirteen repeaters' last names fell in the *L* through *N* group.

I was warned by the principal beforehand that they would be a tough group to handle and that I should be firm with them from the start.

Incident

It was the first day of school. I had gone through the day without incident until I came to my last-hour English class.

I introduced myself and proceeded to call the role in order to associate the students' faces with their names. When I called Chuck Moss's name, no one answered. Thinking him absent, I started to go on to another name when some of the students said that Chuck Moss was here. They indicated he was sitting in the first seat near the blackboard.

I walked over to the boy, who was sitting in a slouched position, his face turned toward the blackboard on the side wall, his hand covering his face. I asked him if he were Chuck Moss. Without looking up, and in a disrespectful tone, he replied, "Yeah, man." At this point I kicked him in the shin with my foot, and as he bent over to grab his shin I took hold of his long hair and pulled him out of the room.

Outside in the hall I gave Chuck a strong lecture indicating that ·if he misbehaved again in my class, he would have to face the consequences. I then took him back into the classroom and had him write his name on the blackboard one hundred times. Since he had not finished when the class was dismissed, I kept him until he had finished and then discussed the previous incident with him.

Discussion

Chuck was vying for power with me in the class. Heeding the principal's warning, I was quick to explode and take action. The harshness I used with Chuck produced very good results—he did solid C work in my class, better than the other repeaters, who all failed again, and he never gave me any trouble after that incident. He failed all of his other classes, however, and was a behavior problem to his other teachers. Consequently he was not admitted to school the following year.

Questions

1. Is it wise to "beat problem students to the punch" and put "the fear of God" into them?
2. Do some students respect only strength and need strong, violent action?
3. Do the methods one uses to obtain compliance and cooperation matter, as long as they attain results?
4. Is it wise to make a very strong example of one student in order to make others conform and to let them know who is in command?

*   *   *

With or without classmates of similar characteristics, a tall, seventeen-year-old repeater in an eighth-grade class would be disconcertingly imposing. If such a person gives evidence that he is a discipline problem, as most such repeaters are, the effect is downright intimidating. Any administrator's assigning any new teacher to an English class with such a pupil, in addition to other repeating students, could not conceivably be justified.

One would expect that other members of the class who were not repeaters were potentially so, since they were probably lower-ability pupils. For administrative convenience, school grouping is frequently done on an ability basis as well as an alphabetical one.

Remedial teaching is clearly required here. Remedial teaching implies individualized attention, which is impossible in a class as large as this one. If large classes are unavoidable, ability grouping appears all the more necessary to provide for the maximum growth of each student. And yet, if all the repeaters in this class except Chuck failed, and the nonrepeaters were promoted, one segment of the class or the other has been seriously neglected and therefore deprived of growth opportunities. Apparently, in more than one area, this school system needs to re-evaluate its philosophy of education in applying that oft-quoted educational aphorism that the public schools should provide for educational differences among all pupils.

Without resorting to sophistry in discussing this critical incident, the faults inherent in the method of disposition of this case can be stated.

In the first place, and germane to other considerations, one must find it very difficult to defend, pragmatically or theoretically, the tenet that to "beat problem children to the punch" is the best possible method of handling them. To be sure, the teacher will be poorly trained, indeed, whose training has not provided an emerging understanding of youth at the age level of specialization. And with understanding comes an awareness of what one can and what one cannot expect from one's students and the ability to recognize symptoms of the social, the asocial, the antisocial, and the inconsistent. But unpredictability is the most predictable characteristic of youth; those who work with young people must guard constantly against fallacious anticipation, interpretation, and rationalization of their behavior. To "beat a student to the punch" assumes a nonexistent clairvoyance into the student's mind and personality. Again, it further implies that in any specific instance, the teacher can accurately generalize from the mass to the specific. The dangers of "beating a student to the punch" when he is punching in a different direction, or if he isn't about to punch at all, are too great and too far-reaching to ignore. Never more relevant than in education is the admonition against jumping to conclusions.

Secondly, a basic principle underlying the educational process is that the success of the process is a triumph of mind over matter, that the educated man is he whose behavior, whose thoughts, whose life are governed by the exercise of his intellect, and who holds, as a corollary belief, that the solution to life's problems through force or violence is reprehensible. One of the most effective means of judging a teacher is evaluating him in terms of the example he sets before his students. It is, therefore, all the more imperative that he adhere consistently to the practice of honing the intellect as a guide and motivator to action, rather than show a lack of respect for the mental through reliance upon the physical, particularly when it is in response to life's frustrations. If students respect only strength and need strong violent action, the teacher has failed in teaching one of the most basic educational concepts.

Similarly, the assumption that the end justifies the means is a false one, inconsistent with a sound philosophy of education, or, for that matter, with a sound philosophy of life. There is no more insidious or rampant threat to principled conduct, in the classroom or in the world outside, than the rationalization that what gets results is good. A teacher who attempts to justify an action on the basis of whether or not it works is indulging in lazy and therefore dangerous thinking. Might does not make right.

All teachers sooner or later use the lesson method of making an example of one student. The stronger the example, and the more dramatic the incident, the more complete and longer unforgotten the lesson. This is one of the fundamental laws of learning. The only occasions in teaching when its use would be unwise would be those in which the student so singled out might suffer humiliation, discouragement, or embarrassment to a serious degree. What is *just* is once again the standard by which such procedures must be evaluated. The constitutionally recognized and guaranteed dignity and worth of the individual make up a concept no teacher has the right to abrogate.

Finally, violent action seldom stands the empirical test of time—even short time. Did beating Chuck to the punch really solve the problem in this critical incident? For the teacher it meant one less behavior problem, perhaps, and for Chuck it meant finally passing the course. But the effect upon the remainder of the class must have been either nil or negative: all other repeaters still failed. And what of their sense of values as witnesses to the treatment of a nonconformist? Might some think of their new teacher as a bully? So many concepts that one carries with oneself throughout adult life are embryonic during the eighth grade. Which students' sense of justice, for instance, were not slanted somewhat as a result of this incident? And was the lesson a truly valuable one for Chuck, one he could apply in other areas at other times in his life? Apparently no carry-over value was there, for he failed every one of his other courses during the same semester and was subsequently dropped from school.

Perhaps no classroom teacher should be expected to handle such a student. Ideally, of course, the Chuck Mosses of the schoolrooms need and should have professional help, highly skilled and highly expensive. In the absence of this specialized assistance, all too infrequently provided for, the classroom teacher must use what means he has at his disposal, including the resources within himself and the classroom, the school, and outside agencies. And always he must strive to break down defensiveness with friendly but firm interest rather than with skepticism or belligerence. Maybe all he can do is to provide a living example, an embodiment of what he is attempting to teach, and to encourage those whom he teaches to apply this example in their own lives.

WILLIS B. INMAN

*   *   *

This incident poses several surface problems. Its major import is its relevance to deeper issues.

One's first impression of the teacher is that he must have been a powerful young man, somehow "heroic"—at least to the boy he won over. At once the question of *identification* arises. Chuck must have seen in him some likeness to an "ideal image" of authority; perhaps his own life lacked such a psychological model. The age of seventeen is late for identification. The time was long gone when his parents should have represented to this child the ethical imperatives of the society as well as more specific sex status within it. Generally the child's acceptance of this joint reference is brought about by reconciliation of his anger against normal prohibitions and punishment with his increased awareness of dependence and growing love. It is a conflict resolved by the acceptance of discipline itself as dealt out in love, through seeing the parents themselves living under the discipline of social law and principle. Same-sex identification must be obtained *before identification with both parents as examplars of the society* can crystalize into "conversion"—acceptance in principle of maturity and its expectations, responsibilities, and rewards.

This reconciliation is not generally understood, much less accepted. People who deal with children do, however, *recognize* experientially (and even light contemporary literature notes) that older children often interpret "permissiveness" of parents as *not caring.* Children are extremely sensitive to problems of right and wrong; the indulgence or over-excusing

7

of "wrong" behavior appears to children as neglect or indifference—lack of love. It would follow that more general understanding of this principle, its dynamics and meaning, might greatly reduce problem behavior at home as well as at school, even in certain learning difficulties. Children resent arbitrary demands and criticisms. They do not rebel at reasonable rules, especially when explained. Thus, overpermissive excuse of transgression *appears* itself as arbitrary, undue, and *unloving*.

In this incident, Chuck had been self-indulgent in rebelliousness for years, as had half the class. Since the punishment of repeating grades had no relation to the reasons for rebellion, these boys continued to fail in school and probably at home as well. It is important to note that the teacher's attack on Chuck was initiated on the grounds of observance of common *courtesy*, learned by children as a matter of course at a very early age. Punishment on these grounds suggested to the boy his teacher's concern that he live up to elementary principles of personal interaction—a "mild" beginning, but one deeply reminiscent and recognized. This felt concern was, moreover, borne out in the teacher's scrupulous "fairness." It appears that Chuck did in fact recognize (or reaffirm) his "duty," that is, some expectations *upon himself*, by acceptance of an identification with the teacher's expectations of him. This tiny episode is a beautiful little model of the over-introjection and assimilation of same-sex identification which takes place in the young child at covert or unconscious levels.

The major question is why did this "encounter" fail, or fall short? This question is asked on two counts: Chuck did not generalize this crucial experience into his total horizon, since he continued to fail all other classes; the other boys were not affected or touched in any way by Chuck's experience.

As regards the others, it is probable that the severity of the attack upon Chuck itself deterred the "rebels" of this classroom from acting out or incurring any risk, even of personal involvement. (A further inference is that its effect on the total situation would be a class "divided against itself.") As for Chuck's "failure of generalization," a major point is involved. Since his identification was only partial, on "same-sex" grounds, it fell far short of *requisite subsequent identification with the larger society*.

Let us look more closely, therefore, at the conditions under which partial identification was achieved. The teacher had been warned that this was a difficult class and that he should be "firm." He saw Chuck's defiance in terms of a power struggle and acted swiftly and punitively to win the first battle. What he found, to his amazement, was that he had won the war. The point is that he did not know what he was really doing nor what he had actually achieved. He won, not mastery, but Chuck—his allegiance and his love. Then, sadly enough, he did not know what to *do* with these gifts, even had he recognized the oblation of "gold, frankincense, and myrrh" . . . to turn them toward the "proper object," the greater goal. The reason was that this teacher himself was standing *not for principle but for power*. Therefore, in the final analysis, he represented only himself.

(So, too, parents who represent "only themselves" in personal requirements of their children can never "let them go," nor be other than manipulators of the destiny of human individuality, untrustful of their children's potential to accept the ethical imperative of the culture toward which they themselves must be desultory or ambivalent.)

Thus, two persons *learned* something of inestimable importance and neither of them realized its magnitude. What began in situational, mastery-won love was arrested at the one-to-one level, perhaps because of the unconscious realization that even this "hero" was standing only for himself and not for larger loyalty.

The behavior involved is clearly that of "shock tactics." It is not *true* that only this teacher, because of his method of "shock assault," could have broken through Chuck's rebellious defensiveness. Any teacher with "caring concern" for the potentials underlying behavior and with faith and belief in the integrity of personality and individuality could have won this boy and others like him, in ways more reflective of his own personality and, perhaps, with more generalized results.

Such an endeavor we cannot require of teachers of large classes; there is not enough staff professionally trained to do this job. Thus, we must credit this teacher greatly for what he *did* do; regardless of motive, it was more than had been done before for Chuck, or for other children, younger or older, who cry out for assistance in entering into maturity and into recognition of responsibility for their feelings and behavior.

Indulgence, "permissiveness" of indulgence, and "pursuit of happiness" for its own sake have never been the measure of man. Rather, it is identification with authority, recognition and acceptance of the ethical imperatives of society, and aspiration and intention to the highest good that have enabled man to grow into the strength and power of manhood—and thus to make the discontinuous shift from the state of being men to the status of mankind.

ELIZABETH Z. JOHNSON

*   *   *

In this incident, we feel that the main issue is the psychological interpretation of anger, or perhaps a better phrase is "anger flooding." Regardless of whether or not the anger is justifiable, two questions need to be kept in mind while we are considering this incident. They are: (1) Is this a strategic or even a suitable time for the teacher to show his anger to the student? (2) Is the anger governing what the teacher says and does, or does the teacher have control over his anger and is he merely simulating wrath to create the image of a man whom it is not safe to bait? With these thoughts in mind, let us react to the material.

At first, it seemed logical to cast the teacher in the role of a hostile villain. We almost inadvertently felt counter-aggressive feelings and wanted to criticize the teacher before we recalled that the teacher himself was a victim of his many unconscious and conflicting motives. Also, we reminded ourselves that the teacher was not only inexperienced—he was also in his first day "in action." In the armed forces, the term *battle anxiety* was coined to explain the behavior of soldiers who were apprehensively facing combat for the first time. We are reasonably sure that there are parallels between the rookie soldier who is preparing for battle and the rookie teacher who is preparing to meet his class. Both are determined to win the battle and return to tell about it. For the teacher, the battle is not a physical one but a psychological one, in which—at least in the episode cited—he is fighting against *feelings of inadequacy, inferiority, and incompetence*. In addition to the impact of these normal feelings of apprehension that all teachers face, there is the principal's admonition to the teacher that he had a very "tough" class that needed to be handled firmly. Against this background of the potential forces acting upon the teacher, let us analyze the incident.

When Chuck Moss did not answer to his name, and after one of the students had identified Chuck, the teacher assumed that he faced a critical test, a battle he must win. He proceeded in his narrative to describe Chuck and others in his class in stereotype-delinquent terms. It is difficult to imagine what alarming associations the teacher had in mind as he described this boy. Perhaps he viewed Chuck as a "Blackboard Jungle" hoodlum, who had no respect for learning, authority, and/or discipline. If this were his interpretation, increased anxiety could have been created in an already insecure young teacher. When the teacher heard the presumably disrespectful answer, "Yeah, man," it was all the verification he needed to substantiate his interpretation that he was dealing with a tough delinquent boy of the zip-gun and switch-blade breed. At this point we are no longer describing a rational process between a teacher and adolescent, of course—we are describing an emotional reaction to a threatening situation. Whether real or fancied, it was "real" to the teacher. The teacher physically attacks the student by kicking him in the shins and pulling him out of his seat by the hair. He then berates him by making him write his name on the blackboard one hundred times. If Chuck were a thoroughgoing delinquent, he would have reacted with counter-aggression at this point and taken a swing at the teacher, refusing to submit to such an infantile and humiliating experience without every show of force he could command.

Let us try to answer some of the following questions: How does one explain why the boy did not answer to his name? It is possible that this seventeen-year-old boy was involved in his own fantasy-life and simply did not hear his name spoken by the teacher. From his perception, he was sitting quietly when this hostile teacher started pushing him around. Yet how does one account for the fact that Chuck reportedly did acceptable work in this class but caused difficulty in the rest of his classes to the extent that he was expelled from school the following year? Within our framework of interpretation, this behavior is understandable; the psychological label for such behavior would be "identification with the aggressor." The psychodynamics behind it is as follows. If a teacher is so aggressive that the child perceives him as having the power to destroy or injure him, one way of coping with the anxiety thus created is to become like the teacher. This is illustrated by the five-year-old who may play the role of a dog that actually frightens him. Some children will, in other words, simulate the behavior of the aggressor teacher as a way of mastering their anxiety.

An important point to remember regarding Chuck Moss is that this kind of identification is based upon fear rather than upon love and does not transfer from one situation to another. This could explain why Chuck acted up in his other classes. An appropriate analogy is a teacher shaking up a warm bottle of Coca Cola and then handing it to another teacher to open. When the second teacher removes the cap, the contents explode and spill out in the room. Further, the "aggressor teacher" may turn to the other teachers, who are having difficulty with Chuck, and note in a supercilious manner that they obviously do not know how to discipline children. This is ironic, to say the least, since the aggressor teacher has unconsciously increased the discipline problem for his hapless colleagues.

Another point that is crucial in analyzing the incident has to do with short-range versus long-range goals of discipline. Only the most indefensible kind of short-range and short-sighted "solution" was realized by man-handling Chuck.

There are some tantalizing questions presented by the writer of the incident. The second one reads, "Do some students respect only strength and need strong, violent action?" In our culture it is safe to say that in some measure we all respect strength. From a psychological point of view, however, we are more concerned with what one does with one's strength than with the amount of strength one has. For example, many teachers do not realize that there is a difference between firmness and harshness and between necessary action and aggression. They feel that they have to intervene violently or in a drastic way in order to show their students that they have direct, physical control of the situation. We know from our work with aggressive children that this is not desirable. Some children may want a teacher to treat them aggressively, just as some children may want whiskey and dope. The point to bear in mind, of course, is that we do not give them these experiences or these narcotics just because they want them. We also know that if a teacher deals with children aggressively, they do not have to feel guilty over their counter-aggression. In other words, children will not have to change their behavior or defenses as long as teachers play the same game and support their belief that *might is right*.

One more point in closing. It is the educator's challenge to avoid creating the kind of classroom milieu that permits stupidity to find expression, and to prevent ill-prepared, problem-ridden, or culturally deprived teachers from working with children and youth. We will forever waste our resources if we are obliged to squander such professional skills as we may have on the frustrating task of repairing human personalities—whether they be the child's or the teacher's—when the social and emotional climate in our schools could be and should be ordered in such a way as to keep most "critical incidents in teaching" from reaching the "critical" state.

NICHOLAS J. LONG
HAROLD G. SHANE

*   *   *

The first problem that this incident presents is an administrative one. Regardless of the basis of division of classes, exceptions can always be made, and the unnecessary concentration of problem children in one group should be avoided. Distribution of troublesome children is due, in justice, both to teachers and to other children in the class. Whenever a class is large enough to permit various sections, it would seem to be an administrative error to permit a situation in which a leader of rebellious pupils is placed in a position where he can make the most of his ability to disturb.

A second problem lies in the fact that seventeen-year-olds were grouped with eighth-grade children. The analysis of a child's background, together with psychological testing and adequate counseling, should make it possible to keep him rather closely associated in classes with children of his own age level. That Chuck was permitted to fail three successive grades without some adjustment being made indicates a lack of several things in the school system: (1) a promotion policy that meets the social as well as the intellectual needs of the individual; (2) provision for appropriate referrals to agencies that might discover the sources of failure and provide counseling that would remedy them at an earlier stage; and (3) a special class or school for pupils who cannot go along in a relatively normal way with their own age group. This would apply particularly should psychological testing indicate that Chuck had a mental ability below low average, for example, an I.Q. in the sixties or seventies. A special class in which a small group was taught by a teacher trained for the retarded could have given Chuck some sense of achievement; a need for achievement may have been basic to the emotional disturbance that caused his antisocial behavior.

These recommendations for the case in hand are all beyond the sphere of the classroom teacher *qua* teacher. Taking the situation as it was, the teacher's actions proved to be a solution to one facet of the problem. He succeeded both in establishing his authority and in teaching a recalcitrant boy. Every teacher has to prove himself before his class in some way, and for some pupils, and at times for all the immature, the way is that of salutary fear. Fear is not the most desirable driving force, but there are times when reason and the more positive emotions are ineffectual in producing necessary effects. This is particularly true where early environment and other circumstances in the child's previous training have failed to develop power to respond to love, hope, and joy. A beginning contact may and sometimes must be made through fear.

But this initial effort must be carried further. In this instance there appeared to be no permanent character change wrought in Chuck. Having met with a teacher strong enough to keep him in check, he performed assigned tasks. Had any other motive besides recognition of power been a causative factor, a difference would have been noted in his relations to other teachers and in his work in general. That this did not occur is indicative of the fact that the teacher who subdued him appears to have done only that. Perhaps he was the only one who could have led Chuck to an appreciation of education in some degree and to a recognition of his leadership qualities and the worthy social ends for which they might be used. His efforts might have been seconded by a guidance counselor and by cooperative steps on the part of Chuck's other teachers. Apparently the teacher did not use his advantage. He failed to see that worthy membership in adult society is one of the goals of his classroom work. He seems to have failed to recognize the misdirected power in a problem boy, a power that was intended for greater accomplishments.

In short, this teacher succeeded in subduing disorderly elements in a class, but he achieved nothing more. The rest of his retarded pupils failed. The subjugation of Chuck did no more for them than preserve order in the classroom. The purpose of that order is learning; the pupils did not learn. For this teacher order was an end and not a means. From that standpoint, its value was less than the teacher considered it to be.

For one reason or another, our country has many boys like Chuck, awaiting the challenge that will turn their energies and enthusiasms into forces for good. Our country also has many teachers who have learned to content themselves with the present subjugation and mediocre achievements of their pupils. Fortunately, the profession knows vast numbers who are ever striving and planning to make of the Chucks of the nation the needed leaders of tomorrow's America.

SISTER M. LOYOLA

*   *   *

Before discussing the issue of "beating students to the punch and putting the fear of God in them," in the case of the teacher who kicked Chuck in the shin, I think that a prior problem has to be considered. Namely, what is the nature of such a "bit" of behavior? For example, in the incident, this unit of behavior included an attempt to call the individual by name, his own attitudinal response, and the teacher's physical response. In a sense, this represents a closed unit having a beginning, middle, and end. What is the role of such a unit in the process of interpersonal transaction and/or (in this instance) the process of teaching? Is this simply an example of "power struggle" between teacher and student?

In an instance of this sort one is dealing with the tail of a long chain of behavioral and teaching transactions in the world of this particular student.

In actuality, Chuck's behavior was quite easily explainable as that of an individual who lacked sufficient socialization. Furthermore, he failed to receive sufficient instruction in assimilating awareness of the "other" and in developing appropriate responsive behavior toward the "other" (that is, any other person). I would not say at all that Chuck was an abnormal individual, but I would like to relate his behavior to several aspects of schizophrenic behavior that I have observed.

When there is a continuum of behavior that apparently has a tendency to go on indefinitely and unchangingly, a sharp and unexpected gesture on the part of another may, at least temporarily, interrupt the "continuity in isolation" and momentarily open the individual to the possibility of a new perception—and this may lead to a new bit of learned behavior. In other words, the sharp blow to the shin may have performed such a service in Chuck's case. This, in itself, would not necessarily be enough to alter behavior. There must be something else. One of the elements of this something else was that the teacher then went on to make clear to Chuck that he expected something more of him.

The second significant element in the reordering of this particular student's behavior similarly calls to mind a phenomenon I have observed in dealing with mental patients. It has to do with an authoritarian, hierarchical or "ordering" bit of behavior. Frequently an element of uninterrupted, perhaps self-cycling behavior that tends in no useful direction, and that is sharply interrupted and commandeered into a particular frame of reference, is followed not only by passive compliance but also by active and progressive devolvement in a positive direction.

Positively directed action, if fearful and executive enough on the part of those attempting to teach a malordered individual, will very frequently bring about surprisingly complete, though often momentary, compliance. Had real work been done with this particular individual to encourage the "spread" of altered behavior into his other scholastic experience at the time, a relatively healthy person would doubtless have been a result.

Absence of positive and coordinated effort of this sort is, I believe, a great failure in modern American teaching. The teacher is geared for promoting the development of appropriate behavior and the encouragement of learning in those students who are *already* motivated. It has not yet evolved an approach to the appropriate *motivation* of those students who have already previously evolved maladaptive behavior. The measure employed by this particular teacher is naturally not something that can be or should be scheduled into usual teaching practices. However, I am sure that it is not rare in terms of the natively impulsive and appropriate response of well-motivated and not infrequently inspired teachers. It is not the particular form of reordering behavior employed here (that is, the kick) that is worthy of note—it is the fact that a message was transmitted to this student. A sharp remark or special attention paid to him over a short or a long period of time might have done as well.

Unfortunately, the kind of support that such individuals need requires an intensity of effort too frequently beyond the possibilities and investments of the average teacher. Furthermore, the usual mass of students confronting the teacher, as well as the usual discouragement in attempting to work with "one-time" and "two-time" losers, in a scholastic sense, is not conducive to the greatest effort on the part of the average teacher. Only the most enthusiastic, devoted, or peculiarly vigorous teachers will make the effort.

Thus we need considerable exploration into the problem of reordering disordered learning behavior as well as the problem of teaching students who are readily accessible to our efforts. Let us hope the day will come when teaching skills will advance to the stage of coping with this unfortunately heterodox, neglected, and taboo area.

JORDAN M. SCHER

*   *   *

The first obvious error in this eighth-grade class is that there were seventeen-year-old boys in it, boys who should have been in high school with their own group. Chuck was a slow learner who had failed several

times. As a result, he had developed negative attitudes toward school
and a rebellious, defiant attitude toward authority. In general, it is unwise
to send a slow learner "back over the same road twice." Rather, he should
be moved along with his age group, his work modified to meet his abilities.
At the junior- and senior-high levels, he should be placed in special classes
for his core subjects and integrated with his peers for shop or home arts,
music, art, and gym. Thus the mental set for failure and feelings of inadequacy and resentment would not be established. In Chuck we observe
attitudes caused at least in part by the nonpromotion policy.

No, it is not wise to "beat problem children to the punch" and to put
"the fear of God" into them. The teacher's approach to this boy was
inexcusable. There is a vast difference between eliminating a problem
by brute force and threat of physical harm and attacking it by helping
a student develop his own controls. It is the difference between superficial obedience and the "will to be good" that comes from understanding.

This socially disturbed boy, who had learned to submit only to force,
threat, suppression, and violence, was a victim of cultural and intra-
personal factors dominating his past. There are many others like him.
By using the same techniques to gain controls, the teacher was merely
causing this boy to continue an attitude and a pattern of response that
might easily lead to juvenile deliquency, or, at best, to personality problems
that would interfere with his social adequacy as an adult. The proper course
would have been to start helping him change his attitude—to help him
develop "the will to be good" through respect and understanding.

The means by which one obtains desired results are very important.
The compliance and cooperation described here are only a temporary and
outward submission to a power that is greater in strength. Chuck's attitude has not been basically changed. He needs to understand and appreciate reasons for certain regulations. It is the "why" that matters.
Regulations have meaning, and life is made up of regulations.

It is unwise to make a strong example of one student in an effort to
secure group conformity and to let them know who is in command. I
hesitate to think what this teacher's action might have done to the boy
and to the other pupils. "Because I said so" is not a reason for conformity.
The real reasons need to be stated explicitly. Everything in teaching
depends upon the reason that motivates the child. The reasons must have
far-reaching effects; otherwise they will probably not have "carry-over"
value. Praise is an important adjunct. It is important for the child to feel
that the teacher is on his side. When force is the motivating factor, on
the other hand, compliance disappears as soon as the force is no longer
present. Future application of the learning is lost.

LOUISE S. SINDERSON

DISCUSSION QUESTIONS

1. Under what, if any, circumstances are teachers justified in using physical force to coerce or restrain children?
2. Should administrators match students to teachers whenever possible, assigning problem children to experienced teachers?
3. Can permissivism be interpreted by pupils as "not caring"? What are the advantages and disadvantages of tough versus easy discipline? What are the implications of styles of discipline in terms of self-direction versus conformity?
4. Can you suggest an effective procedure for enabling prior teachers to communicate information on difficult students to present teachers?
5. Two extremes are possible in teaching elementary school children. Teaching might be completely depersonalized by means of devices such as automated teaching machines and educational television. On the other hand, it might be intensively personalized in the form of tutorial instruction, with the teacher having a deep understanding of and concern for the individual pupil. Can you outline some considerations that might be involved in obtaining an optimum balance of mechanical and personal elements in teaching?
6. What can be done by teachers for children with low academic aptitude for whom school failure is a personal blow?

2

"THE CLASS CLOWN"

CRITICAL INCIDENT

Background

      I was a young practice teacher on my first assignment, a class in eighth-grade history. It was the procedure of the university I attended to evaluate student teachers on the basis of the opinions of a critic teacher and the school principal. When I had been with the class two weeks, the following incident occurred.

Incident

One morning, while both the principal and the critic teacher were in the room observing the lesson (and while I was trying particularly hard to make a favorable impression), the "class clown" decided it was time to strike. An intelligent and shrewd youngster, he was well aware that I was new to teaching, and that I wanted to create a good impression of my teaching ability. He began exercising one of his special talents: while keeping a perfectly straight face he could produce ingenious imitations of various sounds—a growling dog, an air raid siren, a mooing cow. This sterling display of showmanship naturally produced howls of laughter from the other students. The boy continued, with an attitude of "see what I'm doing" and "what are you going to do about it?"

I asked the boy if he would kindly wait with his imitations until after school, whereupon he answered "No," again creating a mass demonstration of hysteria. By this time I was perplexed, losing confidence quickly, and no longer feeling that I was the greatest thing that had happened to the field of education since the development of the blackboard. I then altered my approach by saying that we would all stop for a minute and listen to Jim give imitations of his animal friends. The idea of being asked to perform so took him aback that he ceased his vocal contributions and the class continued.

Discussion

This was the first disturbance of classroom order, the first purposeful misbehavior, that I had encountered. Being new and inexperienced, I was indecisive about what to do; at the same time I felt I had to do *something* in order to show the observers, the class, and myself that "my" class could not have disturbances of this nature and that I could take proper steps to alleviate the situation.

In retrospect I realize that my initial assumptions were not entirely correct. Feeling that I "had to do something" and fearing a loss of prestige had caused me to err in my first reactions to the commotion. I was making a mistake common to beginning teachers, that is, "doing something quick" because my authority had been challenged.

Questions

1. What would have been a better way of meeting the situation?
2. What, in all probability, would an experienced teacher have done?
3. Are there good general principles for dealing with class saboteurs?

*　　*　　*

Clashes with authority figures seem to be common today at the upper grade-school level. Although the clown of this age group has always been in evidence at the most inopportune moments in many classes, recent trends in American culture appear to encourage him rather than to deal with him promptly and firmly, as was the accepted practice formerly. In many cases, repeated experiences of "getting away with it" have built up the clown's self-confidence to the point that he feels he "has the world by the tail," and nobody can really make him do anything or stop doing anything if he does not wish to.

My observation has convinced me that today's teen-agers respect most that rare, flexible adult who can apply a lively sense of humor to emergencies such as the one related to this incident. It is not as easy to come up with an immediate remark that will steal the show from the clown as it is to think of an appropriate comment two hours later. In this instance, the practice gained in meeting a number of similar crises would give the graduate teacher some advantage over the student practice teacher in handling Jim. Since this was a first offense, I think the teacher might have made a real attempt to get a bigger laugh from the group, thus outdoing Jim. To invite him to take over by doing something that, for the moment, is more spectacular than the lecture of class discussion, is to encourage him to satisfy his need for recognition in a socially unacceptable way.

An immediate reaction of being irritated or threatened is not easy to conceal from students, but the teacher's very symptoms of being distracted and annoyed were just what Jim wanted. I agree that the teacher should indeed have "done something quick," but not the thing she did: that was what Jim expected would happen. Giving him an unexpected response before he had time to realize what was happening probably would have made his face turn red, and any further disturbance would not have occurred—or not for some time thereafter, in any event.

There are limits to any mature person's sense of humor when serious purposes are to be accomplished. Some clowns will persist in spite of initial competition for the biggest laugh on the part of the teacher. Ignoring some small distracting disturbances may sometimes be better than making a big issue of them. Yet the point may be reached at which a good learning situation no longer exists, and this failure to maintain order will probably cause students to lose respect for their instructor. Stopping class work to listen to Jim's noises would probably relieve the difficulty only temporarily. On the positive side, it would be sound procedure to try rather often to draw the clown into participating in serious discussion. Recognition achieved in this acceptable manner might relieve the need to attract attention by being funny.

If the class clown feels rejected at home and ignored at school, as is often the case, none of these suggestions will work. Then it appears obvious that sending the boy to the principal's office for the remainder of the period, talking with him firmly in private conference later, and depriving him of privileges he values at school are about the only motivational devices left. Fairness demands making the rules unambiguous to the student and being as consistent as possible in carrying them out whenever an offense occurs.

A final comment seems to be in order on this incident. It concerns the threat of loss of authority that the narrator would certainly feel the first time he had to match wits with a rather defiant teen-age boy. Sociologists and psychologists have written at great length concerning their observations on the increasing ambiguity of the role of the adolescent in our culture. More than ever before, he does not know what he is, child or adult. Actually he is not clearly either one. He does not know what he wants. Perhaps he thinks he wants complete freedom and independence, without fully realizing the inevitable responsibilities that must accompany them. Given more latitude than former generations would have allowed him, he does not know how to handle this responsibility or what to do with himself. Logically it would follow that adults feel more insecure with him, more threatened by him at times, than would have been true several generations ago.

Overcrowded classes, inadequate salaries, and an overload of teaching duties do not help the youth in a public school to feel important as an individual, nor do these factors make teaching at this level attractive to enough of the resourceful, adequate, mature persons needed in these positions. If a boy thinks somewhat as follows: "She (the teacher) doesn't even know I'm back here anyhow and cares less; besides she doesn't even take time to grade my paper correctly," can anyone expect him to do anything but make a desperate effort to be known as somebody? That may very well be what the clown in this class was doing. Such an explanation is not intended as a derogatory comment about the capabilities of the teacher relating the incident. It is offered only in order to point out some working conditions prevailing in many public schools today that make the roles of the teacher and the student both more difficult than they should be.

KENNETH L. BEAN

*   *   *

Ask any new teacher to name the most challenging aspect of her work, and the reply will deal most certainly with problems of discipline and classroom management. Ask any veteran teacher to evaluate the inexperienced teacher, and the answer in all probability will relate to skills of behavior control. Ask pupils to select their "best" teacher, and the choice will undoubtedly be the teacher who gave them the security of controls along with genuine respect.

Essentially the problem in this critical incident is one of classroom management and behavior control. This student teacher is concerned about her ability, and rightly so. Skills necessary to insure a proper learning climate and environment are prime requisites in teaching. I do not believe that this teacher should be worried in this regard, however, for in the present situation, at least, she demonstrated reasonable adequacy. Every teacher is going to have such encounters.

Let us look briefly at three aspects of this incident: (1) the general question of classroom management and behavior control; (2) the relationship between student teacher and supervisor; and (3) the specific problem presented by the "class clown."

A classroom, in order to be an effective environment, must have controls as well as freedom. A teacher, in order to be effective, must be able to sense the controls necessary and appropriate to the maturity of the group and then establish and maintain them. This is essential for effective learning. It is also an important objective of an instructional program that is to help pupils respect controls and to develop self-control or discipline.

Classroom management involves skills that teachers must develop. Often, these do not come naturally, but must be cultivated. Occasionally one does find a beginning teacher in whom the skills seem to develop easily and quickly, but more often competence and security come only after a period of training and experience. Effective classroom management also requires certain specific attitudes on the part of the teacher. In my judgment, attitudes are more important than the techniques that any given teacher may develop to bring about what she feels are necessary controls.

The judge in a courtroom demands and gets respect from all because he firmly respects what the courtroom stands for in our American system of law and government. Also, he is clear about his responsibility and about the responsibilities of all in attendance. The attitudes that operate to establish a proper classroom climate are the same. That is, the teacher must supply the leadership and her approaches must be based on a firm respect, as well as understanding, of what is to be accomplished in the classroom. Furthermore, she is responsible for seeing that pupils understand what controls are to be exercised and why they are important.

I believe that children expect and look for direction from their teacher in determining what is acceptable and unacceptable behavior. This doesn't mean that she need be harsh, unnecessarily demanding, or unfriendly. In fact, the opposite is implied; she must always show respect for the pupils. The teacher who is sincere, and who practices as well as teaches respect, will be secure and humane in her dealings with children. Consequently, she will enjoy a good teaching environment.

There are some useful tips about skills and techniques of classroom management. First, new teachers must think through what they will require in terms of controls before they ever walk into the classroom the first day. Second, specific rules and requirements should be clearly explained to the class. Third, caution should be exercised not to make more rules than are necessary or than can be adequately administered. Fourth, the teacher should remain detached until she has determined the ability of the group and each individual in the group for self-control. Fifth, early in the game, she should look for troublemakers and give them the attention they warrant. Sixth, pupils should be kept busy at some worthwhile activities. If the teacher can't find worthwhile activities, she should just keep them busy. This seems, perhaps, to be a strange suggestion, but I believe a teacher is in a better position if she establishes a mood of industry, even if during the first couple of weeks this means some busy-work.

It is interesting to me that the student teacher felt she erred in jumping to conclusions and in "doing something quick" with the "class clown." Perhaps she was hasty, but I feel she was more hasty in assuming that she was going to be criticized by her supervisors. Supervisors in general do not make judgments on the basis of one visit. A supervisor recognizes the necessity of a series of observations over a period of time in order to make reliable judgments. To fear or suspect a supervisor of anything less in a situation such as the one described indicates insecurity or a lack of understanding of his role.

The question arises as to whether the boy discussed is a "class clown" or a "troublemaker." The teacher needs to answer this question in her own mind in order to deal with him adequately. It is possible, if this boy is a class clown, that he is demonstrating some personal qualities that need to be developed. It is also possible that his presence can be used to advantage by the teacher in establishing a sense of humor in her class. A class, like an individual, has a personality made up of many facets. Each member of the class contributes in some way to both the character and the reputation of the personality. The teacher should be able to identify and develop those facts which contribute to a proper classroom environment and to eliminate those which serve to disrupt the class.

If, on the other hand, the boy is a "troublemaker," the teacher will have to give him some additional attention. A clown generally has respect for his audience, the desire and ability to entertain, and a sense of timing. However, I got the impression that this boy was rather selfish, and that he sought attention through ridicule and rudeness. If this was actually the case, he is a threat to the proper functioning of a classroom situation. He will need to be worked with, or the teacher faces the possibility of continuous suffering and embarrassment, and, perhaps, of losing the respect, and consequently the control, of her class.

DONALD G. FERGUSON

*   *   *

This incident describes a serious situation for an experienced educator, let alone for a practice teacher who is being observed by the university, critic teacher, and school principal. I know competent and experienced teachers who feel uncomfortable and insecure when they are being observed in the classroom. Consequently, when they are under observation they may handle class situations in an abnormal way. This is not to be taken as opposition to observation. Such observation is the best way for administrators to obtain information on how a teacher applies theoretical knowledge to practical situations in the classroom.

I was favorably impressed with the manner in which this teacher handled the incident. She made a significant decision in an acute situation, and took the only action which, under the circumstances, could bring positive results.

I cannot share, however, the practice teacher's fear of acting too quickly when her authority had been challenged. This is definitely related to how secure a teacher feels in her position. If she doesn't feel secure, or if she feels inadequately trained for her job, she will automatically try to "do something" just as a drowning person will try to hold on to a straw in order to save his life. Do something, she must; it becomes a question of *what* to do in order to control a critical situation effectively. Doing nothing may be better than doing the wrong thing, but in most situations, when a child is actively destructive, doing nothing may be a "go ahead" signal and perpetuate the child's mistaken goal, namely that he can be a "big shot" by this kind of behavior.

Before even a secure, resourceful teacher can effectively handle a child who misbehaves, she must know what kind of satisfaction the child derives from his particular kind of behavior. This calls for careful observation of the child in all phases of school life.

We know that a well-behaved child who readily cooperates is a child who feels socially accepted and, therefore, secure. Such a child has status because of his useful contributions to the group and his conformity to the requirements made by his social environment. Every child needs to feel such acceptance and status in the group. Every child tries to achieve this in his own particular manner. The child who is prevented from achieving recognition through constructive contributions seeks proof of his acceptance through socially disapproved methods.

The "class clown" is a maladjusted child who usually tries to conceal his inadequacies. He tries to distract attention from the things he cannot do by putting on a show of his own—one in which he is the main star. If the teacher succeeds in controlling him in one situation, he will soon find something else which will be equally disturbing to her—something that will assure him an audience.

Such a child needs to be helped to understand what prompts him to behave as he does. He needs to be encouraged to achieve recognition in a constructive, socially acceptable manner. The teacher must give him the kind of attention which will make it unnecessary for him to seek it through unacceptable behavior, the kind of attention that brings him prestige. She must maneuver the situation so that he gets recognition from the group. She should let him show off with something he can do well, no matter how trivial and how "unacademic." She must provide opportunities for this child to succeed in something that will bring him the admiration of the group. She must not leave this to chance. A resourceful teacher will find many occasions to let a child "show off" in a positive way. If he can imitate birds, animals, and sirens, as this boy could, why not let him perform openly, in a manner of entertainment, and thereby give him an appreciative audience, and the desired prestige?

I generally refrain from telling a child the cause of his behavior; I merely try to reveal to him the purpose of his action. In most cases children respond favorably and cooperate when we mirror their behavior to them without lowering their self-esteem.

In disclosing the child's goal to him, we may ask him, "Could it be that you do this so that everybody will look at you and admire you?" Or, "Could it be that you behave that way because you feel that nobody thinks much of you unless you show that you have the power to make the teacher angry?" In this particular case, the teacher might have added, "Is it possible that you feel left out and you are jealous of the attention I am getting from the class and from the gentlemen present? I will let you get all the attention as soon as I am through with this lesson. You may then make those noises in front of the class, and we shall listen to you. You're pretty good at it. I admired especially the way you imitate the siren." In this manner, she reveals to the child his immediate goal; she catches him unprepared for her kind attitude and she gives him positive recognition in front of everybody.

In conclusion, a word of caution. The teacher will need to be observant enough to distinguish between the child who clowns for a moment's fun and the one who persists in clowning because he cannot get recognition in any other way.

BERNICE GRUNWALD

*   *   *

This incident, starting so unfavorably for the teacher, nevertheless was eventually handled well under the circumstances. The teacher states that she was trying particularly hard to make a favorable impression on the principal and critic teacher, and her anxiety was probably accurately perceived by this intelligent boy. The fact that he would engage in this attention-getting, defiant behavior in the presence of three authority figures, including even the principal, is an indication of the strength of his need for status with his peers. He was well rewarded by the laughter of the other children.

The teacher then made the mistake of asking him if he would wait until after school to make his animal sounds. Because of the way in which the question was framed, the child was given the opportunity to further demonstrate his cleverness and maintain the focus of attention on himself by answering "No." Questions such as this, requiring a "yes" or "no" answer, are potential traps for teachers and parents because the phrasing implies that the child has a choice. The teacher set the trap by phrasing the question as she did, and the boy sprang it by his answer. The class, of course, appreciated the irony of the situation and the consternation of the teacher. Thus far, the teacher had responded exactly as the boy had expected she would. He had expected disapproval, suppression, and some argument. The teacher made it easy for him to achieve his goal of keeping attention on himself.

The situation was quickly turned in the teacher's favor, however, when she ceased to do what the boy expected. Since he was asking for an audience, she offered him the formal and "legal" attention of the class and the adults in the room. A less intelligent youngster might have accepted the offer and have found himself, after a few minutes before the class, the butt of considerable criticism and even hostility from the rest of the class. This boy unconsciously realized that he had lost his advantage and that the teacher had taken the zest out of the situation by sanctioning his imitations.

This incident shows the effectiveness of a teacher's not doing what is expected of her. The teacher countered this boy's behavior with an unexpected and dramatic action, showing that she was flexible and resourceful enough to meet a difficult situation by other than purely traditional methods. This action undoubtedly engendered greater respect from the entire class for the teacher.

In response to the question as to what would have been a better way of handling the situation, it appears that after a few initial mistakes, the teacher carried off the situation effectively. Even many experienced teachers, I suspect, might have sent this boy to the principal's office or even have punished him personally. Both responses would have meant that the teacher was defeated and the boy would have become a hero in the eyes of the class.

The third and final question—"Are there good general principles for dealing with such class saboteurs?"—is an intriguing one. The first requisite for dealing with situations such as this is to understand that most youngsters who engage in this kind of behavior are not "saboteurs" but "salvageurs," attempting to salvage what they can of their feelings of self-respect. Their feelings of inferiority and self-doubt are eased, if only temporarily, by the attention and interest shown by the rest of the class. Youngsters like this apparently intelligent boy need intensive guidance in finding socially acceptable and more enduring ways of achieving status. There is no simple formula for working with this type of youngster. In order to help him, one would have to identify some of his strengths and his interests, then to encourage him in activities where he can find legitimate success, especially at school.

ORVAL G. JOHNSON

*   *   *

It is worthy of note that this incident occurred in the classroom of a student teacher in the presence of the principal and the critic teacher. Under such circumstances most students feel subdued, and even the more spontaneous and irrepressible "class clowns" usually have the good sense or the decency to wait for a more opportune time. Unquestionably the student sensed the insecurity of the student teacher. When the teacher asked him to do the imitations after school, he must really have felt himself to be in command of the situation to refuse, and therefore he was spoiling for a power contest with the teacher—an awkward situation for anyone who is trying to create a good impression.

Let us analyze what the teacher did. First, it appears that she permitted him to go on after his first demonstration of his talents, hoping, perhaps, he would have the good sense to stop after one demonstration. But no—he gave an encore after obtaining approbation from his fellow students.

I believe that the teacher's first reaction—to do nothing—was exactly proper. The rule goes when you don't know what to do, do nothing! Otherwise one can do something that one may regret.

The next scene in this little play was the encore. The teacher now suggested, and I hope with a smile, that he do his imitations elsewhere—and after school.

This I see as a tactical error. The teacher is setting up the student for disobedience. In strict logic she is telling him to do something which she has no right to do—to do imitations outside of the class. What she really means—but will the student understand this—is that he should not do them in class. If so, it might have been better to have a direct showdown than to lead out in such manner that a direct negative reaction would occur. And, this is just what happened. After the teacher's unreasonable request for him to do his monkeyshines elsewhere, the student said, "no," which he had a proper right to do.

Luckily, the teacher did not misinterpret the "no" to the request to behave in this manner outside of the class as a "no" to her request for him to behave. Some teachers might well have gotten excited at this point.

The next step was apparently to give in, and to ask the class to listen to Jim. This did it. Jim stopped.

In such situations, as I see it, a teacher cannot go far wrong if she keeps in control of herself. Unless she feels threatened she can allow such scenes to take place. She may even secretly admire so bold and powerful a child, and be willing to let him express himself for a while. To have given him the freedom to do what he wanted squelched him.

The teacher realized that in her desire to make a favorable impression she felt the need to do *something* and *quickly*. Too often this is the reaction of the unexperienced teacher when she feels her authority has been questioned. She lashes out too quickly and the result is a power struggle which she is almost always likely to lose, for even if she were to engage the entire power of the school against one child to crush him she would always know she had been unfair.

The wise teacher in dealing with the "clown" or the "saboteur" will recognize his disturbing behavior as a sign of his own disturbance—attention-getting in this case—and she will endeavor to create situations in which the child can receive attention and recognition for useful rather than useless behavior. It is only in this manner that he can be helped toward becoming a useful, contributing member of the class.

ROBERTA MOLTMANN

*   *   *

I cannot become too disturbed about this assumed error in classroom management. To be sure, sarcasm and personal abuse are many times unfair, and neither can be recommended for use in the average classroom situation. Neither approach is a constructive answer. The result in this case was presumably effective, and I doubt seriously that the "class clown" was permanently damaged.

Character inevitably is shown in a crisis; it is not made there. Teaching is consequently more than the sum total of courses in pedagogy. Most teachers can handle the usual classroom situation; the skilled and the professional teacher has the talent to anticipate and solve the unusual situation. The most acceptable criterion of teacher worth is proved ability to make desirable, balanced changes in pupils, particularly in the areas of personality and character. In all human relations, no one finds people exactly as he wants them. It is nice to have everyone smile at you, do exactly as you tell them to, act as you would have them act, but don't count on it. Certainly, you can't command such behavior. Always remember there is no certainty anywhere in human affairs, but mules and teen-agers are alike in that they can be led where they can't be driven!

An experienced teacher probably would not have encountered this particular episode. She would have anticipated it and made plans accordingly. The best discipline is found by removing beforehand those factors that make for problems. An ounce of prevention is decidedly worth far more than a pound of cure. This would be the difference between a capable and experienced teacher in contrast to a new teacher. The former would have arranged relationships so that this problem would not have occurred at all.

In such cases, class time should immediately be taken to discuss the problem with the group. At no time should any pupil be allowed to conduct himself in a manner that creates anarchic class morale and/or a significant safety hazard, nor should the teacher, once the incident has been dealt with, permit it to go by without comment.

In addition, a conversation should take place with the "culprit" outside of class. Listen to the pupil, no matter how convinced you are that he is wrong. You want to know why he misbehaved and you want to prevent a repetition of the incident. Be sure that he understands that the main concern is what is best for him and also what is best for the class. Above all, do not give the impression that you as the teacher are not in control of yourself. He must learn that if he continues to misbehave, he will be penalized. If he behaves, he should be complimented for his maturity.

A smooth classroom organization can be developed without an overuse of rules and regulations. If the proper spirit of cooperation among the pupils is obtained, dogmatic pronouncements can be held to a minimum. This simply means control and responsibility are vested in a pervading self-discipline. Youngsters can do it; they want it; they need it. Getting to know the class members well—their idiosyncracies, their strengths, their weaknesses, their likes, their dislikes—is the first order of business. The teacher must be accepted before his teaching will be accepted.

The teacher must lay down "laws" and be specific about them. Be sure the pupils understand the laws and the need for them! Then, be consistent in applying the rules. Demand a lot, but expect less.

PAUL W. SCHMIDTCHEN

DISCUSSION QUESTIONS

1. When students misbehave, apparently for the purpose of attracting attention to themselves, what are the advantages and disadvantages of:
   a. ignoring the behavior.
   b. making fun of the student.
   c. matching wits with the student.
   d. reprimanding the student.
   e. encouraging the student to continue.
2. Do you agree that contemporary social patterns encourage lax discipline? If so, how can a teacher establish adequate standards of discipline in a classroom? Should schools conform to contemporary social patterns, or should they attempt to maintain independent standards for discipline?
3. What are the implications of the idea that a child who presents disciplinary problems may be revealing positive personal characteristics that should be developed constructively?
4. Do you agree with the notion that a pupil may be motivated to misbehave by a desire to preserve his self-esteem?

3

"A RULE IS A RULE"

CRITICAL INCIDENT

Background

While I was teaching a fourth-grade class, a student whose absence I had not noticed came in ten minutes late. When I asked him why, he replied that he had left his gym shoes in the auditorium and had gone back to get them. Upon changing classes, the children are supposed to stay in line until they enter the next classroom. Knowing this rule, I became angry with him for not getting my permission to return to his previous class; therefore, I made him take the shoes back to the auditorium.

A few minutes later when I noticed that he had not yet returned, I looked into the hall. He was standing there doing nothing. I made certain that he returned the gym shoes, then brought him into the classroom and proceeded to conduct the class. This same child kept annoying other children around him. By this time I was so angry that I put him under the shutter where the students hang their clothes, and I pulled the sliding cover down.

Incident

About one minute before the class was over I raised the cover on the shutter to let the boy out. I was shocked to see that he had urinated on the floor. I looked at his pants to see whether or not it was an accident. It wasn't; he had done it deliberately. Naturally the children in the class started to laugh. This humiliated me—I felt that the members of the class thought the boy had won the battle and had gotten back at me. I thought to myself, "I'll be damned if I'll let him get away with this," and I sent immediately for the assistant principal. I showed him the urine and explained what had happened.

To say the least, I was swept off my feet when he said that the incident was all my fault, since I should not have put the child under the shutter. In justifying his stand he told me that certain students suffer from various phobias and cited several unfavorable incidents that had happened while children were in isolation. He told me to have the boy mop up the urine and then to forget the incident.

Discussion

Perhaps I was at fault, but I felt defeated when the assistant principal took the position that he did. I felt that this was one time when I needed an administrator on my side. I wanted to show the children that they wouldn't be allowed to get away with such behavior. I suppose the thing that really hurt me most was the children's seeing that the assistant principal was not alarmed by the incident.

Questions

1. Was I wrong in making the student return the shoes to the auditorium?
2. Should I have isolated him from the class by putting him under the shutter?
3. Did the assistant principal act properly when he did not discipline the child?
4. Even if he were not going to discipline the child, couldn't he have prevented my appearing discredited before the class?

*   *   *

This incident provides clues about why so many teachers complain about so-called "discipline problems" in the classroom. The perfectly understanding human need of teachers for prestige and recognition is difficult to satisfy in communities that implicitly assign low status to the teaching profession. There are serious implications for education.

The reporting teacher is undoubtedly less healthy mentally, more immature emotionally, and in more urgent need of competent psychotherapy than most teachers. Nevertheless, her plight reminds us of how precariously precious to the maintenance of the teacher's ego is her effective authority over the classroom group. How easily one innocent little late-comer can turn the teaching and learning atmosphere into a battleground for the fulfillment of emotional needs, such as the authoritarian need of the teacher and the frustrated child's need to express hostility! Both teacher and pupil are struggling here to save their self-value in moments of group stress. A four-way clash of emotions develops between teacher, pupil, assistant principal, and class. A pathological interaction between two people instigates a contagious chain reaction, able to engulf the whole school in a group pathology. To contain such neurotic interactions and to prevent the infection of the precious learning and teaching atmosphere, school systems should make psychotherapeutic consulting services available not only to parents and their troubled children, but also—and primarily—to problem teachers such as the one here, whose blind, honest self-description should serve as a reminder of a grave problem.

Why is this teacher so easily distracted from her duty to teach? She has so little interest in her charges that she didn't miss the late-comer, yet she made a great demonstration over the already troubled child. Once publicly embarrassed, what else could this boy do but fight back, albeit in a rather regressed manner? Underneath her overt work, the teacher's own ego needs preoccupied her. This made her forget some of the basic principles of child psychology: "frustration in children leads to regression, retrogression, or both." Certainly frustration never breeds the respect desired and unrealistically expected by this teacher.

The assistant principal's intervention, although a little tough on the disturbed teacher, impresses me as a realistic acceptance of his duty to act protectively toward the youngster who has a bio-social right to show vulnerability in this situation. School administrators cannot be expected to be the all-powerful father-figure to childless teachers who compete with their own pupils for recognition by "higher authority." Teachers who are behind in their own maturation schedule and who therefore have made little progress in solving one of the basic human problems, the authority problem, have the type of discipline trouble illustrated here. For such teachers, children may personify such unresolved authority problems. "Undisciplined" behavior triggers and becomes the target of the anger of a teacher who has "control problems" within herself. Who can find teaching rewarding when it arouses anger, and what child can learn under such tension?

GEORGE B. BACH

*   *   *

Two wrongs never make a right. Making the boy return the shoes to the gym meant that both he and the rest of the class were short-changed in valuable instruction time. It would have been much better to let the student keep the shoes and explain the reason for the rule to him. By such an understanding approach, the incident would have been avoided. Children respect and obey rules that they understand.

Separation from classes should be used with caution and only when there is dire trouble. When you send a child from class, you lose a battle. You risk diminishing your influence with the entire class. You admit publicly to your principal, colleagues, and pupils that you are incapable of managing a class. To isolate a student usually causes embarrassment and resentment or humiliation and hatred. Nothing beneficial is gained by student or teacher through isolation. The student in question is deprived of classroom instruction and becomes a point of ridicule, while the teacher in turn has punished herself by adding individual instruction, review, and makeup work to her already busy schedule.

The isolation in this instance not only shut the student off from the class, but in certain respects perhaps endangered the pupil's health and well-being. Though no special fear or phobia was demonstrated by the student at this time, clear hate was displayed in his action. At that particular moment it was the worst retaliatory action the student could think of. Care should be exercised not to encourage an attitude of resentment. A hasty disciplinary action on the part of the teacher and a hasty retaliatory action on the part of the student could have been avoided if the art of good human relations had been practiced.

I think the administrator acted wisely in not further disciplining the student at this time. An undesirable situation had been created, one that encouraged the child to challenge the authority and test the intentions of the teacher. It is a good policy to allow children to save face when they are in a tight spot.

Righteousness and infallibility are poor qualities in a teacher. I see no reason for a feeling of defeat in this incident. I do see where a very poor spur-of-the-moment idea gave an opportunity for a useful learning situation for both the student and the teacher, if it had only been accepted and exploited.

This was a case of reasoned disobedience, in which the student's own good judgment was contrary to rules and regulations established by the teacher for reasons not clearly understood by the student. A mountain of problems and complications developed from a molehill of misunderstanding. Correction was necessary, but discipline should be educative to be effective. Discipline must be followed by positive actions encouraging a different behavior pattern and understanding. Punishment is otherwise ineffective.

A child's angry feeling directed toward an adult responsible for arbitrary punishment destroys the possibility of maintaining a good relationship. Anger is an immature way of meeting a situation and solves nothing. The study of understanding normal personality among pupils is possibly the most neglected phase of teacher education. Teachers must be sensitive to the world of others, know their backgrounds, and above all, value their values. They must command respect of students by being themselves; they cannot demand it just because they are teachers.

"Blessed are the merciful" might well read "blessed are the understanding." The more the teacher understands herself, the more she, in turn, will understand her pupils. The insecure teacher who has not learned understanding *creates* disciplinary problems.

LELAND J. GRITZNER

*   *   *

This incident touches upon a very important and frequent occurrence in teaching, namely, the power contest between teacher and student.

As one reads it, one doesn't know for whom to feel more sorry, the student or the teacher. This report reflects not only distress, but the frustration and extreme anger stimulated by the impotence of the teacher. It also reflects her lack of understanding of children and the goals behind their peculiar behavior. Most of all, it demonstrates the teacher's own feeling of inadequacy and her great fear of losing her prestige unless she controls every situation that arises in the classroom.

To the reviewer, this is pathetic, for it is impossible to have a proper relationship with children if, as teachers, we flaunt our superiority at them and are afraid to admit that we, too, make mistakes. Children respond to anyone who has the courage to be as he is with all the shortcomings that human beings possess. With better training in interpersonal relationships and interaction, a teacher would not have to be exposed to such threatening situations and, therefore, would not have to resort to such shocking methods. She would know that all efforts to control a child who operates on the basis of power will lead only to a deadlock between them. The teacher has no chance to win in such a struggle, if only because she cannot resort to the fighting methods that a child can when he wants to defeat an adult. There is no limit upon a child, whereas a teacher is restricted not only by prescribed rules and regulations but also by her own sense of responsibility and obligation.

To the reviewer, the significant aspect of this incident is that the teacher was more concerned with her own defeated authority than with the welfare of the child. If this had not been the case, she might have mentioned at least one positive characteristic of the boy; there might have been one occasion when she showed some understanding of the boy's problem, or one time when she tried in a friendly, encouraging way to influence the child. There is mention of no such concern throughout the entire report. In fact, one knows nothing about this boy, except that he was always defiant.

One may understand the teacher's anger when the boy went back to get his gym shoes without asking her permission, since this was a violation of rules. For most teachers, scolding the boy would have sufficed. Not for this teacher. The boy can go back only with "her permission," so she makes him return the gym shoes. Can a young child understand the logic or fairness behind such adult behavior? It makes no sense to a child. Instead of associating the punishment with the action, he associates it only with the punisher, who, in his eyes, is simply a bully. He decides to get even.

Just knowing rules and regulations is not sufficient for children to accept them as necessary and just. Some children may yield and obey them without questioning the reasons for them, but many, especially those who have problems of adjustment to authority, rebel against rules. Such children must be helped to accept discipline as necessary because life can be more pleasant if it is conducted according to certain rules. The basic attitude of such children toward discipline must be changed before we can expect understanding and cooperation from them.

We see that this boy returns blow for blow. When he returns with the shoes, he gets even with the teacher by annoying the students who sit next to him. The teacher could have avoided much unpleasantness if she had merely removed the boy from the group. She could have asked him to do something in a corner of the room, away from the others, or she might have sent him out of the room into the corridor or any place where he could not disturb them. A preferable way of handling such a situation would have been a general, frank discussion of what happened and what this boy tried to achieve by behaving as he did. Shutting the boy up in a tiny, dark closet was, certainly, not the proper way of meeting it.

The teacher claims that the student urinated on purpose in order to humiliate her. This may be so, considering how this child acts and reacts in life. But, is it not also possible that he had to go to the washroom? This would be a most natural reaction under these circumstances. How was he to get out and what else could he have done?

Still, one may also assume that the boy did urinate on purpose, this being the only way left to him to retaliate and to humiliate his teacher. He was quite successful, for the teacher felt completely defeated and enraged. In order to save face, the teacher called for help and protection from the assistant principal.

One can well understand the teacher's further frustration and humiliation when the administrator added insult to injury by putting the blame on her rather than on the child.

The reviewer sincerely sympathizes with any teacher whose superiors do not help her to maintain the respect of their students. It is humiliating and discouraging to a teacher when her superior reprimands her in the presence of his students. Children often take advantage of such situations and expose their teacher to more ridicule and hurt. An administrator should know how to manage such a situation in a way that upholds the teacher's prestige in class and yet does not hurt the child.

At a later time, the administrator should discuss the incident with the teacher alone, and express his views on the matter. An effective administrator would encourage, if not demand, that this teacher receive training in child guidance and group interactions in order to avoid such unfortunate situations in the classroom.

BERNICE GRUNWALD

*   *   *

It is assumed here that the incident occurred in a middle grade, probably fifth or sixth. *Apparently the major issue in this incident centers around the teacher's feelings of adequacy, especially her attitudes toward respect for authority.* In this incident, the teacher became angry when the student did not get her permission before returning to the auditorium to pick up the gym shoes he had left there. Why should a minor incident such as this generate such feelings of anger in a teacher? True, the boy broke a rule and that may have been annoying, but it is not easy to understand why the teacher felt that she had to handle this infraction in this particular way. One possible explanation of her behavior might be found in her own personality structure. Perhaps this teacher had a strong need to control everything in her classroom out of the fear that if she did not control all events, the events might eventually control her. If this were the case, the teacher blinded herself to other alternatives that might have explained why the boy acted as he did. Conceivably, the boy didn't wait for permission because he was afraid that someone might have stolen his shoes.

Let us explain this incident on a deeper level, although we realize that this is not a major point in the incident. The teacher's solution was to tell the student to return his shoes to the auditorium, then return to class and ask for permission to get his shoes. *Psychologically, what the teacher appeared to be doing was symbolically creating reality as she wished it to be, rather than accepting it as it was.* Another way of probing her technique is to ask the question, "What did the student learn by returning the shoes to the auditorium?" The answer to this query would not be found in any textbook on learning theory.

The student's reaction to the teacher's demand was to wait in the hall. We note that the boy was not causing difficulty in the hall. He was not running, shouting, or attracting attention, but simply demonstrating passive resistance. When the teacher discovered that the boy had not returned the shoes to the auditorium, she intervened actively and made sure that he carried out her direction. While the teacher won this particular battle, the boy returned to the classroom only to annoy and irritate his classmates.

What the boy was doing may well have been an illustration of the defense mechanism known as displacement. The boy was displacing the feelings of aggression that he had toward the teacher by directing them to his peers. Like most defense mechanisms it, in turn, created more problems for him and for the teacher. It was at this time that the teacher decided to put the boy under the shutter and pull the sliding cover down.

Once again it is interesting to speculate why the teacher chose this particular action as a way of solving the problem. Our guess is that when a problem becomes too intense for this teacher, her characteristic way of handling her anxiety is to deny the existence of her problem by attempting to remove it visually and psychologically.

Part two of the incident began with the teacher describing how shocked she was when she noticed that the boy had urinated on the floor and how sure she was that it was a deliberate act intended to humiliate her in front of the class. Let's examine her interpretation of the situation. Unfortunately, we are not told how long the boy had to stay in the shuttered locker. It might have been twenty to forty minutes. It is possible that the boy had to urinate but felt so threatened by his teacher that it seemed to him a better solution to urinate on the floor than to face the hostility he might encounter if he were to ask for permission to leave the room. Another tenable interpretation is that his act might have been another example of displacement (that is, the boy was expressing a strong desire to urinate on the teacher for humiliating him in front of his peers, but displaced his aggressive feelings by urinating on the floor).

Another potentially significant point is that the class laughed when they noticed the urine on the floor. This struck us as an unusual response for normally self-conscious, pre-adolescent children. A more typical response would have been one of shock or embarrassment, since the boy had violated an accepted norm of behavior. Since the class did laugh, it is our impression that the laughter was either an expression of the group's aggression toward the teacher, or a nervous expression of accumulated tension, or both.

The teacher, at this time, felt so anxious and threatened by the situation that she turned to authority for help. Unfortunately, the principal's comments were not only inappropriate to the situation but also provided the group with more ammunition to use against the teacher. *The assistant principal, in wanting the boy to mop up the urine and the teacher to forget the incident, again illustrated how many school problems are "solved" by denying their existence.* To us this seems particularly deplorable, because the assistant principal overlooked an opportunity to use constructively a reality situation that could have provided both teacher and child with an insight into why the circumstances had developed as they did.

The teacher accepted some responsibility for the incident, but said that she felt defeated by the way the assistant principal had behaved toward her in front of the class. Here is an interesting example of parallelism. The assistant principal had acted toward the teacher in the same manner that the teacher had acted toward the boy. In both cases, an authority figure berated and humiliated a subordinate person in front of a group, creating in the person feelings of inadequacy and loss of status. From the tone of the narrative it seems likely that the assistant principal, the teacher, and the student failed to recognize this important common event.

NICHOLAS J. LONG

HAROLD G. SHANE

*   *   *

We have here a beautiful example of punitive discipline that backfired with a vengeance. But perhaps more important is the fact that the teacher involved learned absolutely nothing from the entire affair. Whether we are teachers, parents, or administrators, it is important that we recognize a mistake when we make it. G. K. Chesterton wisely said, "The man who hasn't made a mistake hasn't made anything." The teacher in this case seems much more interested in saving face than in learning from her mistake. Face-saving and learning a lesson are, unfortunately, mutually exclusive.

The assistant principal made an equally glaring mistake when he attempted to discuss the incident publicly, thereby leaving the teacher with feelings of humiliation and defeat. As an administrator he failed to see or handle the surging emotions of the teacher that prevented her from learning what she had done wrong. The teacher is naturally preoccupied with her sense of failure and is therefore in no position to accept administrative lectures at such a moment.

To return to the core of the problem, just what did this teacher do wrong? First of all, is it necessary to make a production out of a ten-minute lateness accompanied by a reasonable explanation? If this student turns up in similar situations complete with alibi, it is then worth attention or investigation, but certainly the first offense merits nothing as severe and senseless as insisting that the student return his sneakers to where they do *not* belong. The student's lateness should not have been overlooked, but it should have been dealt with in proportion to the act itself.

A student who responds to discipline by standing and "doing nothing" right outside the classroom where he can easily be caught by the punishing agent, has already given a clue about himself that should be of value in understanding his behavior. A child who behaves in a way that guarantees his being caught is a child with very special problems. It is far more normal to hope to "get away" with one's misdemeanor. The student committed four misdeeds, each successive one more serious than its predecessor: (1) he came into class ten minutes late; (2) he did not follow the instructions to return the the gym shoes; (3) he annoyed the other children; and (4) he urinated on the floor of the shuttered cloakroom. He reacted with mounting tension to the teacher's growing anger. It always takes two to tango. A teacher who pursues a path of successive, backfiring failures provides us with a good example of a person who does not know when to cut his losses.

One cannot, and does not, expect a teacher to have the wisdom of Solomon, the brain of John Dewey, and the knowledge of Sigmund Freud. But a smattering of the less profound ideas of these three men might help a teacher to develop into an inspired and inspiring teacher. A teacher who is constantly punitive, unable to learn from mistakes, as well as unimaginative, had best be encouraged to switch to selling carpetsweepers.

Our concern, in descending order of importance, should be the student, the teacher, the assistant principal. Who should help the assistant principal see where he failed? Let us hope the principal is up to the job; otherwise nothing has been gained for any of the three participants.

ANN TAYLOR MOORE

*   *   *

The pupil, the teacher, and the assistant principal all seemed to be caught in a mental fog.

Of course, the boy was negligent in simply forgetting his shoes. He was disobedient in getting out of line to go back for his gym shoes. But be reasonable: had his mother told him to take good care of his property so that he would not lose anything? Was he caught in a conflict of authorities? Before we make a federal case of something, shouldn't we go through the forms of a "grand jury investigation"?

Why did the teacher become angry? Anger is a sign of insecurity. Must we make a mountain out of a molehill to prove that we are boss? Why on earth send the child back with the gym shoes? He had already been deprived of the joys of being in class for ten minutes in his anxiety to retrieve the shoes. Why waste more time?

Teacher, have a little empathy!

Why did the assistant principal correct the teacher in front of the class? This case has all the earmarks of petty authoritarianism exhibited by a constantly complaining, insecure teacher. But this does not excuse the assistant principal's behavior. The teacher should always be given a show of support, if only by saying, "Let me take this young man with me and we'll find out if he knows how to behave like a gentleman!" Then in a private conference with the teacher the supervisor should explain how a more reasonable approach would have solved the problem. I would have let her take the responsibility for getting rid of the urine.

Let us review the situation from an orientation of teacher-pupil cooperation instead of a series of battles in a semester-long war, battles that the teacher must win.

The establishment of rapport and the maintenance of discipline are not irreconcilable goals. A teacher can be genuinely sympathetic with the pupil and his problems and help him to solve them within the framework of the rule of the society within which they operate. A teacher must earn the right to the confidence and trust of children.

The boy might "know" that his request to go back for his shoes would have been rejected. He might have "known" that he would receive a long lecture on forgetting. If he had not known this, he could not have taken the chance of leaving and getting away with it. One step in breaking down his lack of confidence would have been for the teacher to express happiness that the gym shoes were found. She could have expressed surprise that the boy had slipped out of line. She could have expressed regret that the boy had missed so much of the class but suggested that with hard work maybe he could catch up. At the end of the period the boy could have been asked to remain for a little visit with the teacher about proper procedures to follow in school.

If the classroom atmosphere had been normal, the boy would not have been annoying others. There would have been no tension. One might ask, how was he annoying others? Was he simply trying to "find the place"? Or had he missed so much of the period by being gone so long on a double trip to the auditorium that he saw no point in trying? Or was he responding in a rebellious way to the correction he had received?

The conclusion was that the child was showing off and needed to be removed from the class. One can visualize the boy having a strong need to go to the rest room. Perhaps the need was reinforced by the tension and excitement of being excluded from the class. What is the history of exclusion in this class? It is the next step to being sent to the office? If he had knocked on the shutter to request permission to go to the rest room, how would the request have been received? So, what had he to lose by urinating on the floor?

We must remember pupils react to our actions. We should be above reacting to their actions.

If situations like this arose very often, the administrator would soon lose the teacher's respect. Pupils soon dominate teachers if there is a lack of administrative support. The administrator could have spoken to the teacher outside the classroom, asked the offending pupil to come to his office, and then called a custodian to clean the cloakroom. This would have saved a lot of confusion, which is upsetting and embarrassing to any group of children. (The pupils might have been laughing because they were embarrassed, not because they were engaged in some devious plot to undermine the authority and security of the teacher.)

WARREN W. NIXON

DISCUSSION QUESTIONS

1. What is the essential difference between discipline and punishment?
2. Assuming that it is best for teachers to handle simple disciplinary problems in their own classes, what might be the basic rule for deciding (a) what problems to handle in this manner rather than referring them to others and (b) what forms of discipline to use?
3. What is the proper rule of a school administrator in a pupil-teacher conflict (a) when the administrator thinks the pupil is wrong and (b) when he thinks the teacher is wrong?
4. How can a teacher enforce disciplinary rules in such a way as to minimize subsequent conflict between teacher and pupils?
5. How should a teacher act if she believes that she has made a mistake in disciplining a child?
6. What techniques can teachers use to avoid hasty, possibly incorrect interpretation of disciplinary crises?

4

HOW MUCH CAN ONE DO?

CRITICAL INCIDENT

Background

During my early years of teaching, after school had been in session for about a month, a mother brought her son, Karl, to my sixth-grade room. Karl was an only child and a big boy for his age. He had failed several times in the earlier grades; at the time of our meeting he was thirteen. He wore thick-lens glasses and squinted continually.

In Karl's presence, his mother told me of all the trouble he had caused, both in school and with law-enforcement authorities. She gave me her consent to "beat some sense" into him and to "make him learn." She had the idea that a private parochial school such as ours would serve somewhat as a "reform school." I informed her that this was not true. Then I proceeded to tell Karl in his mother's presence that I was sorry his mother had embarrassed him and that I was ignoring the information. I assured him that he was starting our school with a clean slate—it was up to him to keep it that way. I pledged my cooperation and urged him to take me into his confidence whenever any problems arose. His reaction was very favorable, and he indicated that he was anxious to get started in school.

Incident

For several weeks all went smoothly. Karl responded favorably to his new school environment. He was wholly accepted by the group. Although his class work left something to be desired, he seemed to be making an honest effort and was given credit for his attempt. However, on some days he would seem moody and disturbed. This mood affected his work and his behavior, but such days were few, and it did not seem a major problem to me. I resolved that I would wait for him to come to me if he had something to talk over.

One day a situation arose with Karl in which my authority was questioned in class. In no uncertain terms I let him know that it was about time that he recognized who was "the boss" in the classroom. He was embarrassed and didn't hide his defiance. He slammed his books into the desk and stalked from the room. The room was so arranged that he had to pass through a cloakroom at the back to get to the exit. I immediately rushed to "head him off." He was trapped, except for an open window in the cloakroom, which was on the second floor. When he saw his predicament, Karl exposed a sharp pencil-compass. He seemed undecided whether to jump from the window or rush me with the compass. In either case I felt he was "bluffing." I informed him that I did not intend to stop him if he wanted to "run out" in this situation, but I encouraged him to go back to his seat—we would talk it over later. He began to sob profusely. I tried to comfort him and asked him to compose himself while I returned to the classroom. The incident was dropped then and there, without further discussion. Afterwards I often wanted to speak with Karl, because I felt he needed a friendly adult to talk to, but I kept my distance and did not approach him.

Discussion

After Thanksgiving vacation, Karl did not return to school. Upon investigation I learned that the family had moved suddenly to another part of the state without leaving a forwarding address. Near the end of that year Karl wrote me a letter from the Bean Commonwealth Home for Boys, a reform school, thanking me for my patience with him and expressing his regret that he was no longer at our school.

My conscience bothers me when I think of Karl. I feel that I failed him. I waited for him to come to me with his problems, instead of arranging formal or informal talks to get at the root of his trouble. I never saw his mother again, and didn't even meet or ask him about his father. Our original relationship had been favorable, and I would have had every chance to gain his complete confidence if I had managed it properly. Wherever Karl is now, I hope he will forgive me for failing him.

Questions

1. Why do we teachers always resent having our authority questioned?
2. Should I have let him "run out"?
3. What effect might this incident have had on the rest of the class?
4. Karl accepted religious instruction. What part, if any, can religious instruction play in the guidance process?
5. What are teachers' obligations to disturbed children who behave in class but who evidently need guidance?

*   *   *

Although Karl's teacher is afraid that she failed the boy, and hence is full of remorse, the boy's thank-you letter is definite evidence to the contrary. We have here a teacher whose whole approach is evidently one of long-term tact and kindness; this accepting attitude, more than the specific details of what was done or not done in any one incident, made itself so clear to the boy that he wrote a letter of appreciation.

The teacher's understanding was evident from the initial interview with the rejecting mother. To explain that Karl was being given a chance to start with a completely clean slate was a healthy attitude to present, both to the boy and to the hostile parent. One cannot imagine a much better way to quiet the mother's belligerent accusations against her son and gain rapport with the boy at the same time.

The classroom incident is certainly understandable. Teachers are human beings with tempers, aggressions, and variable frustration-tolerances of their own. Further, a certain amount of healthy authority is absolutely imperative to maintain a smoothly operating class of lively youngsters with their own tempers, aggressions, and frustration-tolerances. Insecure or inadequate teachers probably fear a loss of classroom authority the most—and justifiably, for classes do get out of hand at times for some teachers—and all of us are sometimes insecure.

Actually, the other children in the class probably reacted well to the incident. Children have respect for adults who can manage things, and this teacher managed the episode without any stern, punitive aftermath. It is possible that in the eyes of his classmates the episode tended to stigmatize Karl to some degree as a troublemaker, but it is difficult to see how this incident could have been avoided or glossed over. Underemphasis of the incident was assuredly the kindest way to handle it. One minor criticism here: since the teacher had said to Karl that they would talk it over later, she might have followed through in a gentle way and exploited the opportunity for the more intimate friendship that she felt would help the boy.

Nevertheless a teacher must not feel too guilty about "letting down" specific children simply because so much more obviously needs to be done for them. From the chronology of the story—Karl entered one month late and left after Thanksgiving—we must assume that the teacher knew the boy only briefly. What is surprising is that Karl himself, apparently a rather inarticulate youngster, was so touched by a moment of rare kindness that he even wrote a letter of appreciation for it.

Teachers have obligations to whole classrooms of children. They must try to give fair, kind, and instructive help to all these children, if possible. Beyond this basic minimum, of course, the more help, within limits, the better. But if a child is behaving well within the teacher's own class or if he is in fact exceeding his past records of adjustment and accomplishment in school, as Karl was, the teacher has certainly fulfilled her primary responsibility to the child. A teacher who becomes deeply involved emotionally in the maladjustment of one or two of her pupils may tend to neglect the rest of the class and fall into the Squeaky Wheel Fallacy: the squeaky wheel gets all the oil and attention, the smoothly running machinery takes care of itself—or appears to.

In Karl's case, we cannot be sure that he necessarily wanted more direct attention from the teacher. The delightful new role of being "wholly accepted by the group" and praised for his accomplishments, such as they were, probably satisfied him at the time. But if he had stayed, more could and should have been done.

Surely some chance to talk or to invite friendly overtures after class, before class, or at the noon hour, would eventually have arisen, and would have indicated whether the boy felt a need for further attention and help, or whether the security of a warm and accepting class and adult were enough.

Very soon, some sort of direct contact with the home, simply to praise Karl's progress, would have been most desirable. If a regular system of parent-teacher conferences were customary in the school, so much the better. If not, a note or phone call from the principal or teacher indicating satisfaction with Karl's progress and praise for his gains could hardly alienate even the most hostile of parents, and just might lessen their antagonism to a problem child.

If Karl's adjustment remained reasonably satisfactory, intensive individual study by a school counselor or psychologist might not be called for—his previous episodes of misbehavior had undoubtedly made both Karl and his parents a little wary of too much attention. In many other circumstances, referral to the trained specialist is a teacher's safest and wisest answer to "What should I do for this disturbed child who behaves for me but who needs help badly?" Yet here, perhaps, other avenues should be tried first. One would certainly like to know more about that squint (what could the school nurse or doctor do to help?), about Karl's intelligence (why is he retarded in school?), and whether a big-for-his-age thirteen-year-old really belongs with a regular sixth grade. An individual intelligence test that did not depend on reading would show better whether he belongs in a regular or a special class for slow learners. Cumulative records from previous schools might give invaluable assistance in understanding the nature of his problems—for example, the nature of the home situation.

The more information and understanding the school can obtain about Karl through these and other channels and through the insights of his teachers, the more effectively the school can plan for his future. But when he remains in one school for such a short time; when he has at least one highly unsympathetic parent; when his life history has been one of maladjustment and delinquency; and when some unknown degree of visual and perhaps intellectual deficit is present, we must accept the nature of any single teacher's limitations. Hence to this teacher, not "J'accuse!" but instead "I salute you!" . . . for being sympathetic, optimistic, and sensitive to the possibilities inherent in such a youngster.

GRACE T. ALTUS

*   *   *

In this incident more is involved than Karl's one-time questioning of the teacher's authority. From the background description, Karl's past history contains the roots of problems so ingrained that his disturbing behavior mechanisms, arising out of the damaging experiences of his home environment, would be a long-term job for specialists who are skilled in dealing with such maladjustments.

Here I pose a question: Is it possible for a classroom teacher—or even highly skilled specialists—to effect considerable permanent change from the undesirable to the desirable in the behavior of a growing child, in cases like Karl's, while the child continues to remain in the environment that is the basic cause of the trouble? Sympathy, tact, understanding, and patience can relieve and reduce the problems, but can severe problems be removed or corrected while the environment remains the breeding place?

Karl was under a sympathetic teacher's care and guidance for *less than a dozen weeks*, and she was seemingly making progress in bringing Karl into harmonious relationship with himself and his school world. But was this progress based on extrinsic motivation or natural motivation? Could natural motivation—"the satisfaction inherent in doing good work for its own sake"—be used with a child of such damaged and maladjusted personality as Karl's? In her efforts to build up Karl's esteem and self-acceptance, was there developing a balanced sense of values or only a new self-confidence?

Prestige feelings were brought into play by whatever it was that prompted Karl's challenge of the teacher's authority at the given moment. It could have been a delayed, home-stimulated reaction, a false sense of confidence on his part, a desire to exhibit his new-felt importance to his classmates, or a temporary lapse of his control system for some other reason. Now the teacher, who had been serving as an ego supporter, a helper, a friend-in-need, must have felt momentarily a sense of rejection, futility, and a loss of face before the group. Perhaps unconsciously she felt there was ingratitude. The occurrence could have come at a time when previous situations had built up tensions, fatigue, or strain in the teacher. Even the best of master teachers are subject to these. Surprise at Karl's challenge could have influenced the teacher's reaction.

Once, however, the teacher had reacted by letting Karl know that she was in command and once his resulting defiant behavior was capably settled, the whole matter seemingly was closed until Karl moved away. Had he remained under this interested teacher's care for a sufficient length of time, the groundwork she had done might have produced a number of significant improvements. To say the least, in some areas Karl's problems would have been lessened. Certainly, if he had stayed in her classroom for the remainder of the year, it is most probable that he would not have ended up in a reform school.

Disturbing pupil-teacher clashes in a classroom make for uneasiness and feelings of insecurity on the part of the other pupils. The restoration *by the teacher involved* of an atmosphere of calmness, security, and pleasantness as rapidly as possible following a clash will not impair too greatly good pupil-teacher relationships, provided they do not occur often and provided fairness in settling issues is in evidence. Karl's teacher seems to have adequately performed her role with her class in this situation.

Has she failed Karl in the overall view? Would religious instruction have provided a basic guiding influence for Karl? What are a teacher's obligations to badly disturbed children? Our initial point, that the results of damaging home or environmental experiences make for long-term jobs for specialists skilled in dealing with such problems, is again apropos. Thus, I do not feel that Karl's teacher permanently failed him. I think she provided the one oasis of sympathy, understanding, and personal interest that Karl experienced. He indicated that he felt a loss of these in his letter to her from the reform school. As for not cultivating Karl's confidence in order to give him an outlet for his pent-up problems, is this not also a slow and time-consuming process? Usually, if a child sets the pace for this, the results are more satisfactory than if a teacher takes the initiative.

Religious instruction can prove most rewarding as a stabilizing influence for a troubled youngster provided the child is receptive and interested, and the instructor able, understanding, and skillful. Time is needed to prove the worth of both the confidante approach and that of religious instruction. In the case of Karl and his teacher, time was lacking.

The toll that such behavior problems in the classroom take of a teacher's time, strength, and effort is considerable. Even one child with severe and serious personal problems can impose a strain on a conscientious teacher who is seeking to give quality instruction and to work with pupils on the basis of individual needs. But the Karls need attention, too. They have become children with severe problems through no fault of their own. Here is an area of teaching for those endowed with an abundance of sympathy and understanding, who almost instinctively use humane approaches in dealing with crises, and who are dedicated to this type of work. It calls for the utmost in patience and skill. Whether accomplishment in these special cases is best achieved in homogeneous grouping or through the procedures of the regular classroom is apparently controversial. There seems to be much in favor of grouping children who are seriously maladjusted and placing them under the guidance and instruction of persons whose aptitudes, skill, and training qualify them for this work. Neglected they must not be, for of such are delinquents made.

MARY LOUISE BUTLER

*   *   *

The first thing the teacher might have noted was that the mother needed help and counseling. The teacher should have made an effort to get guidance for the entire family. She should have arranged for a private talk with the mother and gathered more background about the family. This would have enabled her to deal more wisely with the boy.

I believe the teacher erred in telling the boy that she was going to ignore the mother's remarks concerning his past delinquencies. Perhaps at this time she could have suggested some guidance for the boy from a professional source. It seems poor psychology for a teacher to tell a boy of thirteen that she will ignore his mother.

Nevertheless, this teacher eventually won the confidence and respect of Karl; his reactions toward her were favorable. The teacher neglected an opportunity to help Karl by not following through and inviting him to exchange experiences with her. Since she did not extend a definite invitation for a conference, Karl may have felt neglected or unwanted.

When Karl appeared to be friendly and receptive, the teacher should have tried to interest him in some craftwork, such as ceramics or painting, through which he might have released some of his emotional tensions. Situations could have been created through this kind of therapy for better rapport and for the exchange and release of confidences, which might have resulted in Karl's acceptance of guidance.

Karl was thirteen, and in an emotional as well as a physical stage of growing-up. He needed peer contacts and adult friends. He could have been guided to some youth organizations or to a part-time job. Either would have helped fill the vacant hours after school and given him a sense of belonging and security.

Some teachers and parents have strong desires for personal recognition from their peers or from their pupils or siblings. As they fear loss of prestige and respect, they bolster their own ego by imposing their authority upon others. Karl's mother no doubt was such an individual.

The normal child knows who is in authority, and respects the teacher's position. However, an emotionally disturbed child is not always aware of his acts of defiance. The teacher should be alert to this fact and be prepared to ignore or to give guidance or help at a moment's notice.

Sixth-grade pupils are very discerning, and they surely understood the teacher's position with regard to Karl's reactions. She lost no prestige with them for taking a firm stand with Karl. She would have gained Karl's admiration if she had not remarked that she was "the boss, and it was time he understood it." This remark was too similar to what he probably heard at home and must have lessened his respect for her.

The teacher was quite right to try to keep Karl from leaving the building and seems to have handled the difficult episode in the cloak room very competently. This incident might have been prevented if she had been alert to Karl's needs. She might have averted the entire scene if she had sensed his disturbance and had asked him to do a simple errand for her to divert his temporary destructive tendency.

She should have followed up this incident after it did develop by providing an opportunity to talk with him alone; perhaps she would have gained his complete confidence. This act might have been the opening of a new horizon for Karl. A thirteen-year-old boy cannot think straight when he is in a state of confusion. The teacher should have realized this and gone to him when he needed comfort instead of telling him she was the "boss." The fact that she did not even talk with him undoubtedly caused him to feel depressed and unloved, and presumably would make him bolder in his next disturbed state.

The fact that Karl enjoyed religious instruction seems to indicate that he would have accepted moral guidance from the teacher. The moral sense, or the conscience, must be guided and developed when the child is very young; otherwise it never flowers. Karl had missed this home guidance.

Karl's teacher had accepted him for himself alone. He must have felt a sense of security in her classroom and have appreciated her efforts, as is evidenced later by his letter to her. This teacher seems to have been a sincere and conscientious person with a well-developed sense of duty and responsibility. In her later years of teaching, she would likely have approached an incident of this kind with a more mature attitude and would have worked more decisively at the problem.

One thing that has been overlooked in this incident is the part that eye strain may have played in causing Karl to be so tense and to have nervous explosions. He wore thick-lens glasses, yet he squinted. There is no record that the teacher was in possession of information about Karl's eye disorder. The glasses evidently did not correct his visual difficulty. This alone could have caused him to be nervous and jumpy.

The teacher should have arranged for an eye examination through the school nurse or the principal. If other corrective glasses were needed, she would have helped locate some organization to provide the new lenses, if the parents could not pay for them.

The teacher's inexperience with special or handicapped children hindered her, as she was not aware of the possibility of physical strain produced by poor vision. She did not have sufficient understanding of how to handle emotionally disturbed children.

Loving kindness, firm counseling, better attention to the vision problem, and supervised recreation or a part-time job might have provided Karl with a sense of security in the school and in the community. Such a course of action might have saved Karl from the bitter experience of the reform school.

MALINDA D. GARTON

*   *   *

It is axiomatic to say that a teacher cannot know too much about a problem student if that student is to be helped to attain anything approaching a satisfactory adjustment. Karl's case underscores the truth in this tenet.

It is also a truism to say that in modifying the human personality, one attempts to build on the positive elements which are parts of the individual's existing personality pattern. That these common-sense dicta were not followed resulted in Karl's incarceration and a justifiable sense of failure on the part of the inexperienced teacher.

It is unfortunate for both that the very real if modest degree of rapport, so essential to any and all counseling, was not developed through more intimate acquaintance. Most teachers select two or three of their pupils during a given school year to whom they give concentrated personal and individualized attention with the aim of helping each to realize more of his potential. Usually, these "cases" are selected on the basis of need (the child's need, we should hope!), as well as the interest and talent of the teacher. That an auspicious beginning was inherent in the present case is indicated by the initial meeting wherein the mother's negative, destructive attitude was replaced by the teacher's positive, constructive one, and by the extended period in which Karl's role in the classroom was satisfactory. And, of course, the letter from the reform school indicates, however pathetically, that the boy too recognizes that he and his teacher were *sympático*. There existed just too little positive influence to counteract the negative.

To really be effective in helping such a misfit as Karl, the teacher must learn as much as possible, without prying, about what has made him the person he has become. In order to learn what means of control, of influence, of motivation, of encouragement are most likely to result in the kind of modified behavior sought, we must know what has been successful and unsuccessful in his past. As objectively as can be determined, what are the limits of his potential, particularly intellectual and social? What is the familial background he brings with him? What are his attitudes regarding his background, himself in it, and his role in the classroom and in society? Which of these are already positive, to be stressed, enhanced, developed by his teacher? And from this acquired knowledge of not just who is Karl but who Karl is, we should be able to ascertain with greater accuracy what might influence him positively and, conversely, what would constitute a threat to him.

Although strict, rigid, and even harsh discipline occasionally effects the desired result of more socially acceptable behavior, such a punitive philosophy is being questioned in more and more cases. In Karl's situation, this method (apparently subscribed to by the parental figure) failed to deter him sufficiently to keep him out of reform school. It is noteworthy, also, that his animal reaction to being "cornered" in the cloakroom gave way to remorse and tacit acceptance of his own transgression of acceptable classroom behavior. It is especially significant that this realization came as a result of the teacher's calm, rational explanation of the situation, including a suggestion for subsequent positive action. Here also, in a highly permissive setting, speaking relative to Karl's experiential background, there still existed firm limits as to what was and what was not acceptable conduct. These limits must be applied to the Karls of our classrooms—for their sakes, but equally so for the onlookers, the remainder of the classroom.

It is to the teacher's credit that she did not interpret Karl's behavior as refuting her authority on a personal basis. Who among us, particularly during our first teaching experiences, has not felt insecurity in our ability to meet a situation to the point that we allowed it to become a severe personal threat?

Unfortunately, the teacher in Karl's case let the incident of misbehavior rest, rather than using it to build a closer relationship, a relationship unmarred as others had been by fear of threat or retaliation, a relationship in which the boy's ideas and fears might be stated, discussed, and dealt with in an atmosphere of acceptance and maturation. All sixth graders, especially "repeaters" and "troublemakers," need such opportunities. Indeed, don't we all? Karl's teacher could have used the boy's amenity to religious instruction as an invaluable aid to better attitude-building, a tack that is wholly justifiable in a private parochial school and, modified by the elimination of the sectarian concepts, also sound procedure in the public schools.

But, of course, what we as teachers can do for and with the individual psyches we find confronting us in our classrooms must, perforce, be limited by the fact that our function is primarily and basically an educative one, in a fairly narrow sense, and one very often of necessity fulfilled on a group basis. For those disturbed members of our group who obviously need much guidance of a highly professional caliber, we do only what we can to provide a classroom atmosphere most conducive to learning, to see to it that rules and limitations are clear and understandable to the age-group we instruct, and to insure that their application is at all times reasonable, consistent, and just. For the more severe problems, some sort of referral agency must exist in all but the most extreme and isolated instances; these should, of course, be utilized for those whose needs are greatest.

WILLIS B. INMAN

*   *   *

To answer first the specific questions posed: The teacher's authority is indispensable to education, especially in a group situation. Past attempts to conduct classroom education without the teacher's authority have been flagrant failures. We should understand, however, that young people are not always inclined to accept our authority with complete submission and at the expense of their own impulses. Hence we should not *resent* their rebelling against us occasionally, but we should reduce such occasions to a minimum by the wise use of our authority. Yet many of us do resent having our authority questioned because, being influenced by habit, we expect perfection in everything including the acceptance of our position by the students. The resentment results from our inborn habit of perfectionism, of which we should break ourselves.

The teacher definitely should have not let Karl "run out." The trauma would have been deeper for the boy if he had run out and had perhaps gotten into bigger trouble.

If the class was typical and the situation similar to other classroom situations, the effect of the incident should have been slight. Such incidents are fairly common.

The influence of religious instruction is subtle, pervasive, and difficult to measure directly. In a parochial school, religious instruction can play a role in the guidance process, and often does. However, the use of religious concepts in guidance is a difficult process, requiring expert handling. As for Karl, it would appear that he was so completely mismanaged by his own parents, or at least by his mother, that the teacher didn't have much chance. We should always try to be kind and understanding, but we should be conscious of the fact that a teacher's influence is not the only one to which the child is exposed. I doubt that in this case the teacher's influence would have been decisive. Therefore, I believe that the teacher need not let her conscience bother her. The teacher says, "I waited for him to come to me with his problems, instead of arranging formal or informal talks to get at the root of the trouble." The difficulties of such talks might have been greater than she seems to assume. She might have discovered that parental attitudes were blocking any possibility of psychological adjustment. Certainly the mother's instruction "to beat some sense into him" and the later assignment to a reform school indicate that the trouble was of major proportions. I believe that the case was too unmanageable and too far advanced for the teacher to have had a great deal of influence regardless of the affectionate expression received from the youngster after his departure from the school.

"What are a teacher's obligations to disturbed children who behave in class but who evidently need guidance?" This is, in my view, a most significant question. The answer is of great importance to our school system. It is one with which not only teachers but school officials and board members should occupy themselves, because disturbed children deeply affect the effectiveness of the school system.

In an average class, which is supposed to contain a majority of normal children (children without any major emotional disturbances), the first obligation of the teacher is to give the best possible instruction in the subject matter at hand to this majority of normal children. If it were otherwise, if a minority of disturbed children could interfere with this major obligation, the majority would be shortchanged in their education and such a condition would certainly not be in harmony with the democratic premises and promises of education.

However, a few disturbed children are likely to be present in many classrooms; and here it should be pointed out that the borderlines of definition are fluid because sometimes predominantly normal children behave as if they were disturbed while many disturbed children often behave quite normally. To handle such cases properly the teacher should have intelligence, patience, common sense, tact, and an understanding of psychology. If a child is absolutely unmanageable, a psychologist should be consulted and the child, if possible, transferred to a special class. In most schools if the child is moderately difficult to manage, the teacher will be left to deal with the child. But the consulting services of a psychologist may be available. At any rate, although the teacher does have a certain obligation in such cases, it should never become the major obligation.

I doubt that the American school system will ever cope adequately with the problem of the disturbed children in school unless more community pressure is brought to bear upon parents to cooperate with the school authorities and do their share in helping the children. Unfortunately, many parents are irresponsible with respect to the public schools. This need not be so. Much improvement would result if it were an accepted and generally supported community standard that the parents feel themselves responsible for maximum cooperation with teachers and administrators and that they realize that it is not fair to unload the disturbed child on the school.

Our age has lost a sense for standards. To be "disturbed" is nothing to be ashamed of. We know that a disturbed child is often the helpless victim of his condition. To pamper him and relieve him of a sense of responsibility is likely to increase the disturbance. The same thing goes for the parents. Normal behavior should always be upheld as desirable behavior, a model for all. Such an attitude will actually help the disturbed person to find stability.

PAUL R. NEUREITER

*   *   *

Karl had failed the lower grades, he had a physical defect, he had been in trouble both in and out of school, he had been before law enforcement agencies, and he had a mother who did not understand simple principles of human nature. With this background, environment, and record, Karl knew he was a failure when he reported to the school.

The teacher had pledged cooperation and had urged Karl to take her into his confidence, but at the same time told him that it was up to him to succeed. But the teacher failed to give help after promising and instilling hope. Karl had no one to ask for help except his teacher. He needed a lot of help. With the best guidance, and much love, tenderness, and understanding, he would still have had a rough road to travel for a long period of time before noticeable and stable changes in behavior could be expected. Karl was in this school and under this teacher for only a fraction of the school year. Lasting changes in personality could not be expected in this short period.

The teacher took a giant stride forward toward becoming a great teacher when she examined and evaluated her experiences with Karl and admitted to herself that she had not met the situation correctly. Perhaps, for the first time, this teacher began to see the needs of the other students within her group. Perhaps she began to realize that there is much more to teaching than imparting facts and knowledge to students. Perhaps she began to understand that she needed help in solving problems within her own group.

When teachers do not know what to do, it is time to ask for help. If this teacher had recognized the seriousness of this student's problems, she would have gone to her principal or supervisor and alerted him to the potential drop-out who had been enrolled.

What might have happened if the attention of the entire administrative staff had been focused on Karl and his problems?

1. Karl might have been placed in a different section, with a teacher who had a deep understanding of students with emotional problems.
2. The school or public psychologist and health nurse might have been called in an attempt to help the boy.
3. Karl might have been placed in a special class for handicapped or retarded children. Or, he might have been advanced to a higher grade, where he would be closer to his own social group.
4. If the principal had been alerted, he might have asked the staff to give an extra smile to the boy, to stop and talk to him when they met him in the hall. He might have asked the coach to help Karl by making him a waterboy or bat boy, or having him check out baskets from the locker room or some similar simple but prestigeful task.
5. An understanding church officer might have been induced to try to help solve Karl's problems; Karl might have been placed in a church group's after-school youth activities.

Teachers should not take problems to principals and supervisors if they know how to handle them without help. But when they do not know what to do, they should first seek assistance and advice from other teachers. If that fails or is not forthcoming, the principal should be consulted. Every attempt should be made to help the student before giving up on him or evading the problem. Teachers must sometimes give up on students and catalog them as unsolvable problems. Principals have to give up, too. But every person's whole bag of tricks should be tried first.

Once a student is given up as lost and unsalvageable, the teacher or administrator must make a decision or a clean break and leave the problem behind him. Guilt feelings cannot be permitted to remain or they will undermine the efficiency and skill of that teacher. Everyone hates to admit that he cannot solve a student problem and to relegate a student to the derelict pile, but there remain a great number of other students needing help. One's efforts and time should be devoted to those who can benefit by them.

Many teachers have permitted students to "run out" of class or school. Sometimes it is the only answer to an immediate problem. After the student has walked out of class, steps should be taken to return him to the class. Major difficulties between student and teacher should be solved outside the classroom. When a student runs out, he is usually telling the teacher, "I need help." He may actually be saying, "Please help me."

Karl needed help. He felt he was not becoming a member of the class or group. He asked for help when he showed aggression. He was not allowed to save his own face or to reinstate himself. He was finally sent to a reformatory, not because of one teacher but because of the negligence, ignorance, or lack of intelligence of many people.

For a great many students such as Karl, the classroom teacher is the only person left in the world to save them from their own destruction. There are many, many ways to help these disturbed children. But schools are crowded and understaffed. Teachers are often overloaded. Communities will not always provide requested funds. And some communities are more interested in winning ball games than in producing desirable citizens. Consequently, students like Karl continue to come and go, often becoming liabilities to society and thereby filling our reformatories, penitentiaries, and state hospitals. These future inmates can be recognized, identified, and often salvaged.

Schools can do the job when the community desires them to.

ROBERT E. PRICE

DISCUSSION QUESTIONS

1. What is the essential nature of the relationship between teachers and parents? Discuss this in light of some of these following ideas: is a teacher a surrogate mother; does the teacher serve both the child and the family; does a teacher maintain a professional rule in relation to parents as well as to children?

2. Teachers generally spend more time with problem children than with normal children. Do you believe that this is a social problem in terms of its effect on normal, well-behaved children?
3. Under what circumstances, if any, should a teacher counteract the influence of home environment?
4. Under what circumstances are teachers justified in providing counseling for parents in reference to the treatment of children?
5. If a teacher herself cannot handle a problem that involves counseling, what are the advantages and disadvantages of: (a) going up the line to other teachers, supervisors, principals, (b) going to the top and "working down," (c) going directly to the counselors or to other specialists.

SUGGESTED READINGS—PART I

Books

Gould, G. and G. A. Yoakam, *The Teacher and His Work*. New York: The Ronald Press Company, 1954.

Kearney, N. C., *A Teacher's Professional Guide*. Englewood Cliffs, N.J.: Prentice-Hall, Inc., 1958.

Klausmeier, H. J., *Teaching in the Elementary School*. New York: Harper & Row, Publishers, 1956.

Macomber, F. G., *Principles of Teaching in the Elementary School*. New York: American Book Company, 1954.

Redl, F., and D. Wineman, *The Aggressive Child*. Glencoe, Illinois: Free Press of Glencoe, Inc., 1957.

Articles

Adams, J. C., "Teaching the Problem Child in Your Class," *Education* 82 (September, 1961), 46-49.

Bollinger, R. V., "The Social Impact of the Teacher on the Pupil," *Journal of Experimental Teaching* 13 (June, 1945), 153-73.

Brickman, M., "Alice in Thunderland or, the First Days of a New Teacher," *National Education Association Journal* 46 (November, 1957), 517-19.

Cobb, M. M., "Some Suggestions for Preventing Discipline Problems," *High Points* 35 (October, 1953), 1213.

DeLong, A. R. and G. C. DeLong, "How Can You Teach so Many?" *Michigan Education Journal* 32 (February, 1955), 258+.

Gillenwater, V. W., "Problem Child or Problem Teacher?" *Arizona Teacher* 42 (March, 1954), 12.

Long, N. J., and R. G. Newman, "Teachers Handling of Children in Conflict," *Indiana University School Education Bulletin* 37 (July, 1961), 1-62.

McCullar, B., "Your Students Are Watching You," *Journal of the National Education Association* 47 (September, 1958), 427.

Ohles, J. F., "Democracy in the Classroom: The Broad View," *Social Studies* 53 (April, 1962), 144-48.

Resnick, J., "Classroom Maladjustment Can Be Reduced," *Educational Administrations and Supervision* 40 (December, 1954), 489-93.

Rice, H. M., and C. W. Johnson, "What Practices Have Proven Most Helpful in Developing Better Student-Teacher Relationships?" Summary of presentations, *National Association of Secondary School Principals* 35 (April, 1954), 283-84.

Stouffer, G. A., "Behavior Problems of Children," *Mental Hygiene* 36 (April, 1952), 271-85.

Treanor, J. H., "Your Classroom Reflects You," *Clearing House* 31 (May, 1957), 271-85.

II

PROBLEMS OF SOCIAL ADJUSTMENT

II

PROBLEMS OF SOCIAL ADJUSTMENT

5

THE MOTHER SURROGATE

CRITICAL INCIDENT

Background

Mary Ross was in my first-grade room last year and was an active and delightful contributor to the group. She frequently spoke of her family, particularly of her younger sister, Fern. Mary told me at the end of the school year that she hoped Fern would be in my room the following year.

When school began this year I learned that Mrs. Ross had been killed in an automobile accident a few weeks before. I hoped Fern would be assigned to my room so that I could be of some help in her adjustments to school. When Mr. Ross registered the children, he did request that Fern be placed in my room. The request was granted.

During the first days of school Fern did not mention the fact that her mother was dead, and of course, neither did I. As Fern became more sure of her relationship to me, she began to talk with me about the accident. One day when the children were engaged in an art activity, she came up and showed me the picture she had drawn—a group picture of her family, including her mother. As she explained what everyone in the picture was doing, she said, "Mommy is doing the dishes, but she doesn't really do the dishes anymore, because she's dead, isn't she?" I told her, "Yes, she is dead." After this initial conversation, Fern came to me frequently to say such things as, "My

Mommy died in a car, didn't she?" and once, "I don't think that it was very nice of Mommy to leave Mary and Randy and me."

The other children were not aware that Fern's mother was dead; her conversation about it always took place when we were alone. One day, however, I came into my room to find Fern and a classmate, David, engaged in a heated argument. "My Mommy is, too, dead," she said, and David replied, "Don't be silly, everyone has a Mommy." I talked with them and explained that Fern had a mother, just like everyone else, but that her mother was not here anymore because she had died in a car. This ended the argument, but word began to spread to the other children, and Fern began to be able to talk more freely with them about her mother's death.

By this time six weeks of school had gone by, and Fern was having a difficult time with her work. She was left-handed, which may have contributed to her reversal of letters and numbers, but I felt that she was also inclined to use her helplessness to get my attention. She often crawled into my lap and hung on for dear life. On occasion she talked "baby talk." She demanded help from me with every new activity. When she demanded my help without waiting her turn I did not give it, so rather than wait for my assistance, she gradually began to figure out some of the problems for herself. I felt that some progress was being made.

Incident

The mothers of the first graders were having a planning meeting preliminary to the annual spring program for the primary grades. I came into the room on the morning of the meeting to find Fern in tears. I tried to comfort her, but she was crying so hard that I could not understand what was bothering her. The other children did not seem to know either, so I told her that I would leave her alone for a little while, but that when she felt better, if she wanted to talk with me, we would try to solve her problem.

She stopped crying soon. In about twenty minutes she came and asked if we could talk. I asked her what was bothering her, and she replied "I haven't got a Mommy to go to the meeting and I won't get to be in the program now." I told her that it was not necessary for her mother to be there for her to be in the program. I assured her that she would not be the only child whose mother could not come; some of the mothers worked or had little children to take care of at home. Fern was somewhat comforted, but she said, "I won't have a costume like the other kids because my Daddy can't make it, and he won't know what kind to buy." I asked Fern how she would like me to help her, and she replied immediately, "I want you to be my Mommy." I said, "I can't really be your mother, but I will go to the meeting and find out about the costumes and see that you have one. I will do the things for you that your mother would do if she were here. Will that be all right?" Fern said "Yes, you can be my pretend Mommy."

The costume was created, and the program went well.

Discussion

Fern is now doing very well in her work and is liked by all the other children. She realizes that I am not her mother, but she feels confident that I will fulfill the duties of a mother when she needs this service in order to be on an equal footing with the other children.

I feel that as teachers we need to be as concerned with the emotional growth of our children as we are with their intellectual growth. In fact, I would say that we need to be more concerned with the former. Fern was suffering a great deal and felt that her status was at stake. She had needs and recognized them, and I feel strongly that it is a major part of my job to recognize these needs and fulfill them whenever possible. Perhaps I might be criticized for helping to create a fantasy in Fern's mind, but I would counter this by saying that it would be much more serious for me to refuse to meet her emotional needs. My job now is to move her on to the next level of adjustment.

Questions

1. Did I, as a teacher, give in to my emotions and transgress the bounds of classroom ethics?

2. Did I do Fern more harm than good in protecting her from the reality of her mother's death, thereby not helping her to admit and adjust to the loss of her mother?

3. What should be the next step toward making Fern more independent?

4. How important can the mastery of subject matter be if the individual is not equipped emotionally to utilize knowledge?

*   *   *

This case suggests several important principles in working with school children. The first principle is that there is a wide variation in the attractiveness or appeal that children have for teachers and other adults. Some children, like Fern in this incident, are extremely appealing because of their age, their sex, or their circumstances. Fern, a first-grade girl who has lost her mother in a tragic accident, has a tremendous appeal for the average teacher. This does not mean that she is not in need of help. It does mean that because of her attractiveness she is more likely to get it than a less appealing youngster. The defiant, hostile teen-ager with a duck-tail haircut and a leather jacket may be equally in need of help, but he will be much less likely to receive it.

The second principle is that this teacher, while identifying strongly with this girl and showing considerable interest in helping her, is still mindful of the fact that the girl will have to live in a social environment to become a well-adjusted person. Fern would have made the teacher her obedient and willing slave if the teacher had allowed this. She was able to set limits on this girl's appeal for special consideration. It was a necessary part of her social and emotional growth that she learn to wait her turn.

When Fern feared that she would not be able to participate in the program or have a costume because she did not have a mother, the teacher dealt effectively with the situation. She first helped the girl to face reality by explaining that she could not really be her mother, and at the same time she agreed to take on some of the functions of a mother. The teacher agreed to take the role of "pretend mommy," and this is not unrealistic. She could perform many of the functions of a mother for this girl.

The teacher asks whether or not she gave in to her emotions and transgressed the bounds of classroom ethics, implying that the teacher who lets her emotions influence her behavior is unethical. I am sure no teacher in the world could pass *this* ethics test! Sympathy and understanding of children require some emotional involvement on the part of the teacher. Emotions, such as love and anger, are not in and of themselves bad. The danger comes only in the way in which they are expressed, and in what is done as a result of these emotions. In this case the teacher acted with appropriate restraint, and the result is a happier child.

The teacher asks whether or not she did Fern harm in helping her not admit and adjust to the loss of her mother. It is rather clear, as the teacher implies in the discussion, that she has helped this girl both to admit the loss of her mother and to adjust to it. Adjusting to the loss of her mother will take a long time and will require that someone fill, at least partially, the gap that was left in this girl's life when her mother died.

What should be the next step in making Fern more independent? A child of six or seven cannot be pushed too fast or too far toward independence of adults. She has a right to be dependent, and the effort should be made to see that she has someone on whom to be dependent. Next year and in ensuing years she should be placed with teachers who will continue to meet her affectional and dependency needs, while helping her to face reality in a supportive atmosphere.

What about the importance of mastering subject matter if the child is not emotionally ready? The mastery of subject matter, including the teaching of essential skills and understandings, is still (and should be) the primary function of the school. If emotional problems did not interfere with a child's learning ability, school personnel would be on shaky ground in concerning themselves with a child's emotional needs. The objective of a school is to develop a *learning child*. Helping a child to emotional health is a step toward this objective.

ORVAL G. JOHNSON

*　　*　　*

In American culture the mention of death is generally greeted by an embarrassed silence. We have not educated nor have we prepared either the young or the old for its inevitable appearance. Consequent to this, the occurrence of death in a family may be a traumatic affair—especially for the young—who not only may never have been informed about it but may well have been misinformed. For example, if the head of the family has died, the child may be told, "Daddy's gone away for a long time and is not coming back." Is it any wonder, then, that children cry and are afraid and tremulous when the remaining parent tells the child to be good while he or she is away? Although it is true that death has been made more familiar by means of television (even though the motivation is not education), the occurrence of death happens to the "bad guys" and this again indirectly fixates in the child's mind the idea of his immortality. The circumstances described in the present incident concerning death are somewhat analogous to a situation that recently confronted the writer. Therefore his reaction is both subjective as a parent, and objective as a psychologist.

For a child about the age of Fern, the turmoil and upset at home may be quite disturbing, and the only stable factor in her perceived environment that might give her comfort may be the school and the teacher. The latter has in fact (assuming the teacher is a female) become a literal mother-surrogate. Elementary teachers are fully aware of the fact that children frequently call them "Mother" by "mistake." The responsibility of the teacher in a situation such as that described makes her job, as is so often the case, more than just teaching. She has now become a mother-figure, a difficult but much needed role, especially if there is not an older sister, grandmother, or housekeeper at home.

My reaction to the case is that the teacher behaved commendably. She allowed the child to abreact, one phase admittedly, but an important phase, which permitted the child to "get off her chest" the fact of her mother's death. The teacher did not hurry this but allowed it to occur when rapport had been established and the child was "sure of her relationship." As a result of such a situation Fern began "to be able to talk more freely" with other children about her mother's death. It should be noted also that the teacher avoided creating overdependency, by legitimately refusing her help at times. Overdependency is admittedly a problem that exists with all children, but it might conceivably have existed in more acute form with Fern Ross. In her discussion Fern's teacher raised the question of whether or not she had created a "fantasy" in the child's mind. It is difficult to see in what sense this was feared. In the first place fantasy per se may be creative and serve a purpose. Even supposing it was uniformly negative, it strongly appears that rather than having created a fantasy, the teacher in fact filled a vacuum of an emotional need that the child felt and that the surviving father could not fulfill.

With regard to the first question, I would merely say that the "classroom ethics" referred to would be rather peculiar, to say the least, if anything that this teacher did transgressed them.

The second question about whether she did any harm in not allowing Fern to admit to the loss of her mother again is rather puzzling because the teacher in no way encouraged the child to deny that her mother had died in a car accident. If she had done this, it would obviously have been an error and could be thought of as constituting overprotection of the child and in effect denying reality. But, in my opinion, all that is indicated is that the teacher facilitated the adjustment of Fern to the death of her mother.

The third question poses the problem of what can be done to make the child more independent. This, in my opinion, is a problem that *every* teacher faces with *every* child, and although it is true that this problem may have existed to a greater degree with Fern, I do not believe that at present her problem is more or less severe than that of any other child in the class—thanks to an insightful teacher.

The final question raised poses in effect the question of the relationship between emotion and subject matter. This is a large question which cannot be discussed satisfactorily here, except to say that the interactive nature of emotions and intelligence is such that what affects one, affects the other.

My over-all reaction to this "critical incident" is that the teacher acted in a helpful and insightful way. Her actions would have or should have incurred the gratitude of the surviving parent and helped in a situation for which the child was not culturally prepared.

F. L. MARCUSE

*　*　*

The teacher involved in this incident showed remarkable sensitivity in meeting the emotional needs of this child. Only an understanding teacher with much insight into the situation could permit herself to become, in a sense, a mother-substitute, and, at the same time, set the limits so necessary to avoid the obvious dangers of such a relationship. Too sympathetic and pitying an attitude might very well have adversely affected the entire classroom climate, as well as reducing Fern to a complete state of dependency. Rather, this teacher's warmth and support not only gave the child the security and confidence that she lost at the death of her mother, but also created an accepting atmosphere within the classroom as well.

The teacher asks whether she transgressed the bounds of classroom ethics by giving in to her emotions. In the opinion of this writer, this was not a matter of the teacher's having given into her own emotions, even though she undoubtedly felt deeply involved emotionally. Rather, it would appear that she recognized the extreme emotional distress of her student and endeavored temporarily to take the dead mother's place during this difficult period of adjustment for the child.

Apparently the teacher feels that her actions may have prevented Fern's accepting the loss of her mother and consequently affected her acceptance of the reality of the whole situation. On the contrary, Fern's statement to the effect that the teacher is a "pretend mommy" would indicate that she had definitely accepted the loss of her mother and was adjusting to this loss. Knowing that the teacher would act as a substitute mother undoubtedly gave her the courage to accept things as they were.

What should be the next step in making Fern more independent? Certainly of tremendous importance is that she be placed again with a warm and accepting teacher, one who will be sympathetic and give her constructive individual attention to help her maintain the status in the class that she has attained. Another important factor is that she be kept with the same classmates from whom she has gained acceptance and with whom she feels secure.

In this case it would seem that the prime consideration is not how important subject-matter mastery is if the individual is not equipped to utilize the material, but rather this: Is subject-matter mastery even possible in the face of deep emotional disturbance? The time has come when the schools must recognize severe learning disabilities for what they are— symptoms of emotional disturbance. Unless a child feels accepted and emotionally secure in the school environment, unless he gets the attention and support he needs from the teacher, he will not learn what he is ex- pected to learn. Obviously at the beginning of the school year Fern was seriously enough disturbed that her learning was affected. By helping to remove her emotional conflicts, the teacher helped to release her energies for learning.

We must not lose sight of the fact that the main objective of the school is the development of a well-integrated child—one who is both successful in learning and effective in his social relationships. To achieve this goal, we cannot afford to overlook the emotional development of the child, for without emotional security, neither learning nor social adjustment is possible.

ROBERTA M. MOLTMANN

*   *   *

Superficial examination of the teacher's dealing with the described incident could easily lead to agreement with her handling of it. As a matter of fact, the teacher herself seems well satisfied and emphasizes her excellent results. What she professes to be concerned about is the future handling of the case, how to move Fern in "to the next level of adjustment." This concern, and still more the questions that she formulates, give the im- pression that realistically she feels somewhat unsure and uncomfortable when called upon to play the role of Fern's "pretend mommy."

It seems to me that the teacher does not penetrate to the core of the problem: she does not have a well-defined concept of the "role of the teacher" versus the "role of the mother." Doubtless the teacher "needs to be concerned with the emotional growth of children," but what is her part in such growth? A teacher's basic task is to develop in the pupil the skills, attitudes, and knowledge that will enable him later on to do his part as a useful member of human society. Within the framework of this task, emotional problems need proper consideration and handling.

The role of the mother is quite different. Based on a unique relation- ship, it is of such a nature that it cannot be completely recreated. The mother, too, prepares her children for their future, but she does it less through instruction than through encouraging their identification with herself and their father. She is the ever-ready standby of the growing child, continuously adapting her support, her discipline, and her influence to the different age levels of her child. She continues until the child gradually reaches a stage of maturity that makes her continuous support unnecessary. The relationship will continue to be close and warm, but it will have a different character. Mother and child will meet on approximately equal levels of maturity. They will enjoy each other's company, share their interests, their enjoyments, their concerns. The role of the teacher is usually a temporary one and played—in the course of the school years—by many different teacher personalities. A teacher who establishes a very close emotional tie with a student does it often to fulfill her own personal, emotional need; it may jeopardize her effectiveness as a teacher and cause confusion in the student.

In the case of Fern, it seems that the teacher felt strongly challenged by the death of Fern's mother. In the beginning it seems the girl made as good an adjustment as could be expected. Her remark, ". . . but she does not really do the dishes because she is dead . . . ," and similar remarks show how the little girl tried to work out her problem. The dependency and the infantile behavior that she displayed were not necessarily related to the experienced traumatic loss. It is quite likely that the same symptoms would have occurred had her mother been alive. The teacher handled them skillfully but missed the excellent chance they offered to discuss the child's difficulties with her family. Here is an important point: an understanding teacher who is keenly aware of the child's need for a mother-figure could be instrumental in providing for the fulfillment of this need. A discussion with the father could have led to a clarification regarding the child's new social setting: Who was now caring for the physical and emotional needs of the family? Who supervised the children? Whether it was a relative or a housekeeper, she was the person who should have taken on the role of the mother. Tactful counseling by a teacher who has the restraint not to get into the act herself will help to establish the right relationship between the child and her new mother-figure. If this had been accomplished, the described incident would hardly have occurred, since the new mother-figure would have attended the mother-meetings. As it was, Fern manipulated the teacher into playing a role that could necessarily only be a "pretend" role; the result was that she had no real mother, but also no real teacher.

The teacher is rightfully concerned about her possibly having "transgressed the bounds of classroom ethics." There are certainly in every group of children some who suffer from conflicts, often unknown even to the very observing teacher. Blinded to reality, captives of their "private world," they will perceive the teacher's attitude toward Fern only as partiality. It will confirm their feeling that this world is a place of bitterness and unjustice.

The answers to the other "questions" are not too difficult, it seems to me, if one keeps a well-confined concept of the teacher's role in mind. It would possibly harm the child if her adjustment to the loss of her mother were delayed through her teacher's handling. The best help the teacher could render might well consist, as mentioned above, of skillful counseling with the family and a new mother-figure. It does not seem to be necessary that the teacher use some special measures to foster Fern's independence. Since the girl had shown a strong tendency to manipulate the teacher, it might be necessary that the teacher observe her own responses very carefully in order to be able to exercise the needed restraint. Every teacher knows that emotional upset blocks achievement. In such cases, it seems rather futile to force a child to fulfill all academic requirements. On the other hand, success experience has a very positive effect on any disturbed person, young or old, and the understanding teacher will not overlook the right moment when the child is ready for work.

In summary, one might say that no serious harm was done to Fern by the way her teacher handled her problem. A more constructive and far-reaching approach would have been found in the teacher's helping the child and the family toward establishing a good relationship with a new mother-figure, and in filling herself no other role but that of teacher.

REGINE SEIDLER

DISCUSSION QUESTIONS—INCIDENT 5

1. This incident is an example of a teacher going beyond the usual limits of the teacher-role. Although any person will feel sympathy with a child who has a problem, and will try to help, the question arises about the short- and long-term effects of a teacher's spending extra time in a special relationship to a child. What are some general guide lines for establishing the limits on such special relationships.
2. Can a teacher legitimately deny help to school children who request it? What are some general rules (that is, never do for a child what he can do for himself) to guide teachers in such situations?
3. Is subject-matter learning possible in the face of emotional disturbance? What evidence (experimental, subjective, theoretic, practical) is there, pro and con, on this issue?
4. Is your concept of a teacher-role, strictly adhered to, that of a cold and disinterested person? Is keeping to the teacher-role and not lapsing into the mother-role usually wise?

6

"I REALLY LIKE YOU"

CRITICAL INCIDENT

Background

       Phil, one of my sixth graders, tried my patience to the limit every day. He seemed to do everything in his power to irritate me. One minute he would be slumped so low at his desk that only his head showed above the desk top. The next minute he would be sending notes to someone, drawing instead of studying, or throwing paper over three or four heads to see if he could hit the wastebasket. During class discussions he would make funny remarks or odd noises. He was well liked by his classmates and enjoyed a reputation as an excellent ballplayer and pitcher. He was an average student, usually doing his work in a rather careless manner. He had one younger sister several grades behind him in school.

    One day Phil's behavior was so irritating that I became very angry with him. During the afternoon he had been out of his seat countless times and had given sarcastic answers to my questions. At last I threatened him with a trip to the office if he didn't behave. He was angry at first, then sullen, but he didn't leave his desk again. Nevertheless he would not participate in any of the class activities. He sat and pouted for the rest of the day.

    As I was coming down the stairs at dismissal, I could see that he was still angry at me. I felt unhappy about the way things had happened, so I decided to try to patch up our differences.

Incident

We talked for a minute about his behavior, but we didn't make much progress toward an understanding. Then an idea popped into my head, and I asked if he thought I liked him. This startled him; he turned away. When he didn't answer I asked him if the other teachers liked him. He finally said that he guessed that they didn't. Then I told him that they did like him—very much—because they had told me so (which was true). I asked him again if he thought I liked him. This time he wasn't sure how to answer. I told him that I, too, liked him very much (which was also true).

While he puzzled over this, I explained that because I liked him I wanted to be proud of him and I couldn't be when he misbehaved. I told him that I liked to see the corners of his mouth turned up in a smile instead of turned down in a pouting expression. I tried to show him what I meant by imitating his pout, and then smiling. I said that it would be very nice if he could come into class with a happy expression. I told him that when I watched him play after school he hardly seemed the same boy. I mentioned again that I liked him, that it was his behavior that had made me angry. I suggested then that we be friends again. He agreed and left for home.

Discussion

By the next afternoon I had forgotten about the talk, but Phil's behavior made me take notice. He was working hard, volunteering answers to questions, and in general behaving beautifully. I couldn't have been more amazed. His good behavior continued for the rest of the term.

Questions

1. It appears to me that something that I did had a profound influence on this boy. What could it have been?

2. Should a teacher keep her distance and keep out of students' lives? Is classroom instruction our only purpose?

3. Suppose something I said or did outside of my strict duties did not work out well, even though it was well meant. Would I then be considered guilty of improper behavior?

*   *   *

Before the reviewer takes issue with the questions raised here, she would like to point out the principal facts on which this incident rests.

1. Phil did everything he could think of to upset the teacher—not just that day, but always. The teacher felt provoked and angry at him.
2. Phil enjoyed a reputation of being an excellent ballplayer.
3. The children liked him "very much" in spite of his bad behavior.
4. According to the report, one gets the impression that the teacher took no special measures to change or control Phil's behavior in class except for an occasional scolding.
5. When Phil was threatened with being taken to the office, he became angry and withdrew from all participation.
6. Phil's behavior made the teacher feel "unhappy about the way things had happened" and the teacher decided to "patch up" their differences.

The teacher feels certain that something very profound happened when Phil was told that everybody like him "very much," for his behavior changed from bad to "beautiful." The teacher now wonders what brought about this sudden change.

It seems obvious to me that Phil's behavior indicates a dissatisfaction with his position in this class and in his relationship with the teacher. In spite of being a fairly good student, he doesn't seem to have the kind of place in the group that he would like—a place with status. We may assume that he behaves quite differently in his physical education class, where he is the star. Phil evidently needs to be "first" or he feels worthless and neglected. In class, he is only average, and since he cannot be outstanding through special scholastic performance, he manages to get attention by being a nuisance. His entire energy seems to be devoted to disrupting class activities and forcing the teacher's attention upon him.

The teacher's efforts to control Phil result in a kind of power struggle as described in the incident. Phil tries to prove his superiority by his ability to keep the teacher constantly occupied and angry with him. As we see, he is quite successful.

When Phil senses danger, a situation in which he might be the loser, he brings his teacher under control by assuming a hurt look and by withdrawing from all participation. He succeeds in making the teacher feel guilty for the horrible thing she is doing to him. He certainly knows his business, for doesn't the teacher feel "unhappy" and want "to patch up"?

We see that Phil's goals vary with circumstances. In the first place he wants attention, then he wants power, and finally he wants revenge.

There is no doubt that the teacher's handling of the incident had a favorable outcome. It is regrettable, however, that we know so little about the boy's general background, such as his behavior at home, his relationship with his parents and with his sister, how he behaved with other teachers, and so on. Much needed information is missing in order to make a reliable interpretation.

No doubt something did happen to Phil when he was told that the teacher liked him. Perhaps he had always felt disliked by this teacher, and the latter's kind approach and reassurance that he was liked were all he needed. Perhaps he was shocked at the unexpected declaration of the teacher's affection for him, and this took the wind out of his sails. We know that doing the opposite of what a child expects when he misbehaves may often be exceedingly effective.

On the other hand, there is the serious question of whether a single episode would suffice to change a child's basic attitude toward himself and toward others. Could he so readily develop a new sense of belonging without having been helped toward any insight into his basic problem? Might we assume that after this episode, the teacher, unconsciously, began to treat the boy in a different manner from before by now giving him positive attention? If this assumption is correct, we may further assume that the teacher's change toward Phil also influenced the group's attitude toward him, for in addition to liking him, as they did before, they also respected him or even envied him now.

As to whether a teacher should keep out of students' lives and restrict her activities to the teacher of subject matter, the reviewer feels very strongly that an educator should not entertain such thoughts. The function of the teacher is to prepare the child for life so that he will function adequately in whatever situation he may encounter and so that he will realize all his potentialities of growth and development. How can a teacher pursue these goals if she restricts herself to the teaching of subject matter, especially when she is faced with children who have problems?

Potentially normal children who have difficulties in school have difficulties in life generally. These children need to be helped to understand the motives for their behavior and to change their methods of obtaining their goals from destructive to constructive ones. In order to achieve this, the teacher must take the time and the trouble to show a personal interest in the child and his problems. Only then can the teaching of subject matter be effective.

BERNICE GRUNWALD

*   *   *

This incident illustrates what at first glance seems the result of a fairly deep-seated emotional disturbance in a child. It turns out, however, to be a reaction to a disturbed pupil-teacher relationship.

There seems to be a notion, all too prevalent in educational circles, that children who are misbehaving are always rejected children. The magic formula is to show them that you like them, and then their hostile behavior will change. In this case it seems that Phil was rejecting the teacher's querulous and probably perfectionistic strivings. He seems to have sensed that her professional attitude and treatment of him were not genuine. While on the surface she appeared accepting, she was hostile underneath and was showing no effort to understand her relationship with Phil. Phil must have been further confused by the teacher's sudden expression of disapproval after, in a sense, condoning his behavior earlier by nonintervention. He may well have felt that in some way she wanted him to continue to behave as he was, for she set no limits for him.

The incident on the stairs, as I interpret it, was no victory of love over rejection. It was, instead, more a turning point for the teacher than for the boy, but a turning point in which the teacher revealed herself as a human being troubled about her handling of her own hostile feelings. Phil could relate understandingly to the teacher as a human being and proceeded thereafter to do so.

The teacher seems to have made no attempt to study Phil or to analyze any of her own intense feelings of irritation and annoyance with him before she blew up. This nonanalytic attitude seems to have characterized her professional behavior. She apparently did not ask herself such questions as: "What purpose does his behavior serve? Is it tension-reducing or attention-getting? When did it begin? Does he so behave in other classes? Why is he so popular with others and not with me? Am I doing something that encourages this out-of-field behavior? What different approaches can I try or what changes in my attitude can I make?"

Not rational thinking and realistic experimentation, but sudden impulse brought the easing of this teacher-pupil conflict. It seems only fair to point out that such impulses, especially in a person who so little understands her underlying motives, cannot be relied upon for a high percentage of happy endings.

After her impulsive revelation of her human concern, the teacher unhappily used many of the timeworn and judgmental appeals to good behavior that parents find so effective in making their children feel too guilty to be bad. "I like you and I want to be proud of you and I can't be when you misbehave. I like the corners of your mouth turned up in a smile instead of turned down (to make me, the teacher, feel better, you, Phil, had better guiltily take care of this little behavioral matter and then I'll reward you by liking you)." The teacher, like so many parents, was unable to depersonalize a valid concept which distinguishes between liking or loving a person and finding certain aspects of his behavior unacceptable.

In spite of the absence of a mental-hygiene approach and the lack of an understanding of personal dynamics, the classroom situation was eased for both teacher and pupil. We dare hope that this teacher—having courageously faced her own negative emotions—will find it less difficult to check her impulsive reactions in the future. We should like to believe that she would begin to look with increasing fear at the feelings and motives of her pupils, as well as her own. And we wish for Phil that his next teacher be attuned to a nonjudgmental, guidance-oriented viewpoint.

FRANCES R. HARPER

*　　*　　*

Phil's behavior is not unusual. It occurs among pupils at all levels, although it appears to be more accentuated in the early teens. Examples are common of boys and girls seeking attention as a means of compensating for the lack of it in home and community. Bright pupils frequently resort to such devices as Phil did, largely because they finish their work sooner than others in the class and have nothing to do until the remainder of the group completes an assigned activity. Then again, a pupil may become distractive in order to challenge a teacher whom he considers weak or whose limits of patience he wants to establish. There are other reasons for pupils' resorting to annoying forms of behavior; they can usually be determined if time is taken to trace them down.

It is interesting to note that the teacher in this case allowed Phil to continue his annoying tactics for a long time before she lost her temper. When the incident occurred shortly afterward on the stairs at dismissal time, she had already created a somewhat favorable climate for discussion simply because she had put her foot down and had made it clear to Phil that no more nonsense would be tolerated. It is probably a safe guess that Phil had more respect for this teacher as a result of her firm action than he had had before.

The meeting on the stairs also indicated to Phil that the teacher wanted to treat him as a person in his own right and that she was interested in him. This in itself was enough to cause him to regard the teacher differently, especially if the teacher had failed to show this kind of respect and interest at other times.

The teacher did a wise thing at this point, perhaps without knowing it. She associated his good qualities with activities in which he enjoyed some measure of success. It was like saying to him that good behavior pays dividends, as he had discovered, and that similar returns could be expected from better conduct in the classroom.

There is a real question of whether or not the conversation on the stairs was responsible for the change that took place in Phil and lasted during the remainder of the school year. If it was, the chances are high that Phil was ready to undergo a change and that the teacher merely triggered the action. A change in behavior such as Phil made does not come about overnight. It usually takes a long period of careful work. Sometimes a combination of influences outside of the school build up a state of readiness, and behavior only seems to change because of the actions taken by a teacher or a counselor.

There are some other issues deserving consideration. One of them pertains to the matter of how much a teacher should enter into the life of a pupil outside of regular classroom instruction. It is difficult to draw a line separating the responsibility of the school from the private life of the pupil. Certainly the big job of the school is that of changing behavior in ways that are personally and socially more desirable. But behavior changes cannot be effected without some knowledge and understanding of the pupil and the influences which shaped his attitudes, ideas, values, and actions.

Another issue of importance is this particular teacher's competency. It would seem that the principal of the school had been lax in not identifying, and helping the teacher correct, her weaknesses in classroom management and control. Any teacher who knew her business would never have permitted the situation described here to develop. When the pattern of Phil's behavior became evident, she would have examined her own practices to find out if they invited Phil to become a nuisance and a distractive influence in the classroom. If satisfied that her own procedures were sound, she would have instituted a search on her own or through the guidance counselor of the school for facts about Phil's school history and family background. This information would have enabled her to understand him better and to know what she had to deal with in plotting a course of action. Had the principal observed the teacher, he could have offered suggestions and worked with her in dealing with the problem right from the beginning. In some respects this incident brings out more strongly the need for aiding the teacher than it does for solving a problem like Phil's in a classroom learning situation.

LESLIE W. KINDRED

*   *   *

There are several factors omitted from this incident that might substantially influence the reader's opinion concerning the way in which the situation was handled. To name a few, it would be of interest to know the age of this boy, the age and sex of the teacher, the presence and extent of behavior problems which Phil may have displayed with other teachers, and the manner in which his behavior was treated in other classes.

In any event, it would seem to the reader that Phil possessed fairly strong needs for acceptance by his teachers and may also have had related status needs with his peers. He is probably at an age when athletic abilities serve as an excellent status symbol with his associates, but when he has at the same time little knowledge of those matters that will allow him to impress adults with whom he comes in contact in ways satisfactory to him.

For the moment, let us assume that Phil does not present any serious behavior problems but rather that he finds himself in a particular situation with this teacher and in this classroom that causes him to misbehave, promptly and with certainty, in an effort to gain the teacher's attention. It would therefore seem equally evident that the teacher as well was experiencing difficulty in this or her relationship with Phil—both in terms of understanding it as well as in the matter of knowing how to cope with it.

Based on a stroke of insight, and from all we know apparently a correct one, the teacher informed Phil that she liked him and gratuitously added the information that the other teachers felt the same way toward him. The additional point she made with him to the effect that her feelings for him were constant and positive, but that she did disapprove of certain portions of his behavior, was also well taken. There is a probability that Phil had never before had this distinction clarified for him. Undoubtedly his morale was raised considerably by the remainder of her conversation with him, in which she attempted to specify the personal interest that she had in him as a human being. What cannot be dismissed lightly, however, is her perplexity—apparent from the first question she asks—about the manner in which she had influenced the boy.

Apparently this isolated and brief conversation held with Phil brought about a drastic change in Phil's behavior for the better, a change that remained for the rest of the semester. Assuming that the teacher was responsible for this change, her act might well be construed as meddling in contrast to a planned approach. This presents a possibility that chance alone was operating in this particular instance and that the youngster might just as easily have been influenced in one of several negative directions.

Certainly, we would all agree that in the ideal situation a teacher is able to develop and to maintain a genuine depth and breadth of interest in the over-all development of each of her students. The first corollary to this demands that the teacher be able to separate her personal system of values and needs from her role as a classroom teacher. When this is achieved, the teacher will generally find that she has first had to learn the true extent of her own limits as well as of her assets, before tackling those behavioral problems a child may display that are based on that child's emotional makeup. The teacher is then able to offer assistance to a particular student that is in keeping with her abilities and at the same time based on a fairly realistic assessment of the student's needs. A teacher who involves herself with a student's emotional needs in a way motivated by momentary impulse, as may well have occurred in this instance, might find herself in one or another sticky situation. If such an act did not turn out well, quite probably the teacher would find herself in a difficult position if all she could plead in her defense was that her intentions were well meant.

The point being made here is that if the manner in which the teacher met the episode in this instance does constitute an improper approach because of the impetuousness she displayed, then it is improper regardless of whether the results turned out well or not.

I further believe that periodic conferences in which small groups of teachers are encouraged to discuss the treatment of problems in the classroom serve a number of useful purposes. Not the least of these purposes is to allow and encourage the various teachers to discuss matters about which they may have questions *before* they act in a given situation. In this way teachers are able to develop the sense of security that comes from knowing that they are not alone in encountering such problems. Had such an arrangement been available to this teacher prior to this particular incident, the questions she raised after her act might well have never come up.

CHARLES KRAM

*   *   *

The case of Phil is particularly interesting because it is representative of a kind of situation prevalent in classrooms in this country and is being reported more and more frequently from other countries. In this case we see a teacher trying to accomplish the tasks that she believes are her primary responsibilities with little or no functional knowledge as to how this may be done. This is not to be critical of the teacher in her functioning, but rather of her professional training. In all probability she has not had the opportunity to learn how to regard children's behavior in any systematic way. If she has been exposed to psychological principles about why children behave as they do, she has not learned them sufficiently to apply them—unless the principles suggested that one should become confused and use trial and error. Such is not likely.

There is much the teacher did in this case that may be regarded as moving in the right direction. For example, she did want to correct the situation; she did approach Phil in a warm and friendly manner; she did attempt to encourage rather than discourage him ("I told him other teachers liked him very much—which was true").

Yet there is much more here to suggest that this teacher, whatever her successes may be, is far more indebted to her intuition and ignorance than to her knowledge of child development. For example, Phil tried her patience every day. He seemed to do everything in his power to irritate her. "His power" was a clue that the teacher did not realize she had given herself, hence did not know what to do with. She resorted to the futile approach so commonly and ineffectively used: threatening him with a trip to the principal's office. Here the teacher missed an opportunity to see in her own response another clue to the problem: to have sent Phil to the office would have fitted perfectly into his scheme. After all, he believed no one liked him, and what better assurance could he have had than to be sent to the office?

The teacher writes of Phil's becoming angry, then sullen, *but* not leaving his desk again that day. One gets the impression that the teacher's methods of control involve bribes and threats; at best, these serve as but momentary harbingers of peace and at worst set the stage for even greater conflicts to come. That the teacher is "only human" is revealed in her feeling guilty about the way things happened; she decides to try to "patch up" the differences. Few people realize that feeling guilty is a poor reason for undertaking corrective measures.

What the teacher did in winning Phil's confidence was sound. The unfortunate aspect of her corrective measure is that she was without conscious resourcefulness, gaining the idea from some sort of "popping" activity. Had she had some notion as to why Phil was misbehaving, the techniques she used would have readily occurred to her as one of several possibilities.

An important item in the total incident that might have worked against what the teacher was trying to achieve was her telling Phil she liked him and wanted to be proud of him, but could not when he misbehaved. Here we toss out the baby with the bath. It would not be surprising to learn that as a small child Phil had been constantly confronted by his parents with "Mommy (or Daddy) won't love you if you do that!" Many parents and teachers have yet to learn how to distinguish the worth of behavior from that of the individual behaving.

The teacher later stated that she liked Phil and that it was his behavior that made her angry. This is a contradiction of earlier expressions, which could only result in confusion on Phil's part. Such contradictions indicate again that, like so many other teachers, this one had no frame of reference for looking at children.

It is worthy of note that, for the teacher, Phil's response to the corrective measure was nothing short of amazing. Had the teacher any appreciation of the value of mutual respect as revealed in the apparently sincere manner in which she approached Phil, this would have been less amazing and more reasonable. Mutual respect usually has a profound influence on the child who knows little of it but comes to receive it.

In raising the question, "Should a teacher keep her distance?" it appears that she has functioned on the oft-quoted cliché, "Familiarity breeds contempt." This would be more correctly stated, "Familiarity breeds contempt for incompetence." Competent teachers never have to fear knowing their pupils too well or their pupils' knowing them too well. The writer fails to see how teachers who keep out of the lives of their pupils can perform the tasks that are theirs. It is more true than not that the primary task of the school remains that of instruction, but this does not preclude being friendly, understanding, and fair, as well as firm. These qualities can only be exercised intelligently when we know our pupils. Montagu[1] suggests that the primary function of the school is that of being concerned with the fourth R—human relationships. This writer comes to the same conclusion in raising the question with its implied answer, "To what end do we teach the three R's if it isn't, ultimately, to improve the fourth?"

In conclusion, the writer suggests that teachers will come closer to minimizing the number of Phils in their classes when they have some idea of the meaning of this kind of behavior. Further, such meaning will be found less in seeking to understand the *"cause"* of the behavior in question than in seeking to understand the *purpose* of it. There is no question that the greatest weakness in the teacher's approach in Phil's case is that she knew nothing about diagnosing behavior problems. Where this is true, teachers usually resort to trial and error similar to this teacher's behavior. Only when an accurate diagnosis is made can proper corrective measures be taken in an efficient and effective manner. In this instance, it is clear that Phil, because of his feeling that no one liked him, sought to prove his worth by trying to dominate the teacher in getting her upset

---

[1] Ashley Montagu, *Education and Human Relations* (New York: Grove Press, 1958), and *On Being Human* (New York: Henry Schuman, 1951).

and in demonstrating that he could do as he pleased. Only when she conveyed to him that she liked him did he no longer feel the need for gaining status through misbehaving. I would predict that unless the next teacher has some understanding of purposeful misbehavior, together with some idea of how to deal with it, Phil will become a "problem" again.

In reality, of course, the teacher becomes the problem, because she uses techniques intended to improve behavior while, in fact, she encourages the very behavior she is striving to preclude. Most methods used by teachers to correct unacceptable behavior are ineffective because they are based upon principles involving the moral superiority of adults—scolding, punishment, and threats. Since these methods are no longer effective with children, we find many Phils in our schools who are serving notice to their parents and teachers that they won't cooperate except on their own terms. This is an increasing source of bewilderment on the part of both children and adults. Solutions to these problems are not likely to be found in "ideas popping into teachers' heads."

R. N. LOWE

*   *   *

In commenting on the first question, it is quite obvious that Phil's teacher did do "something" to influence Phil. She convinced him that she did not dislike him, but that she disliked some of the things he did and the manner in which he did them. She convinced him that he already had admirers and friends and that it was not necessary for him to resort to purposeful misbehavior to be noticed. She persuaded him to accept the fact that the teachers were on his side, that they were not in conspiracy against him as so many youngsters like Phil tend to believe.

Phil excelled on the playground. This brought him approval and acclaim, and he thrived on the resulting prestige. In the classroom he was thrown into a situation where he was no longer a center of attention. It is possible that here he felt his position was threatened by the teacher and that he resented her. Because of his lack of esteem for her, it followed in his mind that she had a reciprocal feeling of animosity toward him. His classroom maneuvers constituted a means of fighting back and defending himself.

Is a teacher's sole purpose instruction? I would give a qualified but affirmative answer. Any learning process is instruction if it is imparted with competent adult guidance. Phil was receiving instruction when the teacher talked with him on the stairway.

There is sometimes a quarrel between those who say, "I teach English," and those who prefer to say, "I teach boys and girls." Perhaps we should combine the two and say, "I teach boys and girls, and I teach them English." The teaching profession is interested in persons as well as in pursuits.

One would be naïve to expect that everything done within or outside of the limits of "strict duty" will always work out well. Just because some action does not always produce satisfactory solutions, it does not necessarily follow that it constitutes improper behavior. On the other hand, one must never accept the supposition that good intentions produce an automatic license to any procedure. There must be a sound, scientifically valid basis for our actions, and this basis must be arrived at with understanding seasoned by past experience and human kindness.

Phil's teacher in her effort to correct his waywardness did not attempt to reduce him in stature and size to less than those who were no problem. This would only have served to fan the fires of rebellion. She must have made him feel the respect she had for him at the same time she took issue with his inappropriate actions. She convinced him she was basically in agreement with his own unconsciously held assertion that he was not a total scoundrel. She appealed to his previously latent sense of dignity, and he began to make contributions to classwork even though he had only average ability.

The element of surprise in disciplinary action has its virtues. In the after-school discussion on the stairs, Phil's teacher surprised him by saying she and other teachers liked him. Probably no other teacher had so approached him. The overwhelming odds are that worn clichés threatening punishment and rejection had been hurled at him on countless occasions.

Phil's teacher developed in him a sense of belonging to the group within the classroom, just as he already felt he belonged and was needed in his playground groups.

R. CLINTON SCHULZE

DISCUSSION QUESTIONS—INCIDENT 6

1. In view of middle-class emphasis on "being first," how can a teacher prevent discouragement and apathy in a child who does not have the mental ability to excel in his studies?
2. Should the teacher maintain a nonjudgmental attitude (the accepted attitude for psychiatrists and social workers), or should she become emotionally involved with children?

3. How much should a teacher know about a problem pupil's private life in order to deal with classroom problems?
4. If most methods of discipline used by teachers involve "moral superiority" and are no longer effective, as suggested by Lowe, what alternative means exist to obtain necessary cooperation in the classroom?
5. "Is instruction a teacher's sole purpose?" Can you answer Schulze's question?

7

A MAJORITY OF ONE

CRITICAL INCIDENT

Background

       The situation I am about to describe is not unexpected or outrageous, but I think it is unusual because teachers rarely have the opportunity to experience such intense feelings of satisfaction as I did.

In my first week as a fifth-grade teacher, the principal brought in a new student. Bob was new to me, but it was unnecessary to introduce him to the rest of the class. They all seemed to know him; it was also painfully obvious that they did not want to know him better. He was utterly rejected by the entire group from the beginning. Rather than include Bob in a project, the group would pick the class dunce or someone of similar calibre. It was a mystery to me, until I read his cumulative report about a week later.

I learned there that Bob had been a troublemaker since the first grade, so much so that many teachers—and in turn other children—rejected him. It was thought that putting him with another section might cause him to exhibit different behavior. But poor Bob's reputation followed him. He really didn't have much of a chance; he merely clung to his habitual ways.

The immediate cause of the behavior problem was rejection, but deeper than this lay the facts that (1) he was much smaller than those of his age group; (2) he was of a lower socio-economic level than the majority—something of which he was very much aware; (3) he received regular beatings from his father. Perhaps Bob felt that he might just as well do the things that earned him beatings. I am not sure of Bob's feelings in this matter, since he was noncommittal about others' treatment of him, continually playing the "tough-guy" role with an "I-can-take-it" attitude.

Things went from bad to worse those first six weeks. Bob was in and out of trouble as usual. I must admit that I was unable to establish a relationship with him no matter how hard I tried.

Incident

In mid-October the class decided to prepare a Halloween play. I procured several scripts, and we decided at last on "The Timid Ghost." We held try-outs, and Bob participated. I thought he was perfect for the leading role, because he was an excellent reader (he was always reading when others were engaged in group activity), his memory was very good, he was small, and his voice was rather high and squeaky.

Before voting on the casting, I requested that the children really think about it and choose those who they honestly felt were best qualified, rather than let their hearts rule their minds by choosing best friends. I indicated that Bob would fit the part perfectly. Apparently, my talk had its effect. Bob won by a single vote (I voted too).

Bob became extremely enthusiastic. Here was a way he could get the attention he craved, and for a change he was receiving approval rather than disapproval. Everyone in the class was in one way or another engaged in preparations—practicing parts, making costumes, and constructing props. The children even built a realistic imitation mike to be used by the Master of Ceremonies.

In all this buzz of activity, I doubt that the children were really aware of what was happening to Bob. A mutual need had been discovered. Bob needed the group and their acceptance, and now they also needed him. Sometimes I thought that I might be deceiving myself, that perhaps Bob was more aware of what was taking place than I imagined, for occasionally he would seem to delight in taking advantage of his new-found position.

Discussion

There were many times afterward when Bob did not get along well, when his behavior was anything but exemplary. But at least he had got his foot in the door, and an entire classroom had undergone a noticeable change. From that time on there seemed to be an improvement in the conditions under which he had to work out his basic behavior problem.

Questions

1. Should a teacher try to create situations in which a pupil's uniqueness gives him an advantage rather than a disadvantage?

2. I swayed the group to vote for Bob and also voted for him myself. Was this using my authority unnecessarily?

3. Was I wrong to invest so much time in a single child, thus neglecting others?

*   *   *

It is part of the teacher's role in guidance to create situations in which a pupil's uniqueness can come forth advantageously. Obviously, as a completely rejected child who had been experiencing frustration at home and in school, Bob needed the opportunity to be accepted and to excel. From that turning point on, a good teacher could help this young boy to develop his personality constructively. Whether it be a project or assignment, the perceptive teacher can seek the means to bring about a change in a rapidly deteriorating student so that positive steps toward reconstruction in his personality, character, or behavior can take place.

The teacher's appeal to the class to be objective in their voting for the leading part was acceptable. However, it might have been better if she had not singled out Bob herself or voted for him. She should have taken aside a few of the class leaders, brought them into her confidence, and let them present the case in favor of Bob.

A teacher never wastes time when in the ordinary course of classroom events she endeavors to provide for the special needs of any single child. It is easy to accomplish educational goals with the normal child, but the real challenge of teaching comes when the teacher reaches out to the abnormal child and endeavors to bring about some improvement so that the youngster can live a more satisfying life. It is the old scriptural story of going after one black sheep and temporarily neglecting the interests of the ninety-nine white ones who are already "saved." The dignity of each individual warrants concern on the part of the teacher, no matter how repelling or annoying the pupil may be by reason of poor behavior or social inadequacies, and whether or not the pupil's race, color, creed, or origins happen to appeal to the instructor.

PHILIP HARRIS

*   *   *

Children can be cruel and children can be kind. A perceptive teacher can do much to assist children in understanding their own problems and the problems of others. Children in their groping toward maturity are usually uncertain about themselves and their classmates—in fact, about their total environment. Children need security, something that a kind, fair, understanding teacher can give them. Because children like such a teacher, they assume many of her attitudes and this results in better social feelings, the basis for personal security.

The learning of the classroom is dependent upon the materials in the room, the background of the pupils, the community in which the school is located, and other factors. But the most important factor that overcomes lack of materials, that overcomes much of the undesirable outside environment, and that overcomes many parental prejudices, is the teacher. She cannot change the world, but it is amazing what a competent teacher can do in her classroom through her basic attitudes, which can reach every child in the room.

The teacher may have good days and bad days, things may go right or wrong, but when pupils know that the teacher is on their side their respect for her makes all days better days. Her attitudes are received more readily than the best lesson taught.

Teachers teach fairness by being fair. Although this teacher's vote swayed the election for Bob, the important element was her attempt to help him and to teach the other pupils basic fairness and objectivity. It is the duty of teachers, really, to organize and lead classes toward worthwhile academic and social standards. The voting in this case served this end. Bob and the other children probably realized this, or things would not have gone as smoothly as they did in the preparation for the play.

Bob was part of the class group. Although he may have taken up many hours of thought on the part of teacher, she probably would have done the same for some other child with problems. In this case, however, she helped, in addition, to improve the behavior pattern of a very disruptive member of her class. Bob benefited, but so did the class. By being fair to him, she helped the other pupils know she would be as fair and understanding to them.

RICHARD W. HINDS

*   *   *

This incident reveals the therapeutic effect of success experiences on children. Once a child has demonstrated some competence in an activity that has status value with his peers, he has probably changed something vital in their thinking, and more important, in his own conception of himself. When a child sees himself more favorably, he acts more desirably.

Bob's poor reputation had preceded him into this classroom, and as a result he was expected to behave like a problem child. Because of these role expectations, it was difficult for him to be any better in the new situation than in the old. We often unconsciously force others, by our own behavior toward them, to act in ways that will fortify and justify our judgments about them. Children frequently encourage another child to create disturbances and to defy adults, because they enjoy the excitement as a change from the classroom routine, and also as a safe, indirect way of releasing some of their own hostility toward the teacher. It is usually difficult for a child to change the role expectations that others have for him, because his role fits the dynamic needs of the entire classroom group.

Bob's classmates could not accept him initially because it was not politic. They feared the disapproval of their classmates, the teacher, and anyone else who knew Bob's reputation. It was the teacher's obligation, therefore, to lead the way in accepting Bob, thus making it possible for the class to accept him without fear of reprisal. The teacher's acceptance of Bob had to be clearly perceptible to his classmates, which was fortunately the case in this instance.

The incident reveals much about Bob and about the bases for the kind of behavior he showed. As in all cases of this sort, there was a multiplicity of causes for his behavior, although the apparent mistreatment and rejection by his father was perhaps the most cogent. His "tough-guy" and "I-can-take-it" attitude, however, tell us that he was basically sensitive to, and concerned with, what others thought of him. Furthermore, his enthusiastic response to participation in the Halloween play suggests that the "bad boy" role did not adequately meet his needs, and that he could readily abandon it for a socially more acceptable mode of behavior. A severely disturbed child would have adhered more tenaciously to the old pattern, unable to trust the teacher's good intentions and unwilling to give up the limited but proven satisfaction of the former role. Bob could not change his role in the class through his own initiative. He therefore needed the intervention of the teacher, who could set an example of acceptance, making it easier for other members of the class to help formulate a new role for him.

Whether a teacher should try to create situations in which a person's uniqueness gives him an advantage rather than a disadvantage sounds like a rhetorical question. It is, of course, one of the primary tasks of teachers to develop children's unique capacities and assets. Good teaching maximizes individual differences by developing and using the child's pattern of special abilities to his advantage.

Since the teacher swayed the group to vote for Bob and also voted for him herself, she was using her authority unnecessarily. The class would not have had to vote on the children who were to take certain parts in the play. The teacher did influence the vote, and it would have been more honest for her simply to designate who was to have which part. Since it was not really a decision democratically arrived at, the voting might better have been eliminated.

Whether she was wrong to invest so much time in a single child is a difficult matter to determine. Not even a crystal ball in good working order could provide the answer. If one could look into the future of this boy, he might see a stable, responsible, well-adjusted citizen. But he could never know what effect, or how much, this favorable school experience had had on this boy, although he might suspect that it had helped him to greater maturity.

ORVAL G. JOHNSON

*   *   *

The case of Bob supports the notion that teachers are easily discouraged and visit their discouragement upon each other as well as upon children. This is not to say that teachers are any more discouraged than any other adult group. Rather, it is to suggest that teachers seem to learn little in their professional education that helps them gain some functional understanding of themselves as well as of children. All too often students planning to become teachers are exposed to unmeaningful concepts about human behavior. They report this constantly in follow-up studies, and yet departments of psychology and schools of education seldom look at their programs in an attempt to understand the basis for this criticism. The programs of teacher education acknowledged as superior by both students and professional educators have a number of peculiar characteristics, principally the frequent contact with children in an educational setting and the careful analysis of the student's experiences in these contacts. While consensus is high as to the value of such experiences, it appears that the cost is equally so, and here we do not seem to be able to justify in our own thinking the fact that the value derived is worth the price.

For four years Bob has been successful in conveying to his teachers and his peers that he wanted a special place in his various groups; he found it by being highly disturbing, hence alienating all who came in contact with him. While the writer agrees with what the teacher sees in this case, he cannot accept the "causes" cited as sufficient to explain Bob's behavior. The teacher tried to see beneath the "immediate cause," but her attempt at going deeper is really substituting one superficial explanation for another. The three deeper facts to which she makes reference are not to be disregarded; they are, however, secondary factors, not primary ones. Had Bob been Mary or Tom, the teacher might have reported that the student was cooperative, did well in school, and was liked by both teachers and pupils. All teachers have Marys and Toms and are the more perplexed because in the face of the "evidence" they really should be like Bob. Here teachers make a fundamental mistake in thinking that such factors as being smaller than average for one's age group, being from a lower socio-economic level, and having been routinely beaten by one's father cause a boy to misbehave. In reality, they might provide stimulation for the child to feel that "if I'm ever to get out of this mess, I'll have to play ball," and therefore make him proceed to learn the game.

The teacher reveals her lack of understanding of the basis for her diagnosis when she says, ". . . I am not sure about Bob's feelings in this matter since he was noncommittal about others' treatment of him. . . ." Without having more communication with Bob than the teacher apparently had, it is highly questionable for her to have speculated as she did in accounting for his behavior. There is nothing wrong in speculating per se; even the most "scientifically" oriented behavioral scientist does this. What is challenged here is the teacher's speculating about the wrong kinds of information!

Anyone who has taught should have empathy for this teacher as she reports that no matter how hard she tried, she couldn't seem to get through to Bob. The kind of difficulty Bob was presenting is highly discouraging to almost anyone. After all, if one does make a genuine effort to be friendly, kind, and understanding, only to be repeatedly frustrated, he is very likely to be at least as discouraged as the Bobs with whom he is working, unless he has unusual courage and understanding of himself. Some teachers who have had such experiences become the "realists" in the profession and constantly advise the young beginner, "You can't do anything with this kind, so why try?"

The situation leading to the teacher's involving Bob with the group in such a manner as to reveal to him that he could constructively participate is an interesting one. The fact that Bob worked helpfully in the play is indicative of the teacher's skill in manipulating the children in the direction she sought.

The writer sees considerable merit in the direction the teacher was moving Bob, but seriously questions the role she played in promoting Bob to the lead. Teachers are always justified in creating situations in which the unique talents of youngsters are usefully developed and portrayed. In fact, this is an essential technique in good teaching. The same end probably could have been accomplished with more permanency had the teacher been forthright with the group as to what she was doing rather than bootlegging her idea. Actually Bob didn't win by one vote; the teacher did.

The teacher might well have had a discussion with the class about Bob's disturbing behavior, in which she could help both Bob and the rest of the class understand the nature of misbehavior and how Bob used it to get a place of prominence in the group, negative though it was. She might well have asked the class's support in trying out a plan in which Bob would have an opportunity to discover how, through useful means, he could get the attention and feeling of importance that apparently he wanted. No attempt is made, in such a case, to conceal the problem or what the teacher is trying to accomplish; the class realizes that only with its help can anything be done about the problem. Had the teacher used such an approach, she would have known very soon whether or not she had been deceiving herself.

It was noted that Bob's subsequent behavior was not always exemplary and that from time to time he seemed to take advantage of his new role. This is to be expected. For some time Bob will seek to test the limits of his new freedom. In the "testing" process the teacher with the help of the class, or possibly the class with the help of the teacher, will have to help Bob learn to accept the responsibility that must accompany freedom.

The writer is not certain that in giving so much attention to Bob the teacher neglected the others. In the group approach, confidence is expressed in the entire class—confidence that it can be of help to Bob and that its help is needed. In this case, since the entire group participated in the play, and since everyone helped Bob succeed in his new role, one can hardly think of the other students as neglected.

R. N. LOWE

*   *   *

The reporting teacher was certainly not mistaken when she said that the incident was neither unusual nor outrageous. The only unusual aspect of the case was that she had only one "problem child" with whom to contend.

Several items from the background she has provided, however, deserve special comment:

1. *The transferring of children.* To transfer a troublemaker after one week in school will usually succeed in doing only one thing: reinforcing his self-concept of "troublemaker." Apparently Bob had been with his original section since the first grade. He may have been informed of the reason for his transfer. If not, at least he was surely aware of it. One would expect his behavior to be somewhat defensive, even without the reputation he had built for himself. At any rate, one feels that if such a transfer of a student must be made, it is best to make it over the summer so that the newcomer is not faced with the problem of breaking into a new group. One wonders why the school authorities waited until the fifth grade to make the transfer. Granted, a fresh start will sometimes benefit a troublemaker in school, but past experience has shown that to delay doing so until the fifth grade will often compound the problem. By this time many of the behavior patterns have become so ingrained that they are almost habitual. It would be better to attempt such moves at a lower grade.

2. *The cumulative record.* This much-discussed device can be the teachers' best guidance tool, when used correctly. When used incorrectly, its only value comes from the heights, weights, and test scores that may be recorded in it.

The wise teacher will read the cumulative record for each child long before the beginning of the school term. Thus, she will not be "mystified" by actions or reactions of children in her room. In the present case, one should not criticize the teacher for not reading the record earlier, as we do not know when she received it. A cumulative record is only as good as each teacher makes it. Good teachers will attempt to use it to record behavior of children in their rooms through ancedotal reports. Too frequently we find teachers including only adverse information about children. Therefore, as may have happened in Bob's case, by the time the record reaches the fifth-grade teacher we have an accumulation of five or six years of negative comments. There is little wonder that his reputation followed him.

The problem of keeping accurate cumulative records is one of time.

Many teachers have found the daily loose-leaf log a good device in which to keep track of occurrences as they happen. Then, when they compose their ancedotal record they need not rely upon memory alone.

3. *The child who is abused at home.* A fine point of distinction exists between "child abuse" and regular "beatings." Teachers have been known to attempt to interfere in family affairs when it has become apparent that children are being abused. The teacher is within his rights as a citizen to make complaints when he actually witnesses child abuse. However, parents have the privilege of correcting their children's behavior, and the astute teacher will not attempt to interfere unless it is obvious that the child is in physical danger. The teacher can compensate by accepting the child and making his life at school more pleasant than it is at home. When it is felt necessary to intervene in the home, it is best to go through channels rather than to attempt it alone. In this case the adage that there is "strength in numbers" will save a teacher much heartache and worry, or at the least, embarrassment.

4. *The Incident.* The key to the teacher's success in this incident lies in her use of modern methods. It is difficult to envision any success had the class been conducted in a completely authoritarian manner. Several statements lead one to believe that the teacher had accepted the democratic approach to the teaching-learning situation: "The class decided to prepare a play . . ." "Before voting on the parts . . ." "Everyone . . . was engaged . . ." This probably helped the children to practice some of the tenets of democratic living and to try to select the person best qualified for each job.

The teacher did not use her authority unnecessarily. On the contrary, it was extremely necessary for her to draw the children's attention to Bob's qualifications. They had more than likely become accustomed to overlooking Bob in making choices. The action of the teacher was the action of a leader in a democracy. Too often we find a laissez-faire attitude on the part of teachers when they attempt to use the democratic approach. Anarchy is often the result. The teacher's vote counted only as much as that of any other member. Therefore, she could hardly be accused of using her authority unjustly.

One does wonder what the psychological effect upon Bob would have been had he been defeated for the part—and what the teacher would have done. If she had arbitrarily assigned Bob the leading part, the partial acceptance by the class probably would have turned to resistance. His problem could have been intensified.

One of the main jobs of the teacher is to create learning situations in which children can succeed. This incident is a classical example of providing for individual differences among children. Each child in a class has some value and some talent. The wise teacher will build upon those talents to increase the value of the child, both in his own eyes and in society's. It will be well worth the time spent. When the democratic approach to learning is practiced, the teacher actually has more opportunities to concentrate upon individuals than she does when she employs other approaches. In this case, there is little evidence to indicate that the other pupils in the class did not get their share of attention.

ROBERT W. SMAIL

DISCUSSION QUESTIONS—INCIDENT 7

1. Is the teacher responsible for the whole child—his character, his personality, and his increase of knowledge?
2. How much time can a teacher apportion to the needs of a single child who requires special attention if this deprives other children of attention?
3. Do you believe it is a good rule for teachers to be informed ahead of time about children in their classroom who may present disciplinary problems?
4. Discuss the pros and cons of the type of group therapy suggested by Lowe for solving problems of interpupil adjustment.
5. Should personality strengthening, such as the use of learning situations to build pupil's self-esteem, be considered an essential part of teaching?

8

AMBITIOUS PARENT—DISCOURAGED CHILD

CRITICAL INCIDENT

Background

Danny was the only child of ambitious, upper-middle-class parents. His mother was foreign born and believed the European system of education, where the child must "buckle down" and "toe the line," to be the *only* system. His father, a training director in industry, was American. Both parents set high standards for their son.

Because they felt it was very important that their home be clean and uncluttered, Danny could bring other children into his home only infrequently. Furthermore, his being an only child caused him to spend much time with adults. He seldom played with other children in the neighborhood (there were few his age), although on occasion he brought one school friend home to play. At home, he often spent hours at a time alone in his room, occupied with mechanical apparatus, his chemistry set, or anything that he could use to construct things.

Although Danny was a boy of high intelligence, he had not applied himself in school, and performed at about an average level for his grade. Even when he had done particularly well at something, his parents were not satisfied. For example, when it was pointed out to them that as a fourth grader he was reading at the seventh-grade level, they did not feel that this was high enough.

Danny was a virtual isolate in each of his classes, and devised ways of antagonizing other children as much as possible by pinching, kicking, and insulting them. However, occasionally he revealed how much he wanted to be a part of the group, for he was very pleased when a member of the class asked him to his home, paid particular attention to him, or chose him for something. During recesses and physical education periods, he would take part voluntarily in only one game—softball—for in this sport he was a skilled player. For the remainder of the time he would putter about the playground alone or with another boy in the class who also disliked sports. Only at the insistence of his teachers did he enter physical activities, and then reluctantly.

Throughout his school years Danny tried constantly to involve his teachers in a struggle for power within the room. He wanted to show them that he could have his own way. He would challenge their authority in a variety of well-designed ways—wandering about the room when he was to be working, working at what he chose when he did work, deliberately doing what he knew he should not, and so on.

When Danny entered my fifth-grade classroom he fell into his "normal" behavior pattern. He wandered around the room at will. Unless I was standing beside him, he either did not work at all or chose what he wanted to do instead of turning to what the group was working on. During class discussions, films, directions, and student reports, he gave only partial attention while he occupied himself with his hands, painting or constructing.

During the first weeks I ignored his rebellion against order and simply let him do what he chose, for I felt that he wanted to involve me in a contest for power. After a while, I began to realize that Danny was getting nowhere, and some of the children resented his having special privileges. I started arranging matters so that Danny either accepted the group standards or accepted the consequences. As a consequence of playing around at the lunch table, antagonizing others, and showing as few manners as possible, he temporarily lost his privilege of eating in the cafeteria. For irritating his classmates in the lunch line, he was ignored by them (on my advice). He subsequently tried all the harder to upset them but eventually he eased up. (I'm sure that this approach would have been more successful if *all* the children could have *completely* ignored his antics, but for some this was impossible.) As a consequence of not working at all or doing only what he chose, he lost his privilege of remaining in the room. He remained in the hall for a week (with his desk there). *Here* he could have special privileges, for he was not bound by group rules and he could arrange his own schedule in any way.

Incident

Although there was improvement after several of the foregoing incidents, it was usually short-lived. My principal and I knew that something had to be done soon to help Danny break from this pattern before it was too firmly set. With this in mind, we called Danny's parents and asked them to come to school for a parent-principal-teacher conference.

On the designated morning, only the father appeared. We described the situation, and my principal informed Danny's father that Danny was to remain at home for one week; he would do all his school work, would disturb no one, and would not have to abide by group standards. After one week, if he wished to return to the class, he would be *privileged* to do so, and could stay as long as he complied with the standards of the group.

By the close of the week he was anxious to be back. After he returned, he showed marked improvement in the quality of his work and in his behavior and attitude. Occasionally he slumped, as one might expect. Once each week we held a student-teacher conference, at which Danny presented a written self-evaluation, indicating what he wished to improve and what he felt he had done well. I tried, at every opportunity, to let him know that I had confidence in him. All in all, he seemed to have changed his attitude considerably—for the better.

Discussion

I feel that Danny had little confidence in himself. I believe that he wanted to protect himself from being hurt by the other children by building a firm antagonistic shell around himself. He was a very discouraged boy, for no matter what he did, it was not up to the demanding standards of his parents. (He himself had become just as much a perfectionist as his parents were.) He craved and fought for power within each classroom because this was one way in which he could feel important, and he believed that one method to gain power was to rebel against all group order. In a learning situation in which he did not have to abide by group standards he soon found that he missed the group interaction, and that abiding by rules was not intolerable.

I believe that after Danny returned to school, matters would have been more satisfactory if his mother had interfered less. Because she was anxious to see him change, and possibly because Danny's being home a week had curtailed her social life, she did everything in her power to keep him on the right road. Without his mother keeping constant track of his progress, he could have felt that what progress he made was truly his. Instead, each week she called me to confer on the week's events, and if he had taken a slump she would discuss it with him. Danny did much extra school work at home; I often wondered how much of it was motivated by himself and how much by his mother. If it were all to happen again, I would be most happy to see the parents *really interested in Danny*, but other than that, I would prefer that Danny be on his own so that his success or failure could belong to him.

Questions

1. How can one deal with such overambitious parents whose eagerness for their children's success teaches wrong values?
2. Did I meet the situation properly?
3. What else could have been done?

*   *   *

It appears oversimplified to say that excessive parental ambitions were basically at fault in the case of Danny. As long as their aims are not too far out of line with their children's abilities and potential, parents with high goals can motivate their children in a happy and successful fashion. This clearly was not the case with Danny, very possibly because a considerable degree of parental rejection was operating at the same time. For example, his mother did not even show up at the first parent conference when invited to do so (although she was excessively prominent at a later date when her own social life was threatened by Danny's school exclusion); the boy was allowed little social life at home; and there is no evidence that praise was ever given for genuine accomplishment, such as the high reading-test score.

Underachieving in school is often associated with general maladjustment, and should be considered a definite warning signal to parents and school personnel alike, whether or not—as in Danny's case—it is accompanied by behavior that openly upsets the teacher and school routines. Danny's social isolation and aggressiveness toward his peers as well as toward authority symbols confirm the picture of general maladjustment going far beyond mere classroom behavior. Because of his lack of self-confidence and his attention-seeking behavior, he obviously needs skilled help.

Ideally, such help should be secured through a special child-guidance clinic, with trained professional workers. Since Danny's problem has admittedly plagued all of his past teachers, since he has been a social isolate all through school, and since pinching and kicking as regular patterns of adjustment at the fifth-grade level are not superficial in conjunction with the rest of his symptoms, it would seem that no superficial treatment of his problem would be remedial. It is possible that his parents would rebel against the idea that anything could be wrong with Danny emotionally under ordinary circumstances; but faced as they were with his suspension from school, they might become aware of a real need for help. So if the school had guidance counselors, school psychologists, or social workers to enter the case at this point, such measures would be highly suitable.

Barring the availability of specialized help, the school still has to deal with symptoms as such. An aggressive, disobedient boy cannot be allowed to violate class rules indefinitely without a great deal of harm to class (and teacher!) morale, not to mention the harm done to the youngster's habit patterns and perhaps to his inborn need for order, discipline, and sensible limits.

Hence the suitability of such stopgap disciplinary measures as loss of cafeteria privileges and suspension from school. Sometimes, as luckily happened here, they can have a shock effect that will bring about temporary improvements. The parent conference with principal and teacher attending was an excellent measure, as was the idea of having the boy himself report back on his progress—as long as the device was not used to humiliate or punish him (as it regrettably sometimes is).

Once the stage had been set for change by the shock treatment of temporary suspension, it would seem that the time was ripe for accentuating the positive. For example, if Danny had current projects at home with his scientific apparatus that could possibly be related to classroom activities, he could be encouraged to report on them in class. He could in this fashion have legitimate and, let us assume, favorable attention from his classmates, some of whom might be drawn to him more favorably later.

Or, in the parent conferences, his need for social participation or sports skills could be presented—particularly to his father, perhaps—as tactfully as possible. If Danny is good at softball, he might have the coordination and potential skill needed in other sports; it is possible that his father might be able to teach him some sport (tennis, fishing, or swimming) that he could then share with his classmates. Because physical prowess at this age and during adolescence has enormous prestige with boys, Danny's current unwillingness to participate in sports, if continued, could further estrange him from his peers.

The teacher might have found it interesting to attempt a few socio-metric techniques (for example, friendship charts to see if there were any youngsters with a tentative attraction to Danny, and whom Danny liked). Recharting of class committees, seating arrangements, and other subtle devices might have created helpful new friendships for the boy. If his loneliness could be lessened and his self-confidence increased, there would be definite hope that his classroom adjustment, and hence his achievement, would show similar improvement. Perhaps then his parents would be more accepting and the vicious circle would be reversed.

In many ways, Danny is almost the paradigm case referral to the school psychologist: a boy of the middle elementary grades whose overt mis-behavior makes him a classroom problem and who, on closer study, proves to be lonely and emotionally maladjusted as well. The teacher in this case dealt, as often teachers must, primarily with symptoms; ideally the school should have the referral facilities to pursue the boy's long-standing problems more deeply.

GRACE T. ALTUS

*   *   *

Since it is evident from the report that Danny's parents are responsible for the boy's outlook and behavioral habits, the school personnel (teacher and principal) should interpret to the parents the importance of their not setting excessively high academic standards for Danny. They must give him love and encouragement, but the standards they set must be reasonable. In conducting the interview I would present some actual cases similar to theirs, showing quite patiently how overdomineering, standardizing parents have hurt their children even though they meant to help. This might put across one's point to the mother and father, who undoubtedly believe they are doing the best for Danny's future.

I believe the treatment of the case was competent. Rather than hav-ing Danny present a written report once a week for the student-teacher conference, I would have him talk with me in personal conferences. In this way, he could express himself in freer terms; and I could show him, more concretely, my interest, affection, and favorable attitudes. This interchange of confidence would complement the parents' changing attitudes, or replace them if the parents did not actually change their own attitudes.

In addition, after the parents were counseled, I would make certain that the mother was not continuing to put pressure on Danny at home. I would try to follow up the progress of the boy by finding out if the mother was able to keep herself out of the picture as much as possible. It seems highly likely that an ambitious mother would probably continue to pressure her son, and she may need a constant reminder.

I would counsel the parents to allow Danny to bring many friends home, to give him more freedom in their home, and to permit him to act as a normal child. Acceptance by children his own age in his own home environment undoubtedly would help his behavioral patterns in school.

DONALD E. BRENNAN

*   *   *

Danny is a boy with a problem, and consequently he has a teacher with a problem. This bright boy is confused and probably miserable much of the time. In spite of being vigorously encouraged by the school and his parents to do better, he doesn't know how, and despite all the pressure, he isn't highly motivated. Although he is isolated by others in school, there are many indications that he desires better relationships and that he is, in his own way, asking for help.

Danny knows he isn't as good as he could be or should be. Everybody reminds him how much more he is capable of doing and that they expect more from him. Even when he does well, there is the impression that he performed acceptably but not as well as he should have. He may doubt whether he actually can do better—but probably not: he is bright and no doubt has some understanding of his capabilities. How much more does he have to do in order to be doing better? What does he have to do that is different? Danny needs answers to these questions, and he needs consistent adult help in this direction.

One might speculate that the school and the home are not satisfied with each other about the treatment given to Danny. To complicate the confusion, Danny probably is not entirely satisfied with either the school or the home, or for that matter with himself. There exists then a not uncommon but confounding problem, where three parties are presumably working toward the same general goals, yet none of the three appears to be cooperating with the others or showing a consistent effort to improve the situation. No one, to date, has taken leadership for clearly stating the issues or for setting and following through on a course of action.

In my judgment several factors need attention. These are: (1) arriving at clear and realistic goals; (2) achieving more consistency and cooperation among those trying to help Danny; and (3) clearing up Danny's confused and unrealistic self-concept.

Everybody needs the sense of direction that comes from clear, well-understood goals. Danny doesn't know what he is working for nor do those about him. All indications point to a general atmosphere of confusion on the matter of expectancies and goals. I believe that an injustice is being done here by the implication that the adults, to whom Danny looks for direction, know in what direction he should move. An essential step in any remedial scheme will be the setting of some clear, cooperatively developed goals. Danny certainly has a stake in this, but he is by no means independent. The school and the home both have an obligation to set reasonably similar standards of conduct and achievement and to relate these to clear goals. If the parents want perfection and the school will settle for less, all parties will have to recognize that differences are in operation, and work toward some compromise.

Since the goals are to be Danny's, all who are framing them need to become better acquainted with him, his abilities, potentialities, and needs.

Danny lacks social approval and does not know how to get it. He can and does get attention, but often it increases his frustration and tension and does not satisfy his need for approval and support. The parents have been consistently demanding in their treatment of Danny. But they have failed to take into consideration that he needs some warmth along with the demands. They have apparently not paid enough attention to the fact that he is a child and not an adult. Danny would benefit from being allowed to bring other children into his home. This would help him make friends and develop some of the skills needed in relating to other people. These skills children can best learn from other children.

The school authorities have been inconsistent in their treatment. At times their approach is relaxed and permissive, and at other times it is severe and demanding. Danny does not know from one day to the next whether he will be ignored, tolerated, praised, or punished for any given act. Even the children, of their own accord or by persuasion from the teacher, have vacillated in their reactions to him.

The consequence is that Danny not only is confused about goals, but he is also unable to develop consistent and satisfying relations with people.

Danny believes he is a disappointment and a problem, yet he desperately wants approval from adults and children. The fact that he is continuously showing that he doesn't feel successful or valued by others does not imply that Danny is an emotionally disturbed child, for there are no signs of any serious personality disorganization. He is acting out his problems and his concerns, and this is healthy. He is showing a rather normal and healthy reaction to continuously aggravated frustrations. He does, however, need help, especially from a trained counselor, to gain insight into the relationship between his behavior and his desire to be accepted and approved of by others. Furthermore, he can be helped to form a more realistic picture of who he really is in terms of ability, interest, hopes, and so on.

I believe the school must take the initiative for mapping out a plan and assume responsibility for carrying out the plan. Three steps are necessary: (1) a carefully coordinated and executed study of the case, (2) counseling for Danny, and (3) conferences with the parents. A written record of the case prepared by someone trained in the skills of case study would provide, for everybody concerned, a clear and concise description of Danny and his problem. It should also lead to specific recommendations which could be tried out in the school and the home.

If this situation is to be improved, there will have to be some changes in the school, as well as in Danny, and also some clarification of the parents' understandings and attitudes. All too often parents and teachers in cases such as this expect changes to be made by the pupil alone. The solution, more often than not, requires adaptation on the part of the school and the home to the needs of the child (as it does to adjustment of the child). Another point that needs cursory mention is the tendency for school people to think of an acceptable solution as one which completely remakes the child into a conforming, hard-working bookworm. I believe we should look for improvement in Danny, not correction or cure. We must avoid trying to make Danny look like other children. He is an individual, and we should try to help him retain his individuality.

Counseling could be directed toward helping Danny get a clearer picture of himself, his tensions, and some of the things for which he is striving. Being a bright boy, he would profit substantially from some counseling interviews, and probably could reconstruct his concept of himself into one that is more positive.

The counselor should have conferences with the parents also, to: (1) give them a clearer picture of why Danny is behaving the way he is; (2) help them express and clarify concerns about Danny's behavior and his future; (3) give them a clearer picture of the program that the school plans to carry out for Danny; (4) help them become involved—and recognize the necessity of their being involved—in the program; and (5) help them get a clearer picture of the relationship between what they do and what their child is doing.

In conclusion, I would like to mention a bias of my own which I believe is pertinent to this case. It is implied in the description of this case that overambition on the part of the parents had led to some wrong values. We are not dealing here with wrong values, but with confused goals and approaches. If the parents appear to be overambitious for their child, the school's role is to help them better understand these ambitions. Standards need to be established for Danny, and I believe the parents have a right to set these standards. If they are unrealistic in the eyes of the school, then the school's obligation is to help the parents understand and develop some which are more realistic. *I firmly believe that the family is the primary child-rearing body in our society, and that the parents have not only the right, but also the obligation to be ambitious for their children.*

DONALD G. FERGUSON

*   *   *

The teacher in this instance seems to have been trained in Adlerian principles of child behavior, providing considerable information about Danny: the situation in which he functions, his interaction, and something of the goal(s) toward which he is striving. Dreikurs[1] cites the need for gaining information in three areas before adequate understanding of the child's behavior can be had: (1) family atmosphere, (2) family constellation, and (3) methods of training. All three are clearly identified in this report. Diagnosis of the child's goals is an essential phase of the total program of assisting him in changing his behavior. From the first statement, the reader is impressed with the teacher's ability to select significant information that bears directly on the problem.

Unfortunately, Danny is representative of many children in our schools today: a child who has been denied opportunities for developing his social competence by well-intentioned but misguided parents. This the teacher realizes, but unlike many teachers she does not use this fact as an excuse for not being able to do something about Danny's behavior. All too frequently teachers dismiss their responsibility for helping children who are either misbehaving or not functioning up to capacity by stating that there is little they can do because of parental pressures at home. Teachers become doubly pessimistic when they have tried working with parents who won't listen or seem indifferent. In many instances either or both

---

[1] Dreikurs, *Psychology in the Classroom* (New York: Harper & Row, Publishers, 1957).

observations are correct, but neither warrants giving up working with the child.

This teacher apparently has an excellent understanding of the concepts of goal-directed behavior: "Throughout his school years Danny tried constantly to involve all his teachers in a struggle for power within the room. He wanted to show his teachers that he could have his own way . . ." Equally important is the fact that this teacher, although she did not do so immediately, very soon stopped falling for his tricks: "I started arranging matters so that Danny either accepted the order set by the group for the good of the group or accepted the consequences." She then cites how she employed the principle of natural consequences.[2]

There appears to be one contradiction in the background presentation. The teacher notes that while Danny is a boy of high intelligence, he has not applied himself and performs at an average level for his grade. In the same paragraph, the teacher notes that when Danny was in the fourth grade, he could read at the seventh-grade level. This hardly seems to be a child performing at an average level.

The teacher might have strengthened her presentation had she noted that while Danny was being socially crippled because of ambitious parents, Danny himself had accepted the same kind of motivation. Like his parents, Danny must always be first and best. But in this case, since he isn't certain he will be first or best in classroom activities, he declines to participate and turns to activities in which he *can be* first and best—being disturbing to others. Here he has gained unusual skill, skill he is not aware he has developed.

The teacher's use of natural consequences with the other children must have grown out of a strength Danny revealed: "However, occasionally he revealed how very much he wanted to be part of the group . . ." After diagnosis, it is important to begin a program of correction. Here there are no prescriptions one can provide as to what specifically should be attempted. Dreikurs[3] refers to "nonspecific" principles upon which specific methods may be based. Generally, the teacher should appraise the pupil's strengths and build on those. They serve as an excellent basis for encouragement. This the teacher did with Danny.

The teacher misunderstood, to some extent, the application of the principle of natural consequences. Teachers exposed to this principle sometimes do not realize its limitations and try to apply it to all situations. This is a mistake. Actually, it has its greatest corrective effect at the attention-getting level, the simplest level of disturbing behavior. It becomes less applicable at the power level and practically ineffective at the remaining

[2] *Ibid.*, pp. 51-52, 76-88.
[3] R. Dreikurs, *et al.*, *Adlerian Family Counseling* (Eugene, Oregon: University of Oregon Press, 1959).

two levels. Because Danny was engaged in a power struggle, with occasional use of revenge, the corrective technique of ignoring this behavior was not effective. A teacher cannot ignore a child who sets out to engage her in a power contest. The teacher realized this when she noted, "After a while I realized that Danny was getting nowhere . . ." More accurately, Danny was getting everywhere, but the teacher was getting nowhere. The "natural consequences" approach is acknowledged to be weak in this case when the teacher reports that while there was improvement, it was usually short-lived.

An important nonspecific method suggested by Dreikurs involves acting more and talking and reasoning less. The critical incident here took place when a firm and fair course of action was undertaken. Danny knew all along that what he was doing was not acceptable. Only when the teacher and principal demonstrated that they were equal to his pranks did he see the futility in continuing his destructive ways. Here again the teacher realized an important aspect of constructive measures. One doesn't "change" and remain changed in cases similar to Danny's without considerable encouragement from those with whom he must work. The teacher let Danny know she liked him, had confidence in him, and would help him when he demonstrated that he wanted help and would cooperate. He responded to this display of respect by the teacher, and when she served notice that she could not accept his misbehaving, she was able to do the job that was hers.

Some favorable mention should be made of the apparent cooperation received from the principal. This is increasingly, but still all too seldom, the case. Teachers will be able to perform the tasks of instruction at higher levels as their knowledge of human behavior becomes more fundamental and they are able to share this knowledge with parents and school administrators.

R. N. LOWE

*   *   *

Overambitious parents should be invited to participate in a teacher-parent conference so that they may be shown what is happening in school and so that they can see the total picture of their child in this environment. Perhaps Danny's parents were unaware of what was happening to him. The fact that Danny did not get along with the children in his room would indicate to them that something was amiss. A description of him in physical education classes and in the classroom might be sufficient to make the parents strive to correct the matter. Perhaps asking them to observe Danny in action would be helpful. However, this would be useful only if Danny were unaware of their presence.

A teacher-parent conference, of course, should have been held either in kindergarten or first grade when the signs of maladjustment were beginning to show in school.

The teacher handled the situation very competently. Danny was led to feel that rules at school were to be kept, that antagonizing the children was not working out well, that he wasn't going to be accepted in the classroom on his grounds, and that he could not have special privileges in school. At the same time, Danny was able to feel that the teacher was on his side by personal weekly contacts during which he presented a written evaluation of his week's activities. He showed where he was improving and what he wished to improve. He was getting good attention from his teacher about things that concerned only him.

I feel that all that was done at school was proper, sufficient, and wise. However, it seems that more should have been done with the mother and father. For the total approach to be really effective, the parents must understand their part in influencing the boy's behavior. They must realize the importance of Danny's playing with other boys. It is obvious that he wants and needs friends.

This case also illustrates the need for school officials to stress to their teachers the importance of parent-teacher conferences. Conferences should be held at the onset of problems—not when the child is almost impossible to bear. If this were a school policy, the number of problem children would decrease rather than grow.

VIOLET STRIMBU

DISCUSSION QUESTIONS—INCIDENT 8

1. Should a teacher advise members of the class to ignore a pupil who is annoying them?
2. Altus comments that dealing with symptomatic behavior on a common-sense basis is often necessary, and setting realistic disciplinary requirements, even without understanding the motivations, may be helpful to children. Given a situation where professional help is either not obtainable or not desired (for example, by parents), what are the arguments for, and against, the procedure of dropping a child from school for a limited period, even if no positive measures of improvement can be instituted?
3. What are the possible hazards and the potential values of working

out school problems directly with parents and children? Who in the typical school would be most suited to do this kind of counseling?

4. Do schools often treat pupils in an impersonal manner, forcing them to conform rather than letting them develop into unique individuals? How can a school maintain order and yet permit children to develop and improve? Between the conservative philosophy of education and the progressive philosophy of education, what alternatives are there?

5. Dreikurs' "natural consequences" principle (a misbehaver must be made to accept the consequences of his behavior) is recommended by Lowe in this incident. What are the desirable and undesirable elements of the basic attitude of placing responsibility for behavior deviations primarily on the child?

6. Do you believe that present parent-teacher communications need to be changed? What may be the best format to improve such communications?

9

IS LOVE ENOUGH?

CRITICAL INCIDENT

Background

Joan was a fourteen-year-old eighth-grade student at our school last year. She lived with her father and stepmother in a low-income area of town.

From the first day of school it was apparent that the girl had serious emotional and adjustment problems. She seemed determined not to get along with anyone, especially teachers. She showed displeasure and irritability toward any attempt at kindness or friendliness. Her characteristic attitude was one of sneering sarcasm and belligerence. For example, if in gym class I demonstrated a skill to practice, she would swear under her breath and say out loud, "Do you expect me to do that? I might just as well try to fly." To which I would reply that if we all could do it, we wouldn't be practicing, and that I would be glad to help her try. She couldn't understand this attitude. I guess she couldn't bear to have me like her in spite of her actions. Typical of her remarks was, "I hate Jim," or, "I know Marge doesn't like me." I never saw her do or say anything kind.

She had a pretty face, but her expression was usually so twisted and sneering that it was impossible to look at her without feeling that she was hideous. Whenever I tried to speak to her about her behavior, she would twist away and tell me she wasn't doing anything wrong, or say, "All right, all right, I heard you!" No matter what approach I used, I wasn't successful in reaching her, so I simply waited, hoping that perhaps she might begin to trust me.

Incident

I was in charge of the lunchroom and part of my job was to seat the "cold-lunch" people according to classes. As Joan came in with her class one day, she started to go to a table not assigned to her group, and I said, "I'm sorry, but you'll have to sit with your own class, Joan," to which she replied, "Oh shit!" I saw red, and pushed her over to the principal, at which point she repeated what she had said to me. She hung her head as he scolded her. When he finished I walked her to an empty table in the back of the lunchroom and told her to stay there until I personally excused her. Then I said, "If there is one thing I can't stand it is a filthy-mouthed girl. If you are going to continue to act this way, you and I are going to tangle and you are going to get the short end of the stick!" She looked surprised because I was really angry and I meant what I said.

After Joan finished her lunch, she raised her hand to be excused. I shook my head. About five minutes later I saw her coming toward me crying. I couldn't believe my eyes, but I was so relieved to see her express such an honest emotion that I was almost happy she was crying. When she got to me she said, "I'm sorry, Mrs. Grace." I asked if she would like to talk to me and she said, "Yes," so we went into my office.

I said the first thing that came to my mind: "Joan, don't you love anyone?" She started to cry as if her heart would break, and she replied, "Yes, I love my real mother in Kentucky, but they won't let me go to her." I asked if her stepmother wasn't good to her. She said, "Oh yes, she tries, but she's not like my real mother." I did not know what to say at that point, and I let her ramble on through her tears. She said that she knew nobody liked her; her teacher wouldn't even help her understand her lessons. I told her that she was wrong, people did like her but she shut them out and hurt their feelings so they stopped trying to help her. I also said that she must learn to give people a chance, an occasional smile or friendly word from her would change the whole world around her if she would try. In ending the interview, I told her I was sincerely her friend and that whenever she wanted to talk I would have time to listen.

Discussion

I wish I could say that Joan changed overnight, but this was not the case. She had many relapses, but I was now prepared for them and tried to reassure her and help her adjust. I had a meeting of her teachers to discuss a way in which to give her self-confidence. This wasn't especially difficult because she did some things well, and we were able to praise her subtly or include her in prestige groups. Apparently, our approach pleased her because she would then work very hard. For instance, she was skillful in volleyball and I would send other children to Joan for help.

She could not work very hard when the pressure was great. I discovered this when she was selected to be starting pitcher for her class in the class softball tournament. At game time she gave me a feeble excuse for not coming. I tried my best to keep her from backing out, but I believe the fear of failure held her back. I did tell her that I understood how she felt, but pointed out that she would have to face an unpleasant situation sooner or later and the longer she put it off the harder it would become for her.

Soon after this, two weeks before the end of school, Joan moved to Florida with her parents. She came to say good-bye before she left and to thank me for helping her. I asked her to write when she got settled but I haven't heard from her.

There were many problems Joan faced that I know I am not qualified to evaluate. However, I did recognize that she felt rejected and was extremely resentful and vindictive about it. Also she was very discouraged. She was so mistake-conscious that rather than make a mistake she would not try anything at all. Saying that people didn't like her was probably projection, since I don't believe she liked or trusted other people. She most likely had had too many failures in her young life. But for a short time, at least, I feel we did help her to see that she could do something right.

Questions

1. Was losing my temper a factor in getting her to change?
2. How does one go about reaching children who shut themselves off from others?
3. Is it proper to plan a program with other teachers to improve a child's emotional adjustment?

*   *   *

Many staff members find the "Joans," male or female, very disturbing. They arouse our anxiety, challenge our authority, and provoke our poorly controlled aggressive and rebellious feelings. In addition, they often shock our sense of propriety with their forthright and sometimes hostile expressions, which say in essence: "I think you're a phoney! You don't really believe that all people are created equal. You don't even believe that all people should have equal opportunities. You don't love your fellow men or believe in doing unto others as you would have others do unto you. Because I'm not 'nice' like the other kids whose parents you'd like to have for your friends, you don't really give me the same breaks. Everything you do seems to tell me that I don't belong here, that I'm not your kind, and that you hope I'll soon drop out of school, and go to work. Then I can buy clothes, an old car, and the other things 'my kind' wants."

Teachers who pride themselves on being unprejudiced and who bend over backward to be broadminded when discussing theoretical questions in their classrooms often can be led into revealing the worst kind of minority prejudice against low-income and socially handicapped youngsters whose value systems differ from those toward which teachers are striving. Teachers, in general, are an upwardly mobile group who have been able to move away from their working-class and small-business parental backgrounds into the professional middle class through teaching. At the same time, they are often held in bondage by authoritarian principles and Victorian rules of conduct imposed by middle-class mores. They often feel insecure in the conflict between their early backgrounds and their current roles.

Such teachers, striving at all costs to defend themselves against a recognition of their own feelings of inadequacy and low self-esteem, often meet with the very reaction they fear from adolescents of various minority groups. These teen-agers have frequently already learned from the significant persons in their lives a suspicious, mistrustful, and persecuted manner. This behavior may seem to the superficial observer a paranoid projection without basis in reality. A closer study of the social world of such adolescents, however, often shows considerable foundation in reality for such behavior.

Some of these problems seem to have been troubling Mrs. Grace. As a teacher of physical education, she was able to express and tolerate a great deal more displaced aggressiveness in her classes than in the lunch room. She could, for example, be sarcastic in return ("If we all could do it, we wouldn't be practicing") without disturbing her relationship with her class. It is my hypothesis that Joan's sudden and somewhat inappropriate comment of "Oh, shit!" reactivated many earlier unresolved conflicts for Mrs.

Grace. These were unconsciously revealed in her reply: "If there is one thing I can't stand, it is a filthy-mouthed girl. If you are going to continue to act this way, you and I are going to tangle and you are going to get the short end of the stick!" At this point Mrs. Grace abdicated her role as teacher and became a frustrated and hence an angry and threatening "acting-out adolescent." It is pertinent to note that in some circles the "short end of the stick" means the "shitty end of the stick." All objectivity was discarded. Mrs. Grace responded impulsively not only to the verbal, but also to the emotional content.

Here again, as in so many cases where the teacher becomes angry and then tries (out of guilt) to make it up to the student, Joan's life was eased a bit in school. Unfortunately, however, Mrs. Grace did not get any insight into her own or Joan's behavior. Such insight would have increased her understanding of such children and of her own actions and would have made it easier for her to live with herself and with them.

I doubt very much that Joan felt anything deeper for Mrs. Grace than gratitude at having her and other teachers "off her back." Being somewhat relieved of this problem, she was probably better able to utilize the learning situation. In bringing about relief for Joan, Mrs. Grace was doing the best she could with her own present emotional orientation and training. To her considerable credit, we should agree, Mrs. Grace was not interested solely in subject matter, but was deeply concerned about the welfare of her pupils as persons.

This, somewhat comparable to Incident (6), is an example of a teacher's acting on impulse and on the widely held assumption that a child's unacceptable behavior *must* arise out of a feeling that he is unloved and unlovable. Here again, the impulse seems to have led to partially desirable effects. But impulse is much less reliable than understanding. The beginning of understanding for the teacher in a situation like this could be as follows: "To me at this time this child is unlovable and unacceptable in her behavior. Her behavior seems to say that she feels the same way about me. Perhaps if we are both to do the jobs for which we are here, we'd better try to see what we can do to improve our relationship. Since I am the adult and have the leadership role, I must study myself in relation to this child." Herein lies the challenge of teaching!

FRANCES R. HARPER

*　　*　　*

Lacking detailed information about Joan's family history and school record, two assumptions seem warranted by the facts given. The first is that resentment toward her stepmother has been carried over into her relations with other adults, and the second is that she feels that most adults, especially women, are insincere and probably dishonest. These assumptions form the base on which a solution to her problem may be worked out and tested.

Speculating on the home situation, it is probably true that Joan liked her real mother and found security in their relationship. This was changed, of course, when the stepmother entered the picture. Joan no longer had someone to whom she could turn for affection and understanding. She felt uprooted and perhaps unwanted, and she attributed the cause of her distress to her stepmother. Even though the stepmother tried to take the place of the real mother, she did not succeed, judging from Joan's reactions. Obviously the girl's attitudes and feelings toward the stepmother became more intense as time went on and finally reached a point at which the causes of her unhappiness were associated with adults in general.

The teacher with whom the critical incident developed could probably have taken hold of the problem sooner if she had had a better understanding of the home situation. A visit in the home with either one or both parents would have yielded pertinent information. Certainly the stepmother could have shed some light on the girl's behavior and attitudes, and she could have described what was being done, if anything, to gain Joan's acceptance. This case brings up the need for teachers to visit the homes of pupils when they sense serious problems, or to ask the guidance counselor to obtain essential social and family background data.

Because the teacher knew very little about conditions in the home other than what she had learned from Joan, she had to rely on limited information and in effect had to rule out the possibility of working closely with the father and stepmother. She did, therefore, the only thing she could do under the circumstances, namely, try to establish rapport with Joan and hope the girl would begin to trust her.

When the incident arose in the lunchroom, the teacher made one error, although it was not especially serious. She sent the girl to the principal instead of taking her to her own office. On the other hand, her reaction to the girl brought about two things that had not been evident to Joan before. First, the girl discovered that there were limits beyond which she could not go and that those limits would be upheld by the teacher. Second, Joan learned that the teacher was genuinely interested in and concerned with her welfare. Mrs. Grace's anger drove this point home in Joan's thinking and opened the door to a possible solution of the problem.

In recognizing that the teacher was truly disturbed and deeply concerned over what had happened, Joan no doubt interpreted the teacher's reactions and her subsequent willingness to talk as evidence that this teacher was a person who might be trusted. She was the only teacher, so far as is known, who showed any interest in Joan or any willingness to deal with her problem.

The fact that the teacher did not reprimand Joan in public for the remark she made was important. Had she treated the incident openly, denouncing Joan for what she said, Joan would have closed up and would have refused thereafter to discuss anything with the teacher. She would have resented being "put on the spot" before her classmates. Many teachers make this mistake in dealing with pupils who present a disciplinary challenge.

No immediate solution to Joan's social behavior seems possible under the circumstances. New attitudes and values must be substituted for those she has carried into the school, and the process of substitution is a long and slow one, usually. Change would have come about only as ties between the teacher and Joan grew stronger and as Joan gradually learned to recognize the underlying causes of her behavior and to have faith in the teacher's guidance.

After the incident occurred, the teacher wisely left the door open, inviting Joan to come in at any time and to talk freely with her. She realized that patience, tact, and understanding would be necessary before a solution to the problem could be worked out successfully.

The case presents an interesting issue about the extent to which a teacher should go in sharing with her colleagues confidential information received from a pupil. Although it could be argued that the teacher should take her colleagues into her confidence and share such information on grounds that they would work better with the pupil, it would seem much wiser to respect the pupil's trust and not to disclose any personal information that the pupil would refuse to share with other teachers. This would not prevent the teacher from letting other teachers know about the general problem and from suggesting how they might cooperate in helping the pupil to overcome her difficulties. If the pupil had the slightest suspicion that what she was telling the teacher was being passed on to someone else, she would feel that her confidence had been betrayed and would refuse to take part in future discussions. The teacher here had, above all things, to restore this girl's faith in the sincerity and integrity of adults.

Unfortunately, Joan moved away too soon to find out whether or not the teacher's approach was effective. Had she remained in school, she should have been assigned to this teacher for two or three years so that the teacher could establish a solid personal relationship built on a foundation of friendship, respect, and appreciation. Without a doubt, the teacher might have been successful in changing the girl's attitudes and values and in restoring her to a more normal role in society.

LESLIE W. KINDRED

*   *   *

When a teacher loses her temper, she is showing a lack of the emotional control that she is asking her pupils to develop. There is, however, a display of firmness coupled with severity that may resemble anger in its expression but is even more effective because it can be displayed with an accompaniment of love. It moves at the command of its possessor, it does not erupt without his willing it.

Love and attention were Joan's needs. She wanted others to be interested in her for her own sake, not just from a sense of duty or impersonal charity. Because she had felt a lack of genuine concern in the kindnesses of teachers, of stepmother, and probably of all with whom she dealt, her sensitive nature became bitter. Consequently, she struck back at society through each person who thwarted her desires. Mrs. Grace was sincerely concerned about Joan and this became evident, not by her anger, but by her continuous, persistent effort to assist Joan in her emotional difficulties. Joan could recognize that it was not self-interest that was motivating her teacher's attention to her, but real love.

The teacher was successful to a degree; perhaps she recognized that Joan's problems were deep-seated and may have been rooted in rejection from babyhood. It might have required the services of a clinical psychologist or a psychiatrist to reach down into the child's past experience and set right the emotional disorders that had been fostered by early experience. Perhaps this could never have been done, for persons who have been deprived in early life of emotional security seem to have throughout their lives a boundless and unsatisfied desire for affection. At any rate, Mrs. Grace might have been assisted by experts even if they merely guided her rather than attempting to help Joan directly.

Even without professional assistance Mrs. Grace had, perhaps unwittingly, used the one method that reaches children who can be reached in no other way—she loved her. It was this love that gave Mrs. Grace the power to persist patiently in her attempt to win Joan. She was an example of the teacher who knows that in dealing with a disturbed child, failure must be disregarded. Rebuffs must be ignored. If success is ever to be achieved, it comes after a long period of resistance on the part of the emotionally disturbed child.

The fact that Mrs. Grace enlisted the cooperation of other teachers in dealing with Joan is all on the credit side. No good system of guidance and counseling can overlook the fact that the entire school staff is involved in the formation of every child. Although information received in confidence never becomes subject matter to share with others, the judgments made through observation of children should certainly be weighed with other faculty members. The best group thinking should be applied to the needs of each child. Other teachers can contribute their observations and their thoughts on the application of guidance and psychological principles. A joint effort to help children in this manner will contribute to a more consistent approach to the needs of each child than is otherwise possible.

There is another resource that Mrs. Grace might have tapped to assist Joan, and that is the peer group. In one such case of which I know, the teacher had a leadership group of girls that met weekly to discuss what they might do to help solve the problems they had learned to observe. They noted that one girl, Nancy, was continually ignored by the rest and that she was sloppy and unsociable. They knew that her mother had died the summer before, that her crippled father was attempting to support her on a pension, and that she needed money and worked in a local movie house as a cashier. They feared the associations she made at work and decided to attempt to get her another job. At this point Nancy was on the verge of quitting school—she had just turned sixteen. The girls planned their attack carefully, first showing interest and friendliness and drawing Nancy into their conversations whenever possible. Next, they secured an interview for a part-time typing position and coached Nancy for the interview, both about her personal appearance and about her manner of applying. Nancy failed to get the job. But by that time she felt that others were interested in her, and she became a little more friendly toward the group. The girls who had tried to help her continued to draw her out so that she was encouraged to remain in school until graduation.

Today there are many organizations that help to train young people in the social attitudes that this leadership group displayed. Mrs. Grace might have availed herself of such a group to help give Joan the sense of belonging that would have stabilized her emotionally. She needed more than teacher love and guidance; she needed reassurance that she could meet with her peer group on a basis of equality and friendship.

SISTER M. LOYOLA

*   *   *

This is a heart-warming instance of a teacher's effort to teach the total child. It is the sort of service we too often take for granted. All of us are molded by the impact of other personalities on our own. It is possible that Joan will be a more complete, mature, and better functioning woman because of this teacher's devotion to the highest requirements of her profession.

I believe losing her temper was, of itself, no consequence. What was important was this teacher's ability to be concerned well beyond the ordinary, expected limit, and to show this concern convincingly—even to the point of exasperation. It was partly because the teacher reacted naturally that the child was convinced that the teacher cared about her and was sincerely interested in her. Too often we forget that the wisdom of the professional must be imparted with natural feelings. It was partly because the teacher's anger was not an isolated outburst, but an emotion expressed against a background of repeated overtures and efforts to "reach" Joan, that it was essentially a good and relevant thing.

There can be no formula for "reaching" the withdrawn student. One makes one's overtures and tries to show one's interest, waiting, as this teacher did, for something to "trigger" a stronger or warmer response. We cannot make these "triggering" opportunities, we can only be ready to use them if they occur—this teacher acted at the right moment, almost instinctively, to bring home her desire to help.

A personality is often modified by the most unexpected incidents. The interaction between two people may produce results that may affect either in ways not comprehensible to the observer. In part, I believe, this is because there exist at least two levels of communication. The first is on the surface, and is apparent to others. The second, deeper and more important especially in tense, emotionally laden situations, reaches a more sensitive level of feeling. To show emotion is to show concern; it is far worse often to be ignored than to be scolded. It is this that the teacher in the present case showed—a concern, a real feeling.

Awareness of a child's problem *should* be shared among teachers (without an overzealous or unnatural "campaign" to help the child). In addition to patience, firmness, and understanding on the part of whatever teachers desire to help, an intelligent grasp of whatever facts can be learned from wider observation and clinical diagnosis is important. Ideally, the teachers' knowledge of the child should be supplemented by that of other professional persons working with the child or family—such as guidance or welfare workers. The case conference is an effective method of assuring that such knowledge is intelligently used.

DOUGLAS C. RIGG

*   *   *

The problem developed in this critical incident refers to a bit of aberrant behavior developed in an individual who quite deliberately avoided any kind of meaningful communication with the world. The response of

"Oh shit!" that Joan made following the instructor's instruction to sit with her own class represents a very complicated bit of behavior. Joan was an individual who isolated herself from appropriate communication with others. This may have been because of the disrupted parental situation. It may not have been. Certainly, isolated behavior with its inevitable concomitant of ascribing isolation to others, behavior sometimes called "paranoid," is not necessarily a product of disrupted home life. On the contrary, isolation of a particular personality may develop quite within the context of a supposedly "normal" household.

The significance of the teacher's direct remark, which in terms of existential psychiatry would perhaps be called "an encounter," is very significant. The barrier of negative identification with the modes of the world in which she found herself, or with the particular class to which she should have related, was abrogated by the direct, transactional, feelingful expression on the part of the teacher. It was not the teacher's calling her "a filthy-mouthed girl" that altered the relationship and subsequent behavior, so much as it was the student's perceiving the teacher's warmth and acceptance of her as a person, her seeing that she was not condemned as "unacceptable." Furthermore, the teacher followed up her remarks with the apparently disjunctive remark, "Joan, don't you love anyone?" If the student had been in doubt about the teacher's sincerity this remark, which brought forth an affective response, was certainly proof enough.

I do not feel, by the way, that a single incident is productive of great changes in an individual. "One swallow does not make a summer." Instead, a critical incident is the initial "intrusion" into an all-too-fixed and stable system, which must be followed by a great number of other such elements in order to move toward an "enfirmation" (that is, development of a regular or persistent element of behavior). Or, it may also be the final crystallization of a bit of behavior in the same sense that soloing a plane is perhaps the precise moment of most complete awareness of learning. These are, I would feel, the polarities of the "critical incident."

It is my own feeling that no program of reincorporating a proper feeling of emotional relatedness can occur by means of a single teacher's isolated efforts. Of course, there is very definitely the possibility of "spread" of appropriate experiential orientation from one situation to another, but this is more usually a product of an overtly psychotherapeutic situation than it is of a relatively limited and less personally intensive teacher contact. It would, therefore, seem more than reasonable that a group program involving the best effort of a coordinated group of teachers would be most helpful as necessary collusive behavior quite appropriate for such cases. To my mind, such collusion (so long as it is constructively oriented) is not only appropriate but vital to the reordering or reorientation of the isolated individual. Too often the single effort, as in this incident, will have a limited effect. The isolated child must be oriented toward the group whether she likes it or not, and this isolation can be broken by relatively obvious, often neglected, but very simple and common-sense devices.

JORDAN M. SCHER

*   *   *

". . . So I simply waited it out, hoping that perhaps she might begin to trust me."

". . . She looked surprised because I was really angry and I meant every word I said."

". . . I said the first thing that came into my mind: 'Joan, don't you love anyone?' "

These three quotes from the teacher who reports the incident give the clue for the understanding of her success: her ability to reach a girl who up to then could display only aggression and hostility against everyone. Up to that moment fourteen-year-old Joan had not been able to establish a friendly contact with anyone. She provoked by her sarcasm, sneering, and belligerence not only her teachers but also her peers. It seems somewhat surprising that in a group of teen-agers she did not find other rebels to join her. Had she found them, she might have become the leader of a possibly rather dangerous, defiant gang of teen-agers, who would have supported each other in their rebellion. While such a gang can cause a great deal of trouble, the individual members might easily be the victims of a sort of temporary mass hysteria.

Joan's emotional disturbance was a serious and a deep-seated one. Therefore she was rejected by her peers, too; even by those who might have been inclined to rebel against authority.

We know little of her background and since our information is drawn from Joan's own report, it is not free from her projections. Joan's behavior is the more reliable indicator of the measure of her disturbance. We conclude from the severe degree of her hostility that she is a severely disturbed girl. There are behavior signs that give hope for her future adjustment. She says of her stepmother, with an appreciable attempt to be fair, "Oh yes, she tries, but she's not like my real mother."

This remark allows the conclusion that the reality of Joan's life is possibly not so bad as one might assume from her severe symptoms. Therefore her condition might not be of a responsive nature only, but rather might be a true neurosis, a threat from within her own personality causing a conflict that she cannot resolve.

One of Joan's distorted views refers to her contacts with people. She

123

does not trust anybody and therefore is, so to speak, immune toward attempts to help her.

What happened when her teacher was able to penetrate her armor?

The three quotes at the beginning of my comments explain what happened. The teacher at that moment did not play the role of a teacher; she was simply a human being, with strong emotions that she displayed without restraint. She had been waiting her chance for some time, and this seeming indifference made her outburst of genuine anger still more effective. Joan was overcome by the realization that she, this hateful, worthless creature, could arouse such emotion. It made her akin with this teacher; she could almost be one with her. She cried because she had hurt herself in hurting the teacher. Stirred by this deep emotional experience, she was able to respond—at least momentarily. This emotional experience was in fact a mutual one, for the teacher reports: ". . . I saw her coming toward me crying. I couldn't believe my eyes, but I was so relieved at such an honest emotion coming from her that I was almost happy that she was crying . . ." The teacher was stirred, too, and therefore able to respond to Joan with genuine warmth and human feeling.

This incident would have been an excellent initial experience for successful psychotherapy with Joan. It is difficult for a teacher to carry it through. It calls for playing two roles that cannot be completely reconciled. The teacher has to face the student with demands that might often be detrimental to treatment. The teacher has obilgations toward all students that again might occasionally interfere with treatment. Many similar blocks caused by a dual role of the teacher-therapist could be named.

In this case, the teacher certainly did her very best and deserves recognition for her attempts. That she feels her success was only partial shows her sensitivity and general good judgment. She observed Joan's behavior carefully and responded correctly. She didn't pamper her but made her face difficulties without forcing her to solve them. This restraint made it possible for Joan to continue her trust in the teacher.

Children who shut themselves off may do so for many different reasons. The approach of the teacher will be a different one according to the individual case. Therefore it will be important for the teacher to learn all that she can about the child. School records, talks with former teachers, and interviews with the parents will be important steps. It is always safest not to force the withdrawn student into a relationship with the teacher that he obviously fears.

The withdrawn child says: *Leave me alone.* He feels safer when left alone. He sees the world as a dangerous place. Why dangerous? How dangerous? The answer will be different for every withdrawn student. The teacher can approach such a child by giving him little chances to open up, chances that the student may or may not use. The teacher may ask him to do some little job: "Will you please take the paper to my office?" But there must not be too much of this!

When the teacher has reached some understanding of the child's personality pattern, she will find a way to reach the student mainly by her understanding. Then she can create experiences that are needed in the individual case. The child who might have shut himself off because "the world is so unfair" might be occasionally called upon to listen to an argument between fellow students and help to solve or to settle it. He would then experience the concrete idea that fair judgment receives respect. In any case, the best results will be reached by a tactful restraint on the part of the teacher, and by the teacher who gradually offers chances for friendship without any forcing.

The ideal is that all teachers concerned cooperate in helping to readjust a disturbed child. This may not always be easy. But the teacher who understands the child in question and knows how he can be helped should try to win the cooperation of her colleagues. She will be more successful if she does not tell them what to do, but controls her own emotions and gives them a clear picture of the facts that determine the child's faulty attitude.

REGINE SEIDLER

*   *   *

It is evident that Joan's teacher sincerely liked Joan and that in time Joan felt it. When the teacher lost her temper, Joan was shaken by fear of losing someone she secretly liked. Apparently she missed her mother very much and the threat of loss of this person too changed her behavior. Joan's teacher did not just open the door to Joan but actually acted to help the girl. Joan needed more than sincere words to feel accepted.

Joan's teacher was a very understanding person, and Joan needed a friend, someone who would completely accept her. When Joan was fearful of the class tournament, her teacher showed that she understood how the girl felt. If Joan's teacher had been able to speak to the father and stepmother, perhaps something more permanent may have developed and continued. However, I assume time and the situation prevented this step. Had Joan stayed on at this school, she might have become a happier person. If she does not meet an understanding teacher in Florida, little will have been gained.

The idea of getting all of her teachers to work together to build up her self-confidence was an excellent approach. It is always proper to plan an adjustment program with other teachers concerned with a child. Unless one of the teachers has found a way of handling the child, an emotionally unadjusted child carries his problems from room to room. Often a negative approach develops, each teacher probably only scolding and punishing.

Actually, the teachers whom the problem child encounters are *obligated* to pool their resources in order to help the child. The child will do better because she will feel that her teachers are accepting and are trying to help. The full attention she receives from them will build her prestige. Unless all teachers involved work together toward solving a child's problem, one teacher may unknowingly tear down what another is trying to build.

When a school system is without a school counselor, the only recourse a teacher has is to do her best with what knowledge and insight she has. If she is understanding and willing to do this, the school system, the community, and the children are most fortunate.

VIOLET STRIMBU

DISCUSSION QUESTIONS—INCIDENT 9

1. What are the social, political, religious, and familial implications of extending the schools' responsibility to encompass noninstructional functions?
2. Do teachers as a group have middle-class "upward striving" motives? How do teachers with such motives function when teaching underprivileged children who have not been indoctrinated with these values?
3. What are the advantages and disadvantages of a teacher's visiting a problem pupil's home?
4. What are the implications of enlisting the help of other teachers in handling a conduct problem?
5. Apparently in this case, a teacher's ability to display honest anger convinced the student that the teacher cared for her. This raises a question about the proper "role" a teacher should play. Should a teacher always maintain self-control? To what degree and under what circumstances should teachers express their feelings?
6. What should teachers do to help isolated children have a feeling of belonging? What elements should be kept in mind in handling problems of lonely or maladjusted children?

10

"YOU'RE SICK—GO TO BED"

CRITICAL INCIDENT

Background

I am a school psychologist. Problem children are referred to me frequently—chronic truants, mischiefmakers, pranksters, and noncooperators. For very difficult cases I have developed a particular technique that has sometimes resulted in astonishing behavior changes. I would be most happy to obtain informed opinions about why it works and whether it is consonant with respected practices. To illustrate the technique, I shall discuss its use in relation to Joe.

Joe was referred to me because of his mischiefmaking. At that time he was on a "match" kick. He would light a match from a book of matches, using one hand only, then put the lighted match into his mouth, to the amazement of all observers. Among his other pranks were jumping out of the school windows (a drop of about ten feet), setting fires in metal wastebaskets, and throwing blackboard erasers into the air-conditioner duct.

He was small, wiry, and active, with a sly, teasing manner. Teachers were, literally, afraid to turn their backs on this eight-year-old child.

When I interviewed him he was polite, admitted some of the complaints and denied some; he had a cheery, what-the-hell expression. Joe was above average in intelligence; he was working at the third-grade level. His record contained statements about many conferences with his parents, who had been most cooperative. They had admitted that they did not know what could be wrong with him in school, because he was no special problem at home.

Because he was being considered seriously for explusion, which would have meant the parents' having to find a private school for him, I made an alternative suggestion.

Incident

I called the teacher and the parents together and outlined my plan. Instead of expelling Joe, we would try the following experiment.

1. The mother was to remain at home when Joe was at school so that she could be reached by telephone immediately. If she had to go out she was to have someone available to answer the phone.

2. The moment that Joe misbehaved in class, the teacher was to call the mother.

3. The mother was to come to school and take Joe home. There she was to put him to bed, saying, "You haven't behaved well in school. Since you are a good boy, you must be sick, so you must stay in bed."

4. The mother was to keep him in bed the rest of the day and all of the next day. No books, no television, no playing.

5. Joe was then to be returned to school the following day, with the warning that any misbehavior would result in the same procedure.

6. We were to try the experiment for two weeks, or three times. That is, if Joe misbehaved only once or twice in two weeks, then he could stay in school; if he misbehaved three times, he was to be expelled.

The parents and the teacher agreed; I then got the principal's approval. I called in Joe and informed him of the new plan in the presence of his parents and the teacher, and to make certain that he understood, I questioned him about each of the vital points. His replies indicated that he did understand.

The next day, his mother waited in vain for a phone call. Joe behaved properly—for a whole day—something unprecedented in his scholastic career. The next day, he "fell"—the teacher called immediately and the mother took Joe home, not scolding him or even talking to him—as she had been instructed—and put him to bed for that day and the following day. When he returned to school, nothing was said to him by the teacher. He was fine Thursday and Friday. No trouble Monday or Tuesday. On Wednesday he was caught again, and taken home. He returned on Friday. During the next week he was perfect. As of this writing, we have had to send him home a total of three times in a three-month period.

Discussion

The boy was marked for expulsion, which would have been a serious blow to the child and his parents—more than that, it would have meant decided expense and inconvenience. His teacher was a capable, experienced woman, and the school system was progressive. I am certain that this technique saved the boy much hardship.

The experiment also worked in three other cases. In another, it did not. The children, surprisingly enough, agreed in all cases that the procedure was sensible, and they rarely complained or forgot about it.

However, because the procedure is radical and because I have been attacked by colleagues for using this "cruel" approach, I am interested in obtaining comment about it.

Questions

1. Is this procedure logical?
2. Can it hurt the child emotionally?
3. Will the child so dealt with believe that parents and teachers are conspiring against him?
4. Why do some children accept this procedure?

*   *   *

In commenting on this episode, we must consider the motivation for the child's conduct, and the child's needs, which must be satisfied somehow in a socially acceptable way. The fact that Joe was small in size was mentioned, but it appears doubtful that the whole picture of his problems was really known. A very thorough study of the boy and his family would be needed to detect more subtle difficulties in interpersonal relations than were related by the parents. Quite probably, unconscious rejection would be found important in the home situation. Perhaps every attempt to seek approval at home more or less failed, and even undesirable behavior may have been unsuccessful in obtaining much attention. At school it may have been different only in that unacceptable behavior brought a form of recognition that was at least partially rewarding.

There is much to be said for the outlined procedure, which evidently made Joe's spectacular misbehavior no longer satisfying, but the cause of failure to achieve results with one case out of five is not discussed. Indeed it surprises me that success was found to be as high as 80 per cent, because I think that some positive approach needs to be added to this procedure. The fallacy in it lies in the apparent lack of consideration of a need for acceptance, and in the absence of some planning for a more appropriate and socially desirable way of satisfying it. Perhaps the boy found a better solution by stumbling upon it, or perhaps without the teacher, the psychologist, or the parents being aware of what they did, some outlet that worked for the child was provided. The emotional damage that might occur if the child was not helped to find a better way of being recognized is not considered in this case. I have seen withdrawing personalities, in developing stages, who would find the time in bed, without opportunity for much overt action, a welcome relief from a less satisfying reality, and who would achieve the reward of retreat into fantasy by deliberate misconduct when reality made too many demands. The foregoing is merely a plausible hypothesis to explain the failure reported.

Permissiveness has its limits, and acceptance of a person as a good person does not depend upon approval of all his behavior. Children often "test the limits" of the teacher's sense of humor or tolerance. Self-discipline is not learned by growing boys and girls who are treated nondirectively at all times. Fairness of the adult in making and carrying out definite rules consistently wins respect in all but very exceptional instances. Therefore I regard the plan used in this incident as sound in most respects, since the rules were made clear and a total rejection by the school through expulsion was avoided at the time. A paranoid sort of suspicion or resentment of the adults involved would probably be rare. Very important to the child, however, would be the school's and parents' abiding by their part of the bargain and not changing the rules arbitrarily to the disadvantage of the youngster because of fear of criticism, or because of temporary annoyance, or for any other irrational reason.

Making the bargain clear to the child so that he has no misunderstanding of what is expected of him is essential also. Why not add that if he were to do his best to complete a project requiring sustained effort and present a final product representing the best of which he is capable, he would have an opportunity to exhibit or demonstrate it? Not overdone, this policy would motivate him to wait for his turn to be recognized and accepted in a way much more satisfying than creating some temporary alarm or confusion.

A healthy, active, outgoing young personality seldom prefers boredom in bed to real-life activities. No plan will be tailored to fit all cases, but this one does not strike me as too drastic a punishment, provided an element of positive reinforcement is deliberately introduced.

KENNETH L. BEAN

*   *   *

This little incident is charming in its revelation not only of the unusually sensitive intuition of a young counselor in his *honoring* of the student—an aggressive, mischiefmaking little boy who has driven his teachers to such distraction that he was about to be expelled—but also of the counselor's unconscious perception, against all evidence, of a stable child-parent relationship. Attacked as "cruel" by teachers for his means of meeting a situation they could not cope with, he now questions with dismay a procedure that seems to work but that he cannot logically defend. Perhaps the cue lies in its acceptance by the children affected, who alone recognized, with the straightforward honesty and insight of children, what was "happening."

The truism that the home is responsible for children's school difficulties is far from binding. The writer's research on this specific issue[1] pointed out that the tendency of some teachers to ascribe their own problems to children has severe consequences, namely, that *to call a child a "problem child" may be to make him one*, especially a child well identified with his parents and thus vulnerable to felt disapproval in guilt-arousal and reaction. In this instance, the honest bewilderment of the parents, reiterating that Joe was no problem at home, rang true to the counselor, who then *accepted the child-parent relationship as valid*. Had the parents been less undefensive—less loving and less loyal in accepting Joe's problem as their own—the counselor's approach would not have worked.

We pause here to consider how sensitive an issue is the aggressive behavior of young children. Parents who see this anger turned upon them directly greatly prefer to minimize the strength of the "impetus to aggression" rather than to admit its force and try to refocus the *direction* of energy. Let us turn aside from this incident briefly to suggest some possible constructive aspects of anger. Other interpretations may help open a tight little circle and introduce more perspective.

First, much of a child's aggression is "counter-aggression" against demands which seem arbitrary, unreasonable, and even threatening to his growing sense of individuality. Often he may be right. Normally counter-aggression, being punishable, is played out largely in fantasy; the latent

[1] E. Z. Johnson, "The Problem Children of Home and School," *Psychological Reports*, 1 (1955), pp. 371-78.

strength of such a drive is seen in a child's instant recognition of, and turn-ing to account, certain "safe reality conditions" for acting out—as when company comes and the parent is at a disadvantage. Parents fail to follow up this cue: children *are* amenable to discussion and appeal.

Second, we learn to estimate our strength by its impact upon others, per-haps not as "an equal and opposite reaction," but as somewhat indicative of the initial energy. There is no more disheartening experience than the absence of any response to effort. Children subject to affection deprivation, never having learned "relationship," cannot come to terms with the great laws of *transfer*, discernible as antecedent-consequent, stimulus-response, or cause-effect linkages. Children growing up in a normal family environ-ment of love, seasoned with temporary irritation and acting out on the part of their parents, learn that *feelings* are normal responses to reality situa-tions. Thus, although they learn that they can "provoke" their parents, they usually also learn that provocation is less rewarding than other in-volvements. To produce casual effects not only reinforces the "predictabil-ity" of relationships, it also enhances a sense of power—a growing dimension of the self and thus a growing capacity for objectivity. Children are not alone; adults, as parents, teachers, or psychotherapists, "provoke" reactive behavior. We initiate stimuli to discover what may happen—call this curiosity or scientific inquiry. But it was through his power to *predict* that *homo erectus* became *homo sapiens*. Increasingly too we learn that ex-pectancies govern a man's behavior.[2] This "dimension of expectancy" may be a lingering resultant of the "infantile omnipotence" fantasy—never completely fulfilled and so still seeking "power" *to apprehend* and *to order* the mounting accumulation of observations and feelings into hypotheses of lawfulness.

Third, demanding behavior may be a "test of love." A classic cartoon is that of Dennis the Menace saying to his sleepy, barefooted, and shivering father, "No, I don't *want* bathroom water. I want *kitchen* water!" Testing of love is certainly not confined to children. Its occurrence, however, sug-gests the stirring up of the great counter-force of identification—at first glance, incompatible with the driving impulse to aggression. These great forces gather strength, mounting in incremental evidence of love and re-quirement, until tension becomes intolerable and forces the issue of the so-called Oedipal crisis, where the child must "declare himself" for or against his parents (and the society) by introjection or rejection of their standards. The remarkable integrative capacity of children so young is seen in their *reconciliation* of these drives without cancelling out or loss of energy, by accepting *discipline* as an aspect of *love*—in the realization that

[2] G. A. Kelley, *Psychology of Personal Constructs* (New York: W. W. Norton & Company, Inc., 1955), and O. H. Mowrer, *Learning Theory and Behavior* (New York: John Wiley & Sons, Inc., 1960).

parents ask no more of their children than they require of themselves in governance under law. Thus is inaugurated the qualitative change, the discontinuous shift of state, known as latency period (a misnomer), which sets the tenor of the future life of the child.

Returning to Joe, perhaps his teachers were strict; in a permissive school, teachers suppress hostility they cannot ventilate, and they may become more demanding than they know. Joe could provoke them in a "safe" situation, and increased sense of mastery increased his resourcefulness in "acting out" until his "bluff was called."

"If you act naughty, you must be sick," said the counselor, *"because you are not a naughty boy."* In his prescription of bed, trays, and tenderness, he not only answered fantasy with fantasy, "make believe" with "make believe," but, by creating symbolic return to an earlier stage of life, gave the child opportunity to *reaffirm* more consciously the "choice" to which he was already unconsciously committed. This is indeed a "second chance," offered to few of us, and then only under the extreme pressure of psychotherapy after we have in truth become "sick" and recognize our essential "helplessness."

This young counselor's deference to a child of eight—to let him choose his own destiny, in a situation emulating that of earlier unconscious choice, thereby refocusing the effects of his own behavior on him so that he might *experience* his own feelings—is a model of counseling and therapy alike, reflecting (as do all things beautiful) the ideals of creativity, reverence, and devotion.

ELIZABETH Z. JOHNSON

*   *   *

This is a particularly provocative incident. *The major issue seems to be whether one accepts and promotes a particular technique simply because it was deemed to be "successful" by a person whose depth of conviction appears to be greater than his depth of insight.*
The school psychologist provided the background information and the rationale for developing this technique for Joe, a small eight-year-old boy. Joe's behavior was so annoying to teachers that they felt he could no longer be controlled in the classroom. Like many boys, Joe was to be expelled for disorderly conduct rather than for academic failure. If one looks closely at the pranks that Joe initiated in the classroom, they all seem designed to focus attention on him. In the interview with the school psychologist, Joe responded realistically and seemed to be aware of the dubious quality of some of his behavior. The psychologist also commented that Joe's parents

were most cooperative and stated that he was no particular problem at home. Putting these facts together, Joe does not appear to be *an emotionally disturbed boy.*

At the end of the interview, the psychologist decided he would try the experiment, if the parents and teacher agreed. Why the individual designated as a psychologist felt that this was the best or only way to handle this boy's problem is disturbing to us. It seems that before a phychologist makes such a decision regarding the treatment of a boy, he is obligated to do more adequate diagnostic work. Perhaps he did administer additional tests which were not reported in this incident; if so, he was derelict in not recording this fact. In any case, we reject his treatment and feel it was psychologically unsound for the following reasons.

The child is being subjected to manipulation by adults in such a way that the adults do not have to feel unnecessarily guilty. If we take away some of the mellifluous adult words, the message the child hears is: (1) either you cut out your symptoms or we are going to cut you out of school; (2) because you are a nuisance in school, we are going to punish you by "pretending" you are sick; and (3) to impress you with the seriousness of your behavior, we are not only going to pretend you are sick but we are also going to make life reasonably miserable for you at home (by denying you books, television, and so on) so that you will capitulate and accept school as the lesser evil.

Although the psychologist and parents presumably did not intend explicitly to communicate this three-part message to the child, it is our guess this is the way the child really perceived the so-called "experiment." Interestingly enough, the child responded to the plan, making the parents, teacher, and school psychologist happy and convinced that their methods had helped to regenerate the child. Let us examine this interpretation a little more closely.

The psychologist reported that he had used this method in four other cases and stated that it was successful in three of them. It is our interpretation that this particular technique was presumed successful with four of the five boys because the psychologist was working with boys who had rather similar psychodynamics. The four boys were probably intelligent boys, who were going through a developmental stage and/or compensating for certain minor feelings of group rejection. We also conjecture that basically all four of the boys wanted to remain in school. If they had not wanted to remain in school, the technique introduced would have provided them with the coveted opportunity to misbehave three times and then be expelled. The emotionally disturbed boys with whom we have worked would have exploited such an opportunity to the hilt.

Another basic criticism of this technique is that it dealt with the child's symptoms rather than with causative factors. It is known from clinical work that if we put increasing pressure on an emotionally disturbed child to give up his major defense (that is, his characteristic way of handling life situations), then he will substitute another defense that may be more difficult to cope with than was his original one.

Joe may have been attempting simply to win acceptance for himself in his peer group. Unfortunately, this perfectly understandable and healthy desire on the part of the child resulted in his involvement in "a vicious circle." This can be described in the following way. Feeling rejected and striving for acceptance and recognition in his peer group, Joe developed attention-getting devices. While these acts captured the attention of the group and gave him momentary satisfactions, they created secondary and concomitant problems with respect to the teacher. The teacher in turn told him to stop it, to act his age, and so on. The impact of these reiterated comments resulted in more secondary problems. The cycle increased in intensity and magnitude until the teacher was no longer able to accept or even to tolerate the child.

The questions that appear at the end of the incident are written to sample the surface interpretation of the situation and cannot be answered from a dynamic point of view. For example, the second question reads, "Can it hurt the child emotionally?" What kind of a child are we dealing with? A normal child, neurotic child, psychotic child, unsocialized child? The data given here are not adequate for sound professional analysis of such a question.

NICHOLAS J. LONG
HAROLD G. SHANE

*   *   *

As an administrator and a teacher I have several reactions to this incident. First, when someone brings me a problem, I ask myself *why?* To what extent am I expected to contribute to the solution or to what extent am I to sanction the solution? The contributor of this incident seems concerned about having the approval of his colleagues. Is this the problem? Do we lack confidence? Must we always have the approval of everyone with whom we work?

The second reaction I have is that the contributor feels he solved the problem. This person needs praise and approval. Although the treatment or solution of the problem is by no means as radical or as unusual as the contributor believes, he wishes to have confirmation of his own opinion that it is highly successful because it worked four out of five times. Did it? Because something "works," does that mean it is successful? What caused the boy's objectionable behavior in the first place? We still don't know. The symptom of disturbance has been removed, I will agree. But I wonder how he is now expressing his negative feeling. Perhaps Joe was merely testing the limits of his behavior, only seeing what he could do. He tested the limits, found out, and desisted. No harm done.

However, suppose Joe needed desperately to be noticed. Suppose he needed to be a hero. If so, the threat has simply bottled up his feelings. He may obtain release from this tension in many normal ways, including daydreams. Or, he may develop more vicious or subtle ways of satisfying his feelings.

My third reaction is that the use of the ultimatum generally is poor *unless* one is prepared to carry out its provisions. One must have no past history of equivocation in regard to ultimatums. Joe even then might accept the "dare" to misbehave.

My fourth reaction concerns the cruelty or severity of the punishment. The severity of punishment is not the key to effectiveness. More often the certainty of the mildest punishment is more effective than wild threats.

In cases in which a child seems to be seeking the limits of reasonable behavior, this procedure appears to work, as does any measure of punishment that does not delve into basic causes. However, if behavior is too disorganized for this process and it does not appear to work, what then? One must hunt causes in the first place before digging into one's bag of tricks.

One of the procedures used to identify the causes of behavior includes an investigation of the home environment of the child. Certainly our responsibility to the parents of the child is not simply to report to them that their child is creating problems. The parents should always be a significant factor in the solution of a problem. What does this procedure do? It compels the parents to take more part in raising and disciplining their child. It has created a more definite understanding between parent and teacher and cooperation between home and school. The boy must be made to feel that someone is interested in his well-being, and to some children this type of punishment can do miracles if followed consistently.

The child will not think that the parent and the school authorities are conspiring against him if he becomes a part of the solution of the problem. It is important to create a climate of understanding. Verbally and psychologically the child must follow and accept the "solution" upon which parents and teachers agree.

In an oversimplified situation we are not able to determine the logical gaps in this procedure. Perhaps it works because the child is brought in and *not* presented with the conflict, the tension-building ultimatum, or the "dare" to test limits. The child does not understand his own behavior. One of the functions of the school is to help him understand his behavior.

He may accept the explanation that he is sick (as indeed he might be). What is more natural when one is sick than to rest, to go to bed until the "bad" feelings go away? He is reassured that he is a good boy. Perhaps he was frightened by the way he felt impelled to carry out his wild impulses.

Many normal human beings have wild random thoughts. For example, most "normals" reject the psychologically satisfying thoughts of aggressive behavior toward the driver of the vehicle that cuts in front of us. The urge to bump him off the road is resolved into honking our horn vigorously or making acid remarks about courtesy to our travel companions.

What goes on in the boy's mind while he is forced to do nothing but think? We are led to believe that some therapeutic values resulted. Somehow the boy came up with satisfying ways of resolving his aggressive tendencies. Wouldn't it be discouraging to learn that he mentally "boiled his mother in oil" when he was unhappy with her? Could it be that the psychologist was added to the pot? How will the child react when he is old enough and strong enough to carry out these aggressive tendencies? Maybe he will have "learned" that it actually is not necessary to "boil people in oil."

Our responsibility as school personnel is to help each child to understand his own behavior. He must be a significant partner in this solution.

I believe that I would test the idea that understanding his behavior was more significant than the threat to expel him by leaving out the threat. Eventually if he doesn't respond to a short course in practical psychology, the suggestion could be made that he could be helped by going to a "hospital" for a few days. This creates the atmosphere that he (not the psychologist) has the problem, that the psychologist is there to help him find solutions, and that the problems are natural ones that do have solutions.

WARREN W. NIXON

*   *   *

The penalties imposed on Joe in this incident seem unnecessarily cruel, and at no time is recognition given to the possible reasons for Joe's behavior. Since favorable results were received without removing the causative factors, I feel that the results are temporary, and that Joe's behavior will re-emerge at a later date, perhaps with a greater intensity. Certainly, the parents and the psychologist cannot hope to carry out this experiment indefinitely.

The imposition of the adults' authority on Joe and the rigid discipline that he must undergo if he misbehaves will undoubtedly affect Joe's future development, and possibly will give him negative attitudes toward people in authority. The behavior that Joe had expressed so openly in the past has become internalized, and Joe improves out of fear—fear of the punishment to be inflicted upon him if he misbehaves. In school, children misbehave in varying degrees, but Joe is removed from the category of the other children. For him, there can be no variation in his behavior: he is either good or bad.

The mother's silence, the continual confinement of Joe to bed when he was brought home from school, and the repeated warnings on his return to school gave me the feeling that Joe was being treated like a robot and not like a human being. These warnings were inculcated into him until he acted like a "trained" boy with no spontaneity or individuality. Not once in the incident are attempts described in which the psychologist seeks to understand the reason for Joe's behavior and why he has the feeling that me must act the way he does. What does Joe seek to gain from his behavior?

Another negative element in this incident is that Joe may well feel that the adults are against him—his mother included. This leaves him nowhere to turn for understanding and guidance from an adult person. Everyone is against him; no one wants to help him. His improvement gives the adults satisfaction. What does it give *him*? Recognition is important to a child. Was Joe given any verbal recognition for his improvement?

The experiment left me with great concern as to the type of boy Joe will be in the future. I see him as a sulky, withdrawn individual resentful of adults' authority, viewing adults as hard, cruel people incapable of being kind and understanding. Teachers do not want to see children expelled from school; expulsion is usually decided on after all other means of alleviating the situation have failed. But before utilizing an experiment of this nature, I would prefer to see Joe expelled from school with the understanding that he cannot be returned to the school until he can improve. At least when he does improve, it will be because he wants to and has been reached by someone who understands him, not because he is forced to show improvement. Under expulsion, Joe will not have to live in fear of adults and the punishment to which they can subject him. Possibly, special personnel such as the school social worker or someone in the community can aid him in becoming a better accepted boy.

The author asks why children accept this procedure, and whether the child thinks the parents are conspiring against him. These questions are directly related to each other. The psychologist informs Joe about the experiment in front of the parents and the teacher. No one speaks up for Joe. He is a lone boy surrounded by adults. What other feelings can Joe receive except that this is a conspiracy? In the absence of the support and understanding of one who has faith in him despite his behavior, it is fairly certain that a child would have no alternative but to accept the conditions imposed on him. This is why he would accept such a procedure, for this method of imposition removes from him the persons who afford him his greatest satisfaction—his parents. It would have been better if the procedure had been discussed with the parents and Joe individually, and then Joe and his parents could have been brought together for some general talk.

I do not feel that the aims of the school should be met if meeting them involves the possibility of mental harm to the child. The situation should be turned over to other professional people, a psychiatrist or a social worker, or the pupil should be removed from school until he is able to adjust to the school routine. I hope that this experiment does not receive any widespread acceptance. The immediate improvement is not worth the possible future harm to the wholesome growth and development of the child.

WILLYE B. SHANKS

DISCUSSION QUESTIONS—INCIDENT 10

1. Does the fact that a method works justify its use? What are the implications of using a method that is completely successful in, for instance, 80 per cent of cases, but unsuccessful, even damaging, in the other 20 per cent?
2. Do you approve of making a "contract" with a misbehaving child? What are some of the philosophic implications of such contracts as suggested by Johnson and Bean?
3. Under the conditions described, and in view of the proportion of reported successes, would you recommend such a drastic procedure when the only alternate solution is expulsion?
4. Do you believe that it is enough for schools to treat symptoms, that is, do whatever is necessary to stop misbehavior—for the sake of the teacher and the other students—even though the symptoms may reappear in another but less socially destructive manner?

SUGGESTED READINGS—PART II

Books

Averill, L. A., *Mental Hygiene for the Classroom Teacher*. New York: Pitman Publishing Corp., 1939.

Bernard, H. W., *Mental Hygiene for Classroom Teachers*. New York: McGraw-Hill Book Company, Inc., 1952.

Bühler, C. M., *et al.*, *Childhood Problems and the Teacher*. Philadelphia: Holt, Rinehart & Winston, Inc., 1952.

Dreikurs, R., R. J. Corsini, M. Sonstegard, and R. Lowe. *Adlerian Family Counseling*. Eugene, Oregon: University of Oregon Press, 1959.

Hymes, J. L., *Effective Home-School Relations*. Englewood Cliffs, N.J.: Prentice-Hall, Inc., 1953.

Lane, H. T., *Talks to Parents and Teachers*. New York: Hermitage House, Inc., 1949.

Redding, T. W., *When Home and School Get Together*. New York: Association Press, 1938.

Articles

Arbuckle, D. S. and A. V. Boy, "Client Centered Therapy in Counseling Students With Behavior Problems," *Journal of Counseling Psychology* 8(2) (Summer, 1961), 136-39.

Baines, D. L. and J. Slaughter, "Wanted: Better Communications Between Home and School," *National Elementary Principal* 41 (September, 1961), 51-52.

Bevans, C. F., "Parent-Teacher Relationships," *School and Community* 48 (November, 1961), 16.

Cassidy, L., "Emphasizing the Worth of the Individual Pupil," *National Elementary Principal* 34 (September, 1954), 217-20.

Finch, W. H., "Bringing Together Family and School," *Chicago School Journal* 43 (November, 1961), 84-86.

Hoyt, K. B., "How Well Can Classroom Teachers Know Their Pupils?" *School Review* 62 (April, 1955), 228-35.

Johns, W. L., "Guidance Through Parent-Teacher Conference," *Education* 81 (January, 1961), 303-305.

Kvaraceus, W. C., "Teachers and Delinquency," *Journal of the National Education Association* 47 (November, 1958), 535.

Lynch, W. W., "Person Perception: Its Role in Teaching," *Indiana University School Education Bulletin* 37 (November, 1961), 1-37.

Reiss, J., "How Can Parents Help?" *Journal of the National Education Association* 51 (January, 1962), 44-45.

Rotholtz, A. M., "Methods for Improving Parent-Teacher Relationships," *School Activities* 31 (December, 1959), 103-108.

Thalman, W. A., "Child Guidance Clinic: A Mental Health Service Agency and an Aid to Teacher Education," *Journal of Educational Sociology* 31 (November, 1957), 111-16.

III

ACADEMIC ADJUSTMENT

11

READY OR NOT?

CRITICAL INCIDENT

Background

Carol Peters was the second child in a family of four. She and her older sister were the mother's children by a former marriage; the two younger boys were the father's blood sons.

It was immediately apparent when Carol came to us that she was in no way mature enough for school. She was much smaller than the other children; she tired quickly; she was poorly coordinated; she was further handicapped because she was left-handed. Her attention span was very short—three to five minutes—and she was unable to exercise any form of self-discipline. In short, she was not prepared for the readiness work.

I reviewed Carol's records and gave her two tests, a Metropolitan Readiness Test and the SRA Primary Abilities Test. The results follow. Her birth date showed her age to be five years and ten months.

Metropolitan Readiness Test
    Total Readiness Status: Low Normal
    Percentile Rank: 15

SRA Primary Abilities (Quotient Scores)
    Verbal   110
    Perceptual   96
    Quantitative   76

Motor	93
Space	73
Total	90

I was convinced that Carol's slow progress was due to a lack of maturity rather than to a lack of ability. I scheduled a home conference with the mother to request that she remove Carol from school for the remainder of the year.

Carol's mother felt that Carol was so fond of school that she hated to confront the girl with a sense of failure. She asked that I reconsider and keep Carol for the remainder of the nine-week period; at that time we would come to a final decision. I tried to impress upon her that Carol was being faced with failures every day because she could not, and knew she could not, compare successfully with the other children; I said that I was sure this was a much more serious failure than removing her from school. I agreed, however, to keep her for the remaining six weeks and to give her all the individual help possible.

I advised the principal of the outcome of the conference, and he agreed that the correct decision had been reached.

About two weeks later Carol's older sister in the fourth grade said to her teacher "my sister's birthday isn't really the 14th of November, it's the 19th, but Mother said if we celebrate it on the 14th she can come to school." The sister's teacher informed me of this casual remark, and I thought I should inquire about it. I sent a note to the mother asking her to send Carol's birth certificate to school so that I could complete her records. The certificate was brought the next day. It was very obvious that the date on the document had been changed from 19 to 14. I returned it after showing it to the principal, and with his permission I wrote to the Board of Vital Statistics to request a duplicate. When the copy arrived, it confirmed my suspicion that someone had changed the original copy so that the child would beat the deadline stipulated by the state for school-entrance age by one day.

The principal advised the school superintendent of the situation, and the three of us arranged a conference.

Incident

The superintendent asked to see the girl's records, her tests, and samples of her work at the outset of school and at the present time. He asked my opinion of her progress. I told him that I was watching her grow from an immature to a frustrated and failure-struck child. I said that I was sure her behavior was a direct attack on her position in the class and on her peer group.

The superintendent's final determination was, however, that the child apparently was not wanted at home—or the birth certificate would not have been changed—and that, since the incident was rather unpleasant, he wanted Carol to remain in school rather than to have the school risk some unfavorable public relations. Although I did not agree with this decision, I felt that I was obligated to abide by it.

Discussion

In my opinion having Carol remain in school was a grave error in judgment, on the part of both the mother and the superintendent. If education is to be concerned with the welfare of the child, we as teachers should not be forced to jeopardize that welfare. I would never question the legality of a child's school age if that child could function successfully in school, but I will always question the advisability of a child's presence in school when he or she cannot function well because of immaturity—regardless of age. I would definitely advocate the use of some type of testing or screening criterion as an entrance requirement rather than an arbitrary deadline for the date of birth. After all, we are dealing with individuals and not with a group of mathematically compounded entities.

Questions

1. Is there some practical, functional way to screen children for entrance to school—one that would be more workable than present methods?

2. Is a child who is not wanted at home better off in school with an accepting teacher although she is unable to participate successfully in a group situation?

3. Did I as a teacher compromise my ideals and ethics when I agreed to keep a child in school who was totally unready?

4. How can we foster public relations and still not be inclined to use them as a skirt behind which to hide when we wish to avoid unpleasantness?

*   *   *

There should be a practical and functional way to screen children for entrance into school. If schools were not bound by chronological limitations, perhaps a pre-session for children in a general age category, conducted in the summer, could help determine their readiness for school. Judging from my observation some children who have not reached their sixth birthday, or the prevailing age requirement, are ready for school, and some who have are not ready.

A good kindergarten program probably could have been helpful in Carol's case. The kindergarten has done an admirable job in getting children ready for the first grade. Its central purpose is to help the young child adapt to school, to find his place in school life and in the group of which he is a member, and to promote readiness for learning in various areas. It helps him gain independence and social maturity. It works through activities appropriate to a school setting but adapted to the immaturity and restlessness of the young child. If the kindergarten function is not accomplished before the first grade, the necessary adjustments must be sought in the first grade, taking the teacher's time and attention from other matters, including the teaching of reading.

The child is the most important issue at all times. Schools and teachers have provided for individual differences. With that in mind, it would be better for a child who is not wanted at home to be in school with an accepting teacher. If the child is allowed to progress at his own rate of speed and if any progress is accepted, eventually he will mature enough to be eased into some group situations.

I don't believe the teacher compromised her ideals and ethics when she agreed to keep Carol in school. If a situation like that confronted me, I would still believe as I did even if I had had to conform to the regulations.

We can foster public relations and yet not be inclined to use them as a skirt behind which to hide by adhering to these principles:

(a) Interpreting education as an "investment in values."

(b) Encouraging the study and discussion of school needs and pupil needs as a point of departure in school public relations.

(c) Focusing attention on such basic needs as improved curriculum programs, improved grading, honesty on the part of pupils, and honesty on the part of parents and teachers.

(d) Striving to bring about greater recognition of the individual needs of children.

Regardless of how well a school program may be organized, there are times when everyone gets into situations in which he feels inadequate. The administrator should not resort to unethical measures or try to bluff his way out of such a situation where pupils and teachers are involved. Honesty and frankness and a stated intention of getting more information or the right information will serve much more effectively the public relations of the school.

JOHN A. JACKSON

*   *   *

The type of tragic incident involving Carol Peters is unfortunately not infrequent in the public schools. Any first-grade teacher can enumerate cases in which children have been the victims of antiquated entrance regulations which apparently operate on the assumption that through some act of magic all children mature simultaneously if their birthdays fall on or before a certain date. However, it seems unfortunate in this case that the teacher learned of the four-day discrepancy between Carol's birth date and the legal entrance date. Before this, the teacher had had a satisfactory conference with Carol's mother and had agreed to give Carol a longer period in which to adjust to the school environment. Once she learned of the forged birth certificate, she appears to have pursued with a vengeance the opportunity to be rid of Carol legally. Had she not learned that Carol's birth certificate had been forged, she surely should have felt morally obligated to provide for Carol in the group situation. Individual differences in readiness for learning must be considered in any first-grade situation, and needs of all of the children in the class must be satisfied. It is the teacher's task to see that children who are not ready to read and write experience in some way a feeling of accomplishment and the inner strength that comes with accomplishment. The young child can gain this feeling of accomplishment from many sources other than the acquiring of academic skills, and the wise teacher is on the alert for such sources. In the opinion of this writer, no child in first grade, or in any grade for that matter, should be subjected to being "faced with failure every day . . . because he could not *compare* successfully with other children."

Unquestionably there are ways of screening children for school entrance that would be more satisfactory than present methods. However, the practicality of such a change is dubious at present. Certainly a program of parent education would be essential before such changes could be made. A number of school systems have adopted the ungraded plan, in which a child is moved along according to his maturity and readiness with no reference to grade level. This seems to be somewhat more readily accepted by parents than a readiness testing program, since the latter eliminates some children from the school program for a full year, whereas in the ungraded plan these same children would take an extra year to complete the first four grades of school.

The teacher's question about whether a rejected child is better off in school even though he is unable to participate successfully in the group is hardly within the scope of the school. In Carol's case, the only evidence that indicates that Carol may have been rejected or not wanted at home is that the mother sent her to school when the law said she was four days too young. Certainly many mothers have felt their children were ready for school before they were permitted to enter school, but this can hardly be interpreted as an indication of rejection. On the contrary, the mother was cooperative and concerned about the effect of the feeling of failure that Carol would experience upon being removed from school. At any rate, a child's not being wanted at home can hardly be a consideration in whether he should be placed in school. School entrance regulations determine who shall and shall not be admitted to school. In Carol's case, it is unfortunate that the birth certificate was not checked more closely *before* she was permitted to enter school, not *after*.

The teacher questions whether she has compromised her ideals and ethics in permitting Carol to remain in school. This is not the important issue at hand. Of first importance should be the effect of any decisions upon Carol, who hardly seems to have been considered in this respect. What would have been the effect upon her and her sister had Carol been dismissed from school on the basis of the dishonesty of the mother? The teacher had agreed to permit Carol to remain for only six more weeks. What could be gained by the unpleasantness of pushing the illegality of her presence in the classroom?

Perhaps the superintendent was sincere in using "public relations" as an excuse for not carrying out the teacher's wishes. On the other hand, it is possible that he felt that in view of the earlier decision to give Carol a six-week probation period, it was superfluous to make an issue of the four-day discrepancy in the birth date. It is true that it is important for the schools to maintain good public relations; however, in this case, the superintendent was unquestionably not only promoting good public relations, but showing his concern for the welfare of the child as well.

ROBERTA M. MOLTMANN

*   *   *

This incident has almost unlimited facets and raises equally unlimited questions far from simple to answer. Perhaps it is best to deal first with the matter of the legal loophole as an escape hatch for this perplexed, young, unready first grader. Her actual date of birth is of minor importance, give or take in weeks or months, to say nothing of days. What is important is that she is experiencing difficulty in adjusting to a new and strange *modus vivendi*. This is not the first time that she has been faced with a change; she has already switched fathers. The fact that she does poorly on Quantitative (76) and Space (73) scores on the SRA test already gives us an important clue to some of her personal difficulties—her lack of orientation and weakness in number concepts. This little girl may well wonder where she stands in the shifting family (two half-siblings have been added with the advent of the new father) and where she is going as well as where she comes from. A 37-point difference between the Verbal score (110) and Space score (73) is another clue to the fact that something is suspiciously wrong. If one wishes to play Sherlock Holmes, it is better to gather these types of clues than to track down a four-day discrepancy in a birth date. Tangential thinking is not worthy of this teacher, who shows true potential as a sensitive, perceptive person with more than average understanding of pupils as individuals.

The basis on which this little girl does or does not fit into a first-grade classroom must be examined. This incident is all the more remarkable for the fact that no one involved, with the possible exception of the teacher (when she was not busy pursuing legal loopholes), attempted to look at this child's needs and handle the problem of her unreadiness for first grade, either maturationally, emotionally, or educationally. An approach to this type of situation must be primarily child-oriented. The child was hardly considered at all. Perhaps the right thing was decided for the wrong reason. And perhaps the wrong decision was reached by a series of rationalizations. Certainly the child did not have the benefit of whatever scientific knowledge could have been brought to bear on the subject of her needs.

We cannot allow a mother's needs to pressure us into making a decision that is essentially harmful to the child or fails to meet his needs. By the same token school is not now, nor should it become, a place to put children rejected, either totally or in part, by their parents. That problem is a matter for social workers and juvenile-court workers functioning as a team to provide children with their birthright—acceptance and recognition and love and protection from emotional traumas emanating from a variety of negative experiences. A classroom is a place to teach educational material and to help pupils learn to live together in preparation for their adulthood; it is not a dumping ground for the children of mothers who prefer to avoid their maternal responsibilities.

In my opinion, the superintendent's preoccupation with good "public relations" reveals his very limited view of the total situation. An administrative decision based on meeting a student's true needs will automatically promote good public relations.

ANN TAYLOR MOORE

*   *   *

The legal age of entrance into school varies considerably from state to state. At any one time, in any one state, no matter what requirements have been established, one is certain to find children entering the first grade at different ages and stages of development.

By different ages we mean chronological ages, which under most laws could vary by nearly a year. Verbal age, perceptual age, quantitative age, muscular age, and/or carpal age are other criteria that could be used. In fact, an age can be determined for any development facet of a youngster.

Most schools assume, on the basis of past experience and experimental evidence, that to succeed in the first grade a child should have attained an average developmental age of nearly six years at the time of entrance. The developmental age can be found by averaging the various ages for each child, as determined by educational and psychological tests. Carol Peters' developmental age might be determined as follows:

Her partial quotient scores as determined by the SRA test would be converted from a table, such as that found in Terman and Merrill,[1] as follows:

Verbal age	6 yrs.—5 months	Motor	5 yrs.—5 months
Perceptual age	5 yrs.—7 months	Space	4 yrs.—3 months
Quantitative age	4 yrs.—5 months	Total	5 yrs.—3 months

When one compares these ages with her actual chronological age, five years and ten months, it becomes apparent that she is immature for her years. However, one must be careful about jumping to conclusions concerning average scores. What aspects of a child's development contribute most to her success in school? It is observed that she scored at six years and five months on her verbal scale. This, to me, would indicate that the girl had a fair prognosis for success. I would say that the problem stems from the child's *relative* physical-social immaturity when compared to her peers, and the interpretation given to it by her teacher.

The following statements would summarize my analysis of this case.

1. The teacher, in the absence of a kindergarten program, placed too much stress on achievement and on comparing children in the early part of the first grade.

2. The parents, admittedly strivers, probably placed too much pressure on the girl to succeed.

3. The girl, confused by all of the attention and lack of readiness for the structured program, never did get off to a good start.

[1] Lewis M. Terman and Maud A. Merrill, *Measuring Intelligence* (Cambridge, Mass.: Houghton Mifflin Company, 1937), pp. 416-52.

4. The superintendent apparently had made little effort to provide a modern educational program and had no rationale for his actions.

We shall discuss each of the comments, in order.

A first-grade teacher has clear responsibilities that she is expected to meet during the course of the school year. Probably foremost among these is the beginning of formal instruction in reading. Traditionally, many first-grade teachers are judged upon their success in teaching their children to read at a creditable level. This often accounts for pressures placed upon students during the early part of the year. Success in reading is closely related to a child's verbal scores in readiness tests. Therefore, when a child scores well in verbal facility, it can usually be assumed that she can be taught to read. A total mental age of six years is usually considered necessary for success in reading. In this case, Carol could be expected eventually to read, although there might be some delay.

The usual program of studies in first grade includes many activities for building social growth, motor development, perceptual development, spatial development, and eventually readiness for reading. Many of these activities are provided for in the kindergarten program. Where no kindergarten is in operation it is the job of the first-grade teacher to provide them. The reporting teacher probably began her formal readiness program too soon.

The teacher in this case committed a human error. Forgetting the frequently quoted rule, "provide for individual differences," she structured her program for the whole class. This forced the girl to compete unsuccessfully with the other children. It is also fairly apparent that she gave the girl up at the completion of the first three weeks of school.

There is much that the school can do to orient parents to the proper acceptance of a child. Preschool orientation meetings of parents of first graders, pre-enrollment visitation by parent and child, brochures welcoming the child and the parent to the school community, child-study sessions sponsored by the P.T.A. or school administration, and a mothers' club for each grade—all help parents to understand their children. The fact that the parents, or some other individual, had altered the birth record to facilitate the girl's entrance into school indicates that they had some expectations concerning her successful matriculation. Based upon the facts given, the teacher's assumption that the child was not wanted at home may not have been valid. There are many parents who want their children to enter school at an early age, and not all such children are rejects from the home. However, one does get the impression that the child is attending school under some pressure. This pressure for success may actually be contributing to her lack of adjustment and her feelings of frustration.

Carol Peters probably would present problems to a first-grade teacher even if her entrance were delayed for a year. The attention span reported for her is less than that usually attributed to a three-year-old child. One doubts that accurate observation was made in this case.

Leaving the home and entering school calls for a great psychological adjustment. During the first few weeks of school, the teacher should make the greatest attempts to facilitate this adjustment and should continue doing so throughout the year. In Carol Peters' case, insufficient evidence concerning the home background and the teacher's beginning activities has been given to make a complete analysis. Carol's relative immaturity may well have been due to feelings of dependency rather than feelings of rejection. In this case, the maturing influence of the school situation would be desired. Under the guidance of a more understanding teacher the regressive actions might not have occurred.

In the mind of the reporting teacher the incident revolves around a question of professional ethics concerning the superintendent-teacher relationship. Small-town politics can be fascinating, and apparently the superintendent administered his school through politics rather than through policies. When this occurs, the professional-minded teacher needs to have her credentials up to date in the event that she falls into the class of administrative expendables. Only then might she indulge herself in the luxury of questioning the ethics of the superintendent.

The teacher was correct in abiding by the superintendent's decision, even though she felt that he erred in judgment. A teacher's first responsibility is to her superintendent. If she feels that she cannot support the policies of a given superintendent, then she is obligated to seek employment with one whom she can support.

There are many evidences in this case that point to weak administration: the lack of a kindergarten; the absence of preschool orientation and selection; the use of the teacher as the official recordkeeper; the lack of adherence to established policy; the vacillation of the principal and of the superintendent. A teacher owes it to herself to be aware of the degree of administrative support that she can expect. If it is not forthcoming, she should not be surprised.

If I were pressed for an answer to the teacher's questions, I would have to answer as follows:

1. Yes, there are practical and functional ways to screen children for entrance into school, and many of them are in operation now.

2. A child is often better off at school than at home when she has an understanding and accepting teacher. The child would probably benefit more from being in school this year, under the guidance of such a teacher, than she would from being in the home. The teacher, however, will want to have reached an understanding with the parents that the child will repeat the first grade the following year. Frequently we find that repeating

the first grade benefits the immature child more than would her social promotion. This, however, must be accompanied with acceptance, understanding, and activities to promote the proper growth in the child.

3. You may have compromised your ideals, but not your ethics, in abiding by the superintendent's decision. If further facts made you feel more justified in your belief, the ethical procedure would have been to resign.

4. Public relations cannot be fostered if they are used as shields to avoid unpleasantness. "Honesty is the best policy" prevails here. Vacillation from the policy will only earn scorn for the school system in the long run. Whether or not the administrator harmed the child by his actions remains to be seen. One can predict, however, some harm to himself and to the school on the next opening day of school when other parents attempt the same trick.

ROBERT W. SMAIL

*   *   *

The great to-do about Carol Peters' date of birth is unnecessary. The fiasco could have been prevented. The fact that Carol is four days younger than the legal age for admission to school does not by itself make her school experience unsuccessful. If she had been born four days earlier, she would still have been what she is now, "in no way ready for school," but nevertheless, of legal school age. What would the school and the teacher have done then? Probably the same as they did in the account above, held meaningless and time-consuming conferences without attempting to discover why the child behaves as she does.

A practical and functional way to screen children for school entrance is a well-planned and well-executed registration program, generally known as a Kindergarten Round-up. Parents are interviewed and birth certificates are checked. Thus, pertinent information about the child becomes known to the teacher.

After the Round-up, the child is admitted to kindergarten or nursery school, depending upon age and other factors. Readiness is not an *absolute* criterion for being admitted. An adequate preschool program must consider the various levels of development that are always present in this age group. Thus, a preschool program is a readiness program. It is here that experiences are provided for growth and development that the home environment does not or cannot provide. It is during this period that parents can be counseled to provide stimulating experiences to augment the school's program. More important, parents can be counseled in an effort to help them change, in cases where it is indicated, the erroneous methods of interacting with the child that hamper the child's growth and development. The readiness program of the preschool may need to be continued in the first grade for some children for varying portions of the year.

If the school does not provide preschool experiences, a sound registration program should be instituted nevertheless. However, lacking a preschool program, a portion of the first-grade period should be devoted to readiness activities. The amount of time and the number of children involved will depend upon the nature of the individuals who comprise the first grade. Time is not, in itself, an unfailing means of assuring readiness. There are cases of children who have been denied admittance for one year because of lack of readiness and who have been enrolled the next year with very little more readiness, other than being one year older.

Whether the child discussed in this case is better off at home than at school cannot be answered categorically under the circumstances. It is hoped that the superintendent's "not-wanted-at-home" statement was due to an attempt to crawl out of a tight spot resulting from inadequate administration, rather than to conviction. An extremely small percentage of parents reject their children. There is no evidence to substantiate the statement that Carol is not wanted at home. To make such a statement would merely indicate the disrespect in which the parent is held. If the needs of the child were being met in the school—in this case, they are not—there would be no question that the school experiences would be of greater benefit. If the child were accepted at school, provision would be made for the type of education that she needs this moment. Thus it is not a matter of compromising ideals and ethics, which are not involved in this case, but a matter of providing educational experiences at the level on which the child can successfully function, and taking her as far as she can progress during the time the teacher is working with her.

MANFORD A. SONSTEGARD

DISCUSSION QUESTIONS—INCIDENT 11

1. What is the validity of having children evaluated by a committee, on the basis of tests and interviews, to determine their school readiness?
2. Smail believes that the teacher's first responsibility is to her principal. He also implies that a teacher who takes the luxury of questioning the ethics of a principal may fall into the class of administrative expendables. His position in this matter raises ques-

tions about superior-subordinate relationships. What are the areas where a teacher *should* defer to her principal, and what are the areas where she *should not* compromise?

3. Sonstegard's comments in favor of a school readiness program (in contradistinction to readiness testing) implies that a well-constructed program serves as a bridge between the home and school. Does the program as described seem to meet common needs?

4. Should schools be able to adjust to the needs of individual children rather than reject those who do not fit in? What guide lines can you suggest for handling special problems?

12

"POLISH STONES, DULL DIAMONDS"

CRITICAL INCIDENT

Background

The elementary school at which I teach is located in a densely populated district of a large city where first-generation parents are most concerned with their children's progress. When this incident occurred, I was in my first year of permanent-license teaching, although I had been a substitute teacher for the previous two years.

Bertha Astor was ten years old when she entered my fifth-grade class. When her older brother Phil had attended the school several years before, he had won all the school honors. Discussion with other teachers indicated that Bertha was as dull as Phil had been bright. Even before I saw her, I came to the conclusion that in all probability Bertha was not dull but rather discouraged. I hoped to be able to encourage her to do better.

On the first day of school I allowed each pupil to sit where he wished, intending to change seating later according to alphabetical order. In calling role I noted that Bertha Astor had taken a rear corner seat, which further confirmed my suspicion that she was discouraged.

As the semester went on, I found Bertha to be listless. She did not seem to hear and she appeared to be in a constant daze. Although she did what she was told, her work was very poor in appearance, quality, and quantity. Whenever I tried to talk to her, she seemed to be defending herself from me, and despite my trying to win her over, she never responded. Her work continued to be of poor quality.

At mid-semester I gave her failing marks in all subjects. The report card had immediate results: in the principal's office, I was accused by Bertha's hysterical mother of prejudice against the girl. The following week, the school psychologist visited me; I told him of my impression that Bertha was really bright but terribly imposed upon by overambitious parents and discouraged by having an exceptionally brilliant brother. He took Bertha out of my class for several hours of testing.

Later, the principal called me in to discuss the psychologist's report. The psychologist had found that Bertha had an IQ of 72, was reading at the mid-second-grade level, and performing in arithmetic at the third-grade level. In his report he explained that he had considered my impression that Bertha was able but discouraged, but that on the basis of the several tests and his own impressions he concluded that she was mentally deficient; he recommended that she be demoted to a lower grade.

The principal and I, however, after discussion, decided to keep Bertha in my class for the term to see how she would do.

Incident

In spite of my best efforts, Bertha did not respond, and at the end of the school year I did not promote her.

The principal called me into his office and informed me that once again Bertha's mother had come to see him. She was highly distraught and very upset; she cried and even threatened suicide if Bertha was not promoted. The principal asked me to promote Bertha. "It is wrong," he told me, "to promote this girl, but what can we do? You and I know she really belongs in the third grade, but after all, she is quiet and does not make any disturbance. Besides, we have to consider the mother's condition and how she will affect the girl."

I replied, "I resent other teachers promoting poor pupils to my class. Bertha should not have been promoted to the fifth grade. Now, you are asking me to do what I think is wrong."

"I'll leave it to your judgment," he answered, "but please think of all the issues."

Later, I promoted Bertha and she went on to the sixth grade.

Discussion

In my opinion the most basic fault in American education is the assumption that poor and inadequate students have the *right* to diplomas for effort and time-serving and not for accomplishment. Every year I see dozens of Berthas, dull and discouraged, who simply are not capable of advancement and are pushed ahead. These dullards are pushed into high school and even into colleges. American education is being cheapened. Courses are made easier. We polish stones and dull diamonds. I feel that somewhere along the line teachers should be resolute and not be bullied or affected by principals and mothers. With such an accomplishment we can feel that we are doing an honest job.

Questions

1. Would impartial objective tests as criteria for promotion at elementary grade levels be better than subjective teacher judgments?
2. Did I, as a teacher, compromise my ideals and ethics when I promoted a student who simply did not have the requisite ability?
3. How can we get parents to leave us alone so that we can do our job without undue influence from them?
4. Does the promotion of dull students harm bright ones, since it requires that the level of presentation and discussion be lowered?
5. Shouldn't multiple-track teaching be standard?
6. Are these sentiments realistic? Are they undemocratic?

*   *   *

I am in strong agreement with this teacher's discussion at the end of the incident. Furthermore, I have had personal experience with this problem, once while teaching undergraduate students at a college in California and again while teaching in the graduate school of social work at a midwestern university. At the latter institution, a great deal of pressure was brought to bear on me by the director of the school of social work when I told him that I planned to fail a student in one of my courses. In addition, the student himself and some members of the clergy tried to exert their influences on the school of social work and the university president.

This student simply could not do graduate work, and it was unfortunate that he had been allowed to graduate from college, let alone that he had been admitted to a graduate school where he had been in attendance for a year when I arrived on the scene. In other words, he had already completed "successfully" one full year of graduate work when he enrolled in one of my classes. I stood by my decision, and the student was given a failing grade which, coupled with poor but passing grades in all his other courses (my colleagues, even though they knew full well that this student was incompetent, still were reluctant to give him failing grades), resulted in his dismissal from the school. By this time dismissal action was supported by the president, by the director of the school of social work, and by all faculty members who knew the student. I report this item in detail to underscore why I concur with the author of the incident when she states that these "dullards are pushed into high school and even into college." But I would add, yea, and even into graduate and professional schools!

Although I agree with the teacher's conclusions, I have some questions about her judgment. It seems to me that she was determined to be "fair," no matter what the facts might be. Even before Bertha arrived in class the teacher had already made up her mind that the child was not mentally retarded, merely discouraged. And when Bertha sat in a rear corner of the room, the teacher was convinced that this was an obvious symptom of discouragement and that, by implication, it had no bearing on the youngster's intellectual endowment.

Granting that all teachers must be alert in observing the behavior of students, this does not automatically qualify them to make a "diagnosis" in the area of emotional or mental disturbances, which is just what this teacher did. With the possible exception of clergymen, teachers as a whole seem to be especially prone to succumb to the disease known as "playing psychiatrist." Frequently, this disease is called "playing social worker" or "playing psychologist," but whatever its specific syndrome, it is a harmful sickness.

Somehow the notion is abroad that only those engaged in the diagnosis and treatment of emotional problems are doing the really worthwhile work in the service professions. The corollary, of course, is that just plain old garden-variety teaching is not a very important or significant occupation. This is sheer, asinine, unadulterated nonsense. As one who has functioned as teacher, social worker and psychologist, I am convinced that the most important and the most far-reaching activity—in terms of its potential contribution to human welfare and personal satisfaction—is the teaching of children. And the sooner school teachers realize this, the better it is going to be for everybody—teachers, parents, school boards, and most important of all, children.

And while I am at it, I may as well get in a few licks at the psychologist in this case. In the first place, I feel it is unwise to use the Intelligence Quotient as an infallible number or as though it were a result of a fine measuring device such as the electron microscope.

As reported here, the school psychologist gave the child some tests, found out she had an IQ of 72, and therefore made a diagnosis of mental deficiency and immediately "prescribed treatment"—namely, demotion to a lower grade. This patently absurd series of events compels me to point out what I thought was obvious to everyone who called himself a psychologist: that without a careful evaluation of many variables including a physical examination and a social history, the IQ has no value. But apparently, school psychologists (most of whom do not even meet minimum requirements for membership in the American Psychological Association) have not yet learned this very elementary lesson.

Finally, it is shocking to realize that apparently it did not occur to anyone involved in this case—teacher or psychologist—that Bertha and her mother might need psychotherapy or counseling. As far as I can determine, no effort was made to help the mother accept a referral to an appropriate social welfare agency where they could get assistance, such as a Family Service Association (if one exists in their community) or—certainly worth considering—the Child Welfare Services Division of their local county welfare department.

JOSEPH ANDRIOLA

*   *   *

Of the several instances the writer reviewed and chose to reflect upon, he believes the case of Bertha to be the most challenging. In some ways it is challenging less because of Bertha than because of the teacher and the situation in which she finds herself. And further, it is challenging because the writer found it more difficult to formulate his thoughts on this incident than on any of the others. To deal with this problem is more than a matter of expounding philosophical ideals on expedient procedures. Such situations are all too common and illustrative of the heavy price we have paid to attain "public relations." "This policy has tried to please all comers by dilution, compromise, and indecisiveness. It is time that our schools reassert their prerogative, and in fact their duty, of insisting on values that our teachers know are valid and appropriate for teachers."[1]

It seems to the writer that the problem is not that Bertha has demon-

---

[1] R. D. Rabinovitch, "The Hazards of Being Human," in M. I. Rasey (ed.), *The Nature of Being Human* (Detroit: Wayne State University Press, 1959), p. 68.

strated that she was not suitable for promotion, but rather that neither the teacher nor, ostensibly, the community seemed to recognize that the American dream of "equal opportunity for all" is far from being realized. The dream is far from being realized probably because it is a dream, but the writer believes that dreams of this kind are essential to the development of man to his highest potential. Yet from the teacher's description it would appear that in this community, at least, little is being done to provide the kind of curriculum that makes it possible for all children to grow to their greatest potential.

The teacher prepares a careful description of a situation not uncommon in many schools today. Of course, a number of schools have solved this problem by the "automatic promotion" program which precludes the necessity for considering "retention."

First, a few comments about some of the smaller but still important points illustrated in this case. The teacher reveals something of her own personality when she states that, "Even before I saw Bertha, I came to the conclusion that most probably Bertha was not dull, but rather discouraged." This is a human quality and probably is more helpful in working with children than the converse of assuming that all children are dull until they prove themselves otherwise. But even this approach is inadequate in dealing with children. One wonders if the teacher probably wasn't "altruistic" in objecting to the usual negativism of teachers who tend to brand children. The teacher was attempting to give Bertha a "break" in deciding that she wasn't dull, but, rather, discouraged. Of course, there was no actual basis for this conclusion, but at least it was a noble one.

There is no indication that Bertha had a complete physical examination. This might do much to shed some light on her general performance in school. The teacher notes that she was "listless," "in a constant daze," "work was very poor in appearance," and "defensive." What a physical examination might reveal is not known, but certainly Bertha's behavior suggests the importance of one.

As the case description continues, one senses the bankruptcy of education. That a child's mother should not know that her child was failing until the middle of the semester is indicative of the lack of communication characteristic of school-home relations. It appears that the teacher was without benefit of information pertaining to the mother's instability. Even at mid-year the teacher maintains her position that Bertha is bright but is a victim of overambitious parents and an exceptionally brilliant brother. In no instance in the case does the teacher provide any kind of evidence as to why she maintains that position.

The fact that the school psychologist recommended that Bertha be demoted to a lower grade because of her mental deficiency indicates the absence of a comprehensive program to meet the needs of all children.

From the information provided it appears that both the principal and the teacher were wise in the decision not to demote Bertha, but it appears equally unfortunate that there were no resources or facilities in which Bertha could function at her capacity. If Bertha were "discouraged" in *this* class, what kind of a descriptive term could one use if she were demoted because she was mentally deficient?

This kind of thinking denies that individuals continue to grow in feeling and in social awareness even though they may be retarded in intellectual capacity. It is unfortunate that in this case the teacher did not give some indication of what her "best efforts" were. A brief description of these efforts might give some cue as to why Bertha could not or would not respond.

If a mother were as disturbed as is reported in the case, it would seem that some consultation with the father would be in order and possibly even referral to some other community agency: child guidance clinic, mental health clinic, a private psychological consultation. The discouragement of the principal is revealed in his expression that "You and I know Bertha really belongs in the third grade, but after all she is quiet and does not make any disturbance. What can we do?" Here the principal gives primary concern to the mother's condition with little regard to what is happening to Bertha.

It is interesting to note his concept of democratic, school administration when he states, "I'll leave it up to your judgment, but please think of all the issues."

One can empathize with the teacher's feeling and thinking in the discussion aspect of her case. However, she seems to beg the question in her observations. The implication of her remarks is that the dullards should somehow or other be eliminated. Rather than think in terms of impartial objective tests as determinants for promotion, one might better think that impartial objective tests would be used as determinants for total program-planning for this child. In this instance, promotion ceases to be a consideration and program needs become paramount. The writer does not believe the teacher compromised her ideals in this so much when she promoted the student since actually this is an expectation on the part of the community of which she is a member. Here the teacher might better develop some long-range goals as a professional person and make her feelings known in terms of an influence for "broadening the base" of curricula. It is for the people, through its board of education, to decide the kinds of curricula the community wants. Then it's up to the professional person to decide whether or not he wishes to provide what the community wants; the profession itself must decide the method by which it must achieve the desired goals. At the present time, it appears that neither the profession nor the parents are able to make this distinction.

It does not naturally follow that promoting duller students will harm bright ones. Through the use of grouping, team teaching, teaching machines, excellent library collections, and the like, there is no reason why bright youngsters need to be victims of lower levels of presentation.

R. N. LOWE

*   *   *

"Nothing succeeds like success." This cliché could provide us with our text for an examination of the basic problem of organization of groups of children for instruction. We must begin with a philosophy that will provide us with an overview of the entire learning process. Perhaps an analogy will help. Let us compare the process of teaching with that of getting an automobile to operate. The battery (teacher) provides the spark which ignites the mixture of gasoline and air (assignments) which causes the engine (pupil) to function. How many stalled engines (pupils) do we have by pumping too much gas into the mixing chamber (classroom)? We could carry this analogy to ridiculous extremes and point out that dirty plugs (principals) and sticking valves (parents) are quite unnecessary impediments. However, we do suggest that the profession of teaching is concerned with determining the proper dosage that will enable each pupil to function successfully. Just as some engines run on a thin mixture of regular gas and some on a rich mixture of high octane, so do pupils vary in their capacity to master assignments.

We could get overenthused about our analogy to the point of believing that teaching could be a mechanical process. Are we not somewhat wishful in suggesting that we rely on "impartial objective tests—as determinants for promotion at the elementary level—"? Certainly, objective tests may be valuable tools in aiding the teacher to make assignments, evaluate pupil progress, and interpret to parents the relative status of the child. However, I would be reluctant to base promotion on tests alone (particularly on the elementary level). Teaching is not mechanical. Teaching is a profession that depends on a delicate judgment blending many factors of pupil capacity, group status, home background, and needs of society into a diagnosis of the educational needs of the pupil.

Often we find the educational needs of the child tied closely to other basic needs. Critical incidents do develop when these needs are unsatisfied. Bertha did not respond to the educational dosage given to her in the fifth grade. We are not given details on the degree to which differentiation of assignments is made. Regardless of how capably the instruction was carried out Bertha did poor work. (I am unmoved by the temptation to say that a more experienced teacher would make flexible assignments because many do not.) An outside authority, the psychologist, then determines that Bertha has low capacity. This stage of the critical incident is important, because it involves an outside-of-school factor in the learning environment, the mother.

How do we inform the parent that the performance of her child is below average without threatening her sense of adequacy? This is the core of the critical incident. The parent needs to be informed. If the parent is part of the problem, facilities in the school or the community should be available to aid the parent. Guidance and counseling services are often helpful in enabling parents to reappraise their role and their expectations. The procedure calls for psychological skill of a higher order and degree than the school can provide at this stage of the critical incident, since improvement depends on modification of the self-concept of both pupil and parent.

Did the teacher compromise her ideal and ethics by promoting a student who did not have the requisite ability? Yes, she did so under pressure. However, the basic question really returns to our original compromise. We failed in the educational dosage administered to Bertha. Our failure is that the child has not taken educational dosages for some time. No wonder she is retarded! We continue to fail as long as we continue to force dosages on pupils who do not seem able to handle them.

Promotional policies and placing children in rigid grade levels are educational techniques or devices that are undergoing constant evaluation and research. Each school system should be vitally concerned with this problem. The ungraded elementary school may be the answer. Very flexible grouping practices may be called for if the community is not ready to accept the ungraded elementary school.

What about the community? Does anyone hire a doctor, a lawyer, or a broker without evaluating his service or consulting with him? Stating the position that parents should leave teachers alone is unrealistic. The lines of communications between parent and teacher should be open. Some schools have adopted the conference technique as a supplementary way of evaluation of pupil progress, and a way of suggesting to the parent how he can reinforce the teaching of the school. Bertha's mother is not the only one who must face reality. Teachers are hired to do a job. We owe our employers an explanation when we label a child as a "reject." It is our responsibility to find out whether the home is reinforcing our educational dosages or (consciously or unconsciously) neutralizing our efforts by unrealistic, tension-producing incidents, and in some cases indifference. An experienced teacher often traces lack of success of a pupil to the indifference, if not the antagonism, of the parent to the value of the school program.

Yes, it is undemocratic and foolish to consign those who do not meet standards to an educational junk heap. Just what are standards? The American dream has been to develop the individual to the fullest of his capacities. Education for all is within a framework of dignity and self-respect. With compulsory education we have accepted the challenge of "polishing stones."

WARREN W. NIXON

*   *   *

In addition to the basic problem of what to do with students who attend but do not achieve, several specific questions arise about the situation described in this incident.

Why was not psychological testing for poor Bertha utilized earlier? Since she was ten years old when she entered fifth grade, she must have been promoted regularly through the first four grades—although other teachers considered her quite dull.

On what evidence did the reporting teacher judge Bertha "not dull, but rather discouraged?" She states that she came to this conclusion even before she saw Bertha, and there is no apparent basis for the conclusion except that Bertha had a brilliant brother. Although the child's taking a rear corner seat might indicate discouragement, that does not necessarily mean she was bright. A dull child is even more likely to feel discouraged, especially if parents and teachers are expecting more than the youngster can deliver.

Certainly, without psychological testing or any other evidence that the child had the necessary ability, the teacher was almost criminally complacent in her dependence on kindness and encouragement. This is not to deprecate kindness and encouragement. But "kindness" is not really that if it is based on the expectation of miracles. Earlier, and if necessary long-continued, counseling with the parents might have enabled them to accept the truth about Bertha's ability. Not to tell parents as soon as possible any such unhappy truths is a cruelty to both the continued hopes of the parents and the hopeless efforts of the child.

The teacher's (and the principal's) naïveté *after* the test reports is even more incredible. Why did they seek professional guidance and then not be guided by it? How could they expect a child with an IQ of 72 and a reading grade of about 2.5 (plus, undoubtedly, emotional handicaps because of comparisons with her brother) to pass the last half of the semester when she had failed the first half?

At this point, the child should not have been retained in the class unless principal and teacher had already determined to *give* her the passing grade she could not possibly earn. She might have been set back a grade right then after vigorous counseling with the parents, who could have been given the choice of accepting that decision or of withdrawing the child from school for the balance of the semester and then entering her at a lower grade. Or the teacher and principal could then and there have decided that the child would continue to be passed and in due course graduated.

Surely the end-of-the-semester to-do could have been avoided—and, in particular, the tailoring of the grade to the parents' wishes. In some cases, school officials may decide, and I think quite justifiably, that the psychic injury to the child of nonpromotion would be more serious than the possible injury to education and to society in general. Even under the strictest scholastic standards such deviant judgments may be made—but they should be the judgment and decision of the teacher assigning the grade, not a bowing to parental pressure.

The underlying problem, of course, is what to do with the ever-increasing number of children coming to school and to high school (where Bertha will doubtless land some day) who are not capable of earning a high-school diploma for achievement but whose parents insist that they must get a diploma. At present these pupils attend high school for ten or twelve semesters instead of eight, occasionally finding courses that do not demand more from them than they have (or teachers who "pass through pity") and get other credits by scraping through summer school for three or four semesters. Eventually, if they are persistent, they get a diploma identical to that of an honors student.

Two classes of diploma have been suggested as a solution, but the awarding of "attendance diplomas" would not really solve the problem. After a few years the industries and trades now insisting on high-school diplomas as a condition of employment would be demanding high school *achievement* diplomas—and then we would be back in the same old dilemma.

DOROTHY E. SPARKS

DISCUSSION QUESTIONS—INCIDENT 12

1. Education is the major means for upward advancement and for social acceptance. The discrepancy between parents' aspirations and children's abilities can lead to conflicts between parents and children and to inner conflicts. Thus, emphasis on education can

create a serious social-psychological problem. Accepting the thesis above, can you suggest a program to maximize the positive value of education and at the same time avoid emotional problems?

2. Andriola suggests a total social-service approach which would include an integration of all professional services for every failing child—possibly for all children. Would you be in favor of such a procedure?

3. What procedure would you recommend for a principal who is required to inform a parent of a pupil's academic inadequacies?

4. If a certain percentage of pupils are not capable of earning elementary or high-school diplomas, how can they be enabled to develop to their full capacity in a way that will satisfy their parents and not interfere with the progress of brighter children?

13

A COMEDY OF ERRORS

Background

During the first quarter of last semester, immediately after grading, one of my better students came and asked me why I had graded her as I had. I explained to her that she had not completed all of her assignments, and showed her the record book. She agreed that the mark seemed fair enough, but before she left she muttered, "My father won't like it." After she had gone, I dismissed the conversation from my mind.

Incident

About a week later our assistant principal came to my room and began questioning me about this student. I showed him the record of her work and gave him an account of her, explaining what I thought were her relative strengths and weaknesses. When I had finished I asked why he was so concerned. He gave me an innocuous and noncommittal answer. By the next day I had quite forgotten his visit.

Several days later, as I was teaching a class, the same assistant entered my classroom looking considerably perturbed. He asked if I were willing to talk to this girl's father. "Why, certainly," I replied. After class had been dismissed and I was sitting at my desk arranging some papers, I looked up to see a huge, florid-faced man enter the room with our two assistant principals. He approached and belligerantly stated his name. Pounding on my desk, he demanded to know why his daughter had not received a top grade. I noted that both the assistants were perspiring profusely. The father, on the verge of apoplexy, was about to strike me.

I took out my record book and showed it to him. He calmed down considerably when I explained that his daughter, although she was an excellent student, had missed several of her assignments and had not earned a top grade. Somewhat mollified, he left the room sheepishly with the two assistant principals on either side.

Discussion

The entire affair left me with a vague feeling that I was one of the chief characters in a comedy of errors. All the characters had played their role; all of us, it seemed to me, had committed sins of omission that allowed the play to go to its climax. The girl had apparently neglected to tell her father that she had missed several important assignments. The father had neglected, evidently, to check on the girl's story before precipitating action. The assistant principal had failed to approach me as a professional associate and to discuss the case on that level. And as for myself, I had not recognized that an unhealthy situation was developing nor detected it in time to use preventative measures.

Questions

1. Is it possible that this girl is an overachiever because of parental pressure?

2. What is the best way to behave in such a situation?

3. How could similar incidents be prevented? Might a different type of grading help? Perhaps grading by parent-teacher conferences, or having grading books with comments?

4. Could frequent parent-teacher conferences help prevent such developments?

5. What is the role of the administration in such situations?

*   *   *

It is wishful thinking, perhaps, to believe that every such "comedy of errors" as this incident describes can be anticipated and prevented. However, we can urge the teacher to be more sensitive to comments, facial expressions, and other behavioral clues provided by each student, for learning better the possible conflicts or problems that may be affecting the student. Such sensitivity might uncover a need for counseling by the teacher or for referral to the guidance department for a more intensive evaluation of the nature and extent of the student's difficulties.

Certainly tests of intellectual ability and academic competence are indicated when overachievement is suspected. Such information, when integrated with data concerning the student's family background, school history, physical and mental health, interests, and leisure-time activities will assist a counselor in ascertaining whether or not the student is trying to achieve at a level above that which might reasonably be expected of him. In addition, a psychological study can do much to delineate the relative influence of parental pressure, intellectual curiosity, imitation or identification, peer-group pressure, or other factors in the personality functioning of the suspected overachiever.

I believe that the teacher handled effectively the "big scene" of this incident. How such an experience (and the learning that may have occurred) will affect the future attitudes and behavior of the participants is nevertheless problematical. The teacher may henceforth be inclined to be unduly doubtful and disparaging of the administrator's contribution to home-school relationships, and thus contribute to mistrust and tension in subsequent situations. And no administrator enjoys "losing face" in this manner, even though the number of parents demanding to confront the teacher for a showdown may be very small.

An incident such as this should indicate clearly to all school personnel the need for more effective communication (including greater frankness), even at the risk of imparting information that may be somewhat unpleasant.

Frequent parent-teacher conferences might well serve to reduce the possibility of incidents of this type. Such conferences could "take off" from a grade book or report-card basis and proceed to discuss aspects of the student's achievement or personality and the school's program that might be difficult or impossible to deal with adequately in the "comments" section of a written school report.

But in fairness to the teacher (and to the parent also, perhaps), teachers should not be expected to hold such conferences without first receiving some orientation and instruction in the "art" of conducting them. In-service training programs probably will be needed for those teachers whose formal preparation included no textbook study or practicum experiences in the theory and techniques of interviewing and counseling. Such knowledge and skills must be a part of the repertoire of the professional teacher. We could note here that this "goes double" for administrators who may no longer have a great deal of contact with classes of students but who spend much time in conferring and consulting with students, teachers, parents, and others on a one-to-one basis or in small groups. Their need in this area is probably even greater than that of the classroom teacher, and their preparation is usually no more adequate.

WILLIAM J. FIELDER

*   *   *

A comedy of errors would certainly be the proper title for this incident. The matter was handled rather strangely by the school administration throughout. The primary role of the school administration is to facilitate the teaching function—the main concern of the public schools. As a management function, school administrators should certainly develop a policy for dealing with parents. A number of incidents may arise in which angry parents feel a need to vent their spleen on the public schools and on one teacher or administrator in particular. It is at times like these that school administrations should have previously framed, clear policies on how contact shall be made with these unhappy parents. Some intelligent means of communication should be established so that the teacher will have an opportunity to present information to the parent in a fashion that is appropriate. Certainly a planned meeting is vital in each case to give all parties an opportunity to participate and to present their points of view.

One of the best ways to handle situations of this nature is by planned counselor-parent conferences. It is the responsibility of the elementary school counselor to have available some type of report on student progress. In most well-organized guidance programs, the counselor has an opportunity to discuss all phases of the student's instructional program, not only with the youngster's parents, but also with the teachers concerned with the child's academic progress and performance. The counselor has an obligation to be the liaison between the school and the home. Many schools will make sure that liaison between home and school is routed through a single person, who thus establishes an identification and a bridge of relationship. It is my feeling that the person best suited for this task is the counselor who, through his training and experiences, has had to come face-to-face with parents in varied situations.

The question arises whether the child could be an overachiever because of parental pressure. We have inadequate data to answer this question. The teacher's statement that the youngster was one of his better students would seem to point out that he considers the girl to be academically talented. Also, the teacher, in his discussion of the case, pointed out that the youngster was an excellent student, although she had missed several of her assignments and had not earned a top grade. If this youngster were a so-called overachiever, and this term is used quite loosely, we would probably find that there were other areas where she had been having difficulty. At times the overachieving youngster achieves success at great cost. The pressures and strains on these adolescents are excessive, and often they tend to display certain signs of maladjustment.

Another question that has been posed is that of how to act in such a situation. It is difficult to attempt to point out that one should act in any one way in response to a concrete situation. The situation should call for the type of behavior best designed to cope with the demands of such an interview. One does not try to adopt a best way of acting and attempt to make this appropriate for each situation. Such a course may very well be disastrous. It is somewhat similar to a youngster who, in the very early stages of learning, performs an action which resolves his problem. The next time a problem evolves, the youngster attempts to use the problem-solving solution he used previously. If it is successful, this tends to reinforce the pattern. However, more often than not, this solution is not applicable in the new situation. This produces frustration in the child. Then through trial and error, he must once again seek out a new solution that will be appropriate for this one situation. So it is with how one would tend to act in a situation of this nature. One would have had to have previous experiences of a similar nature and to have developed some basic techniques of being able to communicate with people, to be able to establish a bridge of relationship over which there would be a flow of information and an acceptance of the other party to the discussion.

How could similar situations be prevented? The establishment of a procedure of parental contacts with the school is one basic step. Certainly one gets the impression here of administrative persons ill-equipped to handle their jobs. If administration is to serve its major purposes of facilitating the educational program of the school, it cannot allow the type of conduct exhibited by these two assistant principals. This matter was handled most unprofessionally by the administration and their conduct left much to be desired. The day the assistant principal came to talk with the teacher regarding the student's grades, he should have discussed the matter on a professional level. He should have stated to the teacher his reasons for the visit. If there was to be a conference, he should have given the teacher adequate notice so that plans could have been made for a successful conference and for a meaningful sharing of information.

ALVIN GROSSMAN

*   *   *

I hardly believe the girl described could be classified as an overachiever, but, from all the evidence, undue parental pressure seems to have been applied. Seemingly, it was the wish of the father that his daughter make good grades, and from all indications the girl either wasn't concerned about good grades or she wasn't mentally able to make them. There is also the possibility that other teachers more familiar with the father's attitude or influence had simply avoided such encounters by giving the daughter undeserved good grades.

As to the best way to act in such a situation, the first thing is to maintain an open mind. The second is to be willing to listen to whatever the other party has to say, and even go so far as to ask for suggestions from him, although you are sure of the fact that you have done no wrong. It is often effective to inquire of a parent if he wants his child crippled by good grades as a reward for poor work or neglect.

Similar situations could be prevented by cultivating a better home-school relationship. The teacher, with assistance from the principal, might set a meeting for parents at the beginning of each reporting period. In this meeting, the teacher could explain to parents how much material is expected to be covered during this period, the quality of work she expects of the students, and also the anticipated achievement. The teacher may also give a general report of the progress of her pupils in the previous period. This general meeting should be followed by individual parent conferences about pupils with problems as well as about pupils without problems. Then too, the teacher could have individual conferences with her pupils, in an effort to find out whether they want to spend their time and energy to make good grades and whether they have the ability to accomplish more than they are actually accomplishing.

A different type of grading system may have prevented such a situation. However, with some parents and with some children, there will always be the feeling: "I have not been treated justly." The one thing most helpful in this situation was the fact the teacher was able to produce a progress record of her pupil's work. This was an evidence of the girl's day-to-day progress. Teachers should always be in a position to refute arguments or defend themselves in this type of situation with proof of the reasons for a pupil's grades.

The teacher must take the initiative in promoting cooperation with the home. Parents are sensitive. They seldom take the leadership; however, they are usually glad to cooperate with the teacher when the center of attention is focused on the individual child.

The parent-teacher conference is an effective means of communicating desired information about pupils to parents. It may include planning, recording, and evaluating, but it explains pupils' progress, pupils' status, and the objectives of the school in a manner not possible in any other way. To gain a better knowledge of the home background of the pupils, the teacher should attempt to learn through conference:

a. The status of the child in the home.

b. The general economic status of the home.

c. Parental attitude toward education and the school.

The role of administration in such a situation is to:

a. Serve as a good public relations agency.

b. Create a wholesome attitude toward the teaching staff.

c. Give individual support to each child.

d. Organize the community (parents) in such a way that there will always be a two-way flow of information. The administration must do extensive planning with parents, with teachers, and with pupils. In planning with any of these three groups, the administration must always show a willingness to accept suggestions as well as a willingness to make suggestions.

The administrator should never be so noncommittal and vague as to give the impression that the teacher must be on the defensive and is not entitled to enlightenment concerning an unpleasant situation. This particular assistant principal was not professional in his dealing with the teacher, and he doubtless did not enjoy the loyalty of the staff.

JOHN A. JACKSON

*　　*　　*

In this episode we have an excellent lesson in how NOT to listen to storm signals. Such warnings, in the form of rumbling thunder still in the distance, are not difficult to hear. The amazing aspect of this particular near-crisis is that all three school personnel, a teacher and two assistant principals, failed to have one ear (among their collective six) to the ground. Even more astonishing is the fact that one of the assistant principals further failed to be aware of an approaching crisis when he was personally pressured by the student's father for an "explanation" of a mark he considered unjustified as well as unfair. At the time the teacher was asked to explain the questioned mark by his immediate superior, the supervisor should have been more insistent in pressing for information. This was a point at which there was still time to prevent the eventual explosion.

In tracing the problem back to its origin, why had "one of the better students" failed to complete all of her assignments? An alert teacher would have discussed the student's incompleted work with her, exploring the reasons for and consequences of her actions, stressing the fact that she was potentially a good pupil. Such a student of ability who fails to respond to this sort of approach may well be struggling with some problem. The present student has obvious difficulties revolving around her relationship with her father, since she is only too aware of the fact that her father "won't like it." The student's muttered comment upon receiving her grade was the first obvious signal of a coming storm. A mutter or mumble should always receive more attention than a forthright statement; a mumble is a loaded item, loaded with some variety of emotion, such as fear, anger, resistance, or anxiety. It is not a wild guess that we are confronted with a pupil who is reacting to parental behavior with Ghandi's highly effective "passive resistance." It is one certain way to get a reaction out of her father and this she well knew. She indicated, by muttering, that she knew the scenario before the curtain went up. Yet her foreknowledge did not prevent her from behaving in a fashion that would displease her father, and hence it is safe to assume that this was her intention, conscious or unconscious.

In the teacher's discussion of the incident, he assumed that the student had neglected to tell her father the reason for the lower grade. But it is important to understand that this sort of father would not control his impulsive, aggressive behavior because of "logic" or "explanations." A man of this type brushes aside explanations. Was he satisfied after his first contact with the school's assistant principal? So little so that a few days later, in spite of proffered explanations, he was back for another round, this time with the one whom he felt was the original offender, the giver of the lowered mark. Of course the original offender was actually his own daughter who had earned the lowered mark by her behavior, offending and enraging her own father. No one at the school, alas, seemed to have an inkling of the fact that the battle was actually between father and daughter. The other participants were mere observers.

ANN TAYLOR MOORE

*   *   *

This incident is a representative example of the manner in which report cards and grades are used as pseudo-motivators, attempting to pressure a student to achieve and inciting the parents against the student. The exception in this case is that the teacher, at least for the moment, became the victim.

The teacher is correct on one point. It is a comedy. However, he does not realize the full implication of the farce. The picture of two administrators conducting an irate parent to the teacher merely to prove the girl's inadequacy, and then conducting him away after his defeat, is pathetic. It illustrates vividly the lack of leadership on the part of the administration in helping the teacher become an effective educator and in helping the girl in her educational growth and development.

The incident is not entirely the teacher's fault. There are two mitigating factors. In the first place, the teacher's college education, which was supposed to educate him to become a teacher, has left much to be desired. In the second place, the administration has obviously made no effort to help the teacher learn effective means of motivating the student and to guide her to optimum application of her abilities. The teacher senses, vaguely, that there must be a better way, or he would not have written the incident.

The student depicted is not living successfully in school. Her behavior, just as that of all human organisms, has a purpose. Unless the purpose of her behavior is uncovered, whatever action is taken merely treats symptoms.

Failure on the part of the girl to complete the work in a manner in keeping with her ability is symptomatic behavior—not causal. There is a reason for it. In this case the symptom was treated by giving a low grade, and the teacher "explained to her that she had not completed all her assignments, and showed her the record." The sins are sins of commission, not of omission as the teacher wants to believe. The committed error is typical. Teachers will spend long periods of time going over with a child or student the things she has done or failed to do. The procedure is unnecessary and consequently a waste of time. The child knows what she has or has not done. What she does not know is the purpose of her action.

The teacher, to function as a guide in the educational process, should have set out immediately to discover what purpose the girl had in not completing her assignments and in not performing as her ability indicates she should. The lack of application to assignments is a signal, a warning light, that something is wrong—she is not able to handle the problems of everyday living. The teacher did not understand the signal. Not recognizing the girl's behavior as a signal, he took punitive action.

The indicated procedure should follow several definite steps. First, the teacher should observe the girl's relationship to her peers. How does she get along with them? Does she belong to a subgroup that does not achieve well? Is she a lone wolf? Does she give up easily? Is she overly dependent? Does she require an undue amount of attention?

Second, the teacher should interview the parents. The interview should be structured to reveal the family constellation (order of birth of the children in the family), the relationship with the parents, relationship with siblings, relationship with other adults, routine of daily living, and methods of discipline. The outcome of the interview provides the thoughtful, experienced teacher with an hypothesis as to why the girl may be doing what she does.

The hypothesis should then be tested by an interview with the girl. The background of data obtained in the interview with the parents determines the structure of the interview with the girl. In other words, the purposefulness of the girl's behavior is determined.

The teacher is now ready to take the fourth step. He helps the parent understand why the girl is not developing educationally as she should. He may need to recommend some changes that the parents should make in their relationship with the girl. It would be a unique case if the parents were not using improper methods or were not responsible in some way for the girl's dysfunction, albeit with good intentions. The teacher then does what he can do to help the girl re-evaluate her useless goals through an interpretation of the purpose for her behavior, that is, not completing her school work. Steps to ascertain what lies back of the surface manifestations are mandatory. To fail to take them leads only to instituting expedients with discouraging results.

MANFORD A. SONSTEGARD

DISCUSSION QUESTIONS—INCIDENT 13

1. This "comedy of errors" seems to raise the issue of professional relationships between teachers and other staff members. Do you feel that the assistant principal behaved in a proper professional manner?
2. The overachiever may pay too high a price for academic success. What does this involve, and how can this concept be best explained to ambitious parents?
3. Do you see a need for regular parent-teacher conferences, such as the type outlined by Jackson, for every child?
4. Sonstegard, as do several others, stresses the importance of trying to discover motivation and then pointing out to the person the reasons for his behavior. Assuming this procedure to have positive value, do you believe teachers should attempt to treat behavior problems by pointing out possible goals? Should teachers receive training for this purpose?

SUGGESTED READINGS—PART III

Books

Del Solar, C. F., *Parents' and Teachers' View of the Child.* New York: Bureau of Publications, Teachers College, Columbia University, 1949.

Frampton, M. E. and E. D. Gall (eds.), *Special Education for the Exceptional.* Boston: Porter Sargent, Inc., Publishers, 1955.

Heck, A. O., *Education for Exceptional Children,* New York: McGraw-Hill Book Company, Inc., 1940.

Ingram, Christine P., *Education of the Slow-learning Child.* New York: The Ronald Press Company, 1953.

Witty, P. (ed.), *The Gifted Child.* Boston: D. C. Heath & Company, 1951.

Articles

Bolz, G., "Student Participation in Acquainting Teachers to Parents," *National Association of Secondary School Principals* 45 (October, 1961), 195-97.

Bucher, C. A., "What Can Parents Do?" *Journal of the National Education Association* 51 (February, 1962), 39-40.

Erickson, L., "Parents: Meddlers or Partners?" *California Teachers Association Journal* 55 (December, 1959), 13 ff.

Jacobus, E., "Parent Looks at School Grade Teacher," *Grade Teacher* 75 (October, 1957), 146.

Kitch, D. E., "Will the Individual Get Lost?" *California Journal of Secondary Education* 29 (February, 1954), 95-97.

Perkins, H. V., "Nongraded Programs: What Progress?" *Educational Leadership* 19 (December, 1961), 166-69.

Primack, R., "Child Who Demands Excessive Attention," *The Instructor* 71 (September, 1961), 52.

Seidman, J. M. and L. B. Knapp, "Teacher Likes and Dislikes of Student Behavior and Student Perception of These Attitudes," *Journal of Educational Research* 47 (October, 1953), 143-49.

Venn, G., "Superintendent's Role in Improving Instruction," *Education Digest, School Executive* 23 (December, 1957), 16-18, and 77 (September, 1957, 21-23.

IV

EXTRA-CLASSROOM RELATIONSHIPS

14

"ON BEING ONE OF THE BOYS"

CRITICAL INCIDENT

Background

As a teacher, I was invited to accompany our youngsters on their annual eighth-grade picnic. We went in buses to a nearby park, and a free lunch was supplied by the P.T.A. In the morning the youngsters played, had lunch, and went swimming. The principal felt that since this was a holiday especially for the graduates, the teachers should not interfere unduly with their activity.

Incident

An irate park-department employee came up to the principal and announced in my presence that some boys had stolen the keys to his park-department jeep and had broken a lock on a storehouse. He had no clues to the identity of the boy or boys concerned. The principal apologized and said that he would try to find the culprit. Among the boys of this school a peculiar code of honor prevails, namely that they do not "snitch" or tell on each other. The principal and vice-principal were unable to discover who had taken the keys.

Two hours later the lunch gong was sounded and we sat down. I was on the outside of the group, talking with Dick, who shortly before had given me a pack of cigarettes to hold for him. He did not want to be caught with them. With some misgivings I had accepted them, but I was glad he trusted me. I had always tried to be especially friendly to him. Dick often went without lunch to save his money for cigarettes, and several times I had begged him not to be so foolish. He invariably behaved well in my art class, better than in his other classes.

Suddenly Dick said to me in a low tone, "I'm going to light a firecracker." I was too surprised to say anything, but I stood where I was. The firecracker went off with a loud bang. Immediately the vice-principal approached my group and asked who had done it. No one answered for several moments. Finally, when the vice-principal threatened to punish the whole group, Dick confessed, "I did it, Mr. G.," and added that I had known but had not forbidden his setting off the firecracker.

I verified Dick's statement that I had not objected. I further stated that I did not know whether or not throwing firecrackers was against the law in this state. The vice-principal took Dick and me aside. Dick apologized, said he would never do it again, and was dismissed. The vice-principal asked me again if I had condoned the throwing of the firecracker, and I repeated that I had not forbidden the boy. I think the vice-principal's thoughts toward me were slightly uncharitable, to say the least, but he did not pursue the subject.

Then Dick asked me to go for a walk. I did so, and he informed me that if I would hand him back his cigarettes, he would tell me who had stolen the keys. I was anxious to discover who the pranksters were, so with misgivings, and after making him promise not to smoke in the park, I agreed.

After receiving the cigarettes, Dick told me the names of the boys. He offered to give the same information to the vice-principal, so we walked over to him. Dick said, "Mr. G., you have done me a favor, now I will do one for you. Larry stole the keys, Tom took them from Larry, and now James has them." The vice-principal thanked him. "Please do not tell them I told on them," begged Dick. The vice-principal agreed and went to recover the keys.

Discussion

Dick wished to gain attention by active-destructive means in the quickest and easiest way, so he threw the firecracker. He also wished to gain attention by talking with me alone, and to feel a sense of power over a teacher by making a bargain. In addition to the desire for attention and power, he had a strong sense of fair play and justice, evidenced by his saying that he would give the vice-principal a "break" for not having punished him for throwing the firecracker. Dick is a boy of lower economic status than our other students; his goal in life is to be a garage mechanic; he probably will not finish high school. But he was following the code of conduct that dictates, "Do unto others what they have done unto you."

Questions

1. Did I act properly in accepting the cigarettes in the first place or should I have informed the principal at once?
2. Should I have sharply forbidden Dick to throw the firecracker?
3. Was I right in backing Dick up when he confessed to the vice-principal?
4. Was my entire behavior during this picnic proper?

*　　*　　*

Two things impressed me about this incident: (a) the apparent inexperience and/or naïveté of the teacher, and (b) the teacher's basic warmth and positive feeling for this boy. I shall discuss both of these.

There is no question that we are dealing here with an inexperienced and unsophisticated teacher. This is manifested in a variety of ways. For example, the teacher states that among the boys at this school a "peculiar code of honor prevails . . ." An experienced teacher would know that there is nothing "peculiar" about "not snitching" and that peer-group loyalty is a common and natural phenomenon among boys in pre-adolescence and early adolescence.

The teacher states that he "begged" this boy not to spend his lunch money for cigarettes. He also reports that Dick struck a bargain: ". . . if I would hand him back his cigarettes, he would tell me who had stolen the keys." A mature, experienced teacher simply would not "beg" a child to do anything for a variety of reasons, among them being the practical one that such an approach is ineffective. Nor would he place himself in a situation where one of his pupils literally bribes him. And, incidentally, the teacher's remark in front of Dick that he didn't know whether it was against the law to explode firecrackers impresses me as lame excuse that compounds naïveté with poor judgment.

On the other hand, this teacher's positive feelings for Dick (and by psychological extrapolation we can assume this feeling extends to his other students) are an extremely valuable asset. *This teacher apparently really likes youngsters.* I place this statement in italics because it is a quality that unfortunately is frequently conspicuous by its absence in many teachers. What I am suggesting is that many teachers simply don't like children, and that perhaps it is this dislike for children that motivates them to enter the teaching profession. After all, what better opportunity, short of being a parent, can one have to punish, denigrate, humiliate, and otherwise emotionally cripple children, than to become a teacher?

The trick, of course, for the teacher who really likes children is to retain and develop this quality of liking in such a way that it becomes a catalyst for good teaching. That is, if one can avoid becoming stilted and/or indifferent, and if one can retain a warm, positive feeling for students despite some of the drudgery and frustrations of daily classroom teaching, the battle is half won. In addition, if one can learn how to set limits and also earn and maintain the respect of one's pupils, then one will be in an enormously better position to help them to learn. Used improperly, however, this positive feeling can degenerate into a type of identification with the student that frequently brings out one's antisocial proclivities. In this case, I think the teacher was close to just that.

A few words should be said about the teacher's discussion at the end of the incident. I think his interpretation that the episode with the firecrackers and Dick's desire to talk to him alone were attention-getting devices has little meaning. Virtually all children in this age group, unless they are emotionally withdrawn because of a mental disorder, are constantly involved in antics that draw attention to them. Among the drastic revisions needed in the formal education of persons who wish to become teachers is a sound preparation in the psychology and physiology of normal human development from zygote through old age. Unless we really understand what constitutes normal behavior, we have no frame of reference for estimating abnormal behavior.

JOSEPH ANDRIOLA

*   *   *

A teacher-student relationship should contain, among other things, mutual respect and a sense of propriety. For this relationship to be of benefit to both parties, it is helpful for the teacher to behave in a mature manner, at all times aware that he is an adult and that he is dealing with youngsters. Ideally, therefore, the teacher should possess sufficient knowledge about, as well as understanding of, any particular youngster with whom he is establishing an especially helpful relationship; he should have an adult scale of values to guide his actions and a sense of security along with an adequate amount of self-respect in his work with the child.

In this incident, the teacher behaved toward Dick in a manner more to be expected from another student. He was motivated by a need to gain Dick's trust at the cost of blinding himself to all else. To win Dick's affection, especially when other teachers failed to do so, seemed to him to comprise an important achievement. Actually this gaining of trust yielded little benefit to either of them. Dick may have needed from such a relationship to learn how to relate to an adult, how adults relate to each other, a respect for the welfare of others, the reasons for rules and regulations, and generally the answers to more specific questions that he may have had about himself and his future. He could hardly be expected to obtain this help from an adult whom he could easily bribe, who freely entered into secret agreements with him, and who could offer little real help when the going got rough.

The teacher should have learned that winning a child's affection is not always synonymous with earning his respect; that it may be more important to work for the long-range goal of really helping a youngster than to seek the immediate one of pleasing him for the moment; and that a teacher who is primarily concerned with having his environment satisfy certain personal and immature needs is not yet ready to offer help to another person.

CHARLES KRAM

*   *   *

If the instructor was trying to understand Dick and win his confidence, then he would not inform the principal about his cigarettes. The principal has enough to do without worrying about each little infraction of every student. Good discipline, especially with students like Dick, starts with confidence in the fairness of the disciplinarian, and to run to the principal about every little infraction does not build a good relationship.

According to the case history, the teacher was too surprised about the firecracker to say anything. Hence he was neither right nor wrong in not sharply forbidding Dick to throw the firecracker. Whether there was a law or not, if he had had his presence of mind, he should have forbidden such behavior. Accidents have been known to happen from what seemed to be a harmless firecracker. If the boy had threatened to throw a match into a can of gasoline, the teacher would not have stood by idly, unless he had no presence of mind at all.

Since Dick neither waited for the teacher to forbid his action nor asked permission, I see no reason why the teacher should have backed him up. As it was, he told the objective truth when he stated that he had not objected.

The term "proper" is relative. Since the teacher had been told by the principal that the students were not to be unduly interfered with, he was in a sense following these instructions. Whether or not it is proper for a teacher to hold a pack of cigarettes of an eighth-grade student depends on what relationship has been established.

The relationship between teacher and student, especially in a quasi-social gathering, depends on the particular teacher and student. Teachers do not have to become pals of their students to gain their respect. Others seem to be able to get down to the level of their students in order to win their confidence. What seems most important is the students respect the good intentions of their teachers and believe that they have their best interests at heart.

JOSEPH MERSAND

*   *   *

Basically, the incident involves the question of whether a teacher is ever right in giving tacit approval to an infraction of "the rules." The answer is *almost never*. The exceptions would have to be extreme indeed, to warrant a course of action that places the teacher in a questionable relationship with others charged with enforcing the rules and with the majority of students who obey them.

Wherever the teacher is responsible for a group of students, on a picnic or in a classroom situation, that responsibility requires that respect be maintained for the laws of safe, proper, and ethical conduct. Dick in this instance learned that a teacher might overlook an infraction of the rules of his peers. He learned that one teacher might keep his cigarettes for him and then return them, in spite of the fact that teachers were charged with the responsibility of prohibiting cigarettes. He learned, too, that he could even escape punishment from other teachers by placing an "easy" teacher in such a position that some responsibility for his action in shooting the firecracker would seem to have transferred to the teacher.

The teacher did not have the ethical right to condone an infraction of the rules prohibiting the possession of cigarettes. The cigarettes should either have been reported to the principal, after first explaining to Dick the reason for doing so, or they should have been thrown away or destroyed in Dick's presence. This was a time for learning on Dick's part: learning the reasons for rules and the inevitable responsibility of those charged with enforcing the rules to act consistently and honestly, regardless of opportunities for accepting bribes—even a bribe in the form of a pupil's special confidences. Friendship between teacher and pupil is certainly possible; a certain degree of friendliness in the relationship is almost essential for good teaching. But many acceptable means exist for forming such friendships. The friendship of a pupil that depends upon special favors from the teacher is seldom a satisfactory solution to any problem.

The teacher should have been aware of the rules governing firecrackers. Obviously, however, a new teacher will seldom have had the opportunity to learn all the rules until such incidents occur. A quiet tactful suggestion should have been made in time to prevent the action. If the teacher was caught completely off guard, however, the arrival of the vice-principal should have reminded him of his duties to accept his responsibility for the affair at once. Dick was wrong, and Dick probably was fully aware of this when he shot the firecracker; his means of warning the teacher of his action was probably a trick to involve the teacher. The teacher should have made a quick and clear explanation to the vice-principal at once, without waiting for the boy to confess. This would have demonstrated that the teacher, like the vice-principal, believed in the enforcement of rules. It would have helped the vice-principal's position and would have served notice to the pupils that the teacher was not to be taken in by tricks. It is not at all important that the keys were discovered in return for the teacher's mistaken actions; the keys could have been found in any case.

An honest explanation to the vice-principal of what had happened in the firecracker episode was all that was necessary. Dick had no reason to expect the teacher to defend him. He had not asked permission to shoot the firecracker but had asserted his intent to do so. This is like following up a statement of intent to kill by immediately murdering a fellow student. Such an action would likely leave an inexperienced teacher in a state of shock, but it would make the crime no less important.

Evidently the teacher had no clear understanding of his duties at the picnic; quite possibly no one had thought to explain them in detail to him. Trial-and-error methods frequently are the basis for learning such special responsibilities. Nevertheless, the teacher's behavior was not proper, and careful preliminary analysis of the potential of such an expedition would have given the teacher a much better guide to action.

During field trips, picnics, parties, or other functions sponsored by a school, attending teachers have an automatic responsibility to observe carefully and prevent incidents that may threaten the safety of others. They have an obligation to enforce rules governing student conduct and an equal obligation to know the rules in advance. Opportunities for friendly relationships should be developed, but never at the expense of responsibility for doing a job properly. Literally millions of fine teachers have found it possible to be liked, respected, and obeyed, whether in the classroom or on picnics. The teacher can never expect to become "one of the gang."

DON H. OTTO

*   *   *

Such an incident as this is complicated. I would wonder very seriously about the teacher as a person, to say nothing of his role in this experience. The naïveté of the teacher who holds cigarettes (apparently a prohibited item for students), or what may be this teacher's overwhelming wish to be accepted by the student, makes me wonder about his confidence in his role with students in general. I do not at all follow why the teacher could not have taken a stand regarding the throwing of the firecracker. I get the impression that since the teacher was, more or less, "along for the ride," he did not feel constrained to speak authoritatively one way or the other. The "bargain" or deal made between teacher and student confuses me completely. I do not understand the "pact of silence," or collusion, between vice-principal and student, either.

My own feeling is that neither bargains, protective silences, nor covenants should be made with students. I think it is important that each individual understand his own responsibility, independent of such confounding expectations. Evasions of teacher responsibilities, or avoidances of student responsibilities, cannot be useful in this context.

Through this experience Dick might have learned to acquire more appropriate relationships with his own group and with persons of authority; however, I wonder whether he had not discovered instead that collusive pacts with authority figures were useful "dodges."

This would seem to mean that neither teacher nor vice-principal were quite sure of their roles in the situation, nor sufficiently concerned about the entire structure of the student social group on holiday. The problem is not a matter of permitting Dick to throw the firecracker nor of accepting the cigarettes from him—it is a matter of awareness of accepted mores on the part of the teacher in this situation. Obviously the teacher plays a different role in a primarily social gathering of students than he does in a classroom. Nonetheless, he must differentiate his role as teacher or "cultural carrier" for the student in such an essentially disordered setting. The teacher should have shown the student how to behave and should not have played the role of peer, compatriot, and willing conspirator. From the general pattern of this incident, I am sure that authority lines, role structures, and status supports were almost, if not totally, absent. It is interesting that this incident took place on a picnic. I would be considerably interested to know what manner of incident occurs in the teacher's classroom.

A teacher should be able to handle a social role with a student without demeaning himself, losing face, or feeling a compulsion to be "one of the boys." The teacher is not "one of the boys," and I would seriously wonder whether, in this instance, he is one of the teachers.

JORDAN M. SCHER

DISCUSSION QUESTIONS—INCIDENT 14

1. Should a teacher attempt to establish a "one of the boys" relationship with his pupils?
2. To what extent should a teacher be a buffer between an errant student and other people? What are the limits of his social responsibility to students?
3. Andriola suggests that many teachers simply do not like children. Discuss (a) the probable reasons why people who do not like children gravitate to teaching or (b) why people with no preconceived negative attitudes begin to dislike children as a result of teaching.
4. What are the principal means by which teachers can gain both respect and liking from their students?
5. What are some rules you might recommend to guide teachers in their relationships with students at social gatherings?

15

"DON'T BE CRITICAL"

CRITICAL INCIDENT

Background

Superintendent X was a dynamic leader in a small midwestern prairie community. He had reason to be proud of his twenty-year administration in the city. He had run the school system with efficiency and an iron hand (having been a captain of infantry in World War I). In his locality, his was the "last word" when it came to educational procedures. Among fellow administrators he was well known and popular. He knew how to tell a good story and could please an audience.

His formality with his faculty, however, had a tendency to "put the fear of God" into his teachers during the conferences that followed his routine observation tours. Generally he was more friendly off duty, but for a system in which the faculty tended to have close relationships, he was not easy to know.

Teacher A of the same community had had ten years of successful experience and held a recent M.S. in Education from a nationally prominent university. This young teacher was well thought of wherever he appeared, was a dynamic speaker (and willing to fill a spot on any civic program when needed), a brilliant and well-rounded personality, cultured and poised. He developed an interest in writing

educational articles. To his amazement every article he wrote—about
the teaching of government, the direction of debates and plays, or
research on historical topics—was published in a national periodical.

Incident

Imbued with missionary zeal, he began to delve into educational
philosophy. He wrote a provacative article entitled "Are Your Teachers Happy?"—a piece based not necessarily upon personal experience,
but upon general observation and reading. It was illustrated and published in an important education magazine, and a reprint appeared
in the state educational journal.

When Superintendent X read the article, he was aghast. Formerly
he had appeared quite pleased that a teacher of his district had published in national journals. This achievement had been reported, with
a photo and a personal interview, in the local newspaper. The present
article, however, was of a critical nature. It cleverly stated that teachers
were the forgotten people, that stage curtains, swimming pools, band
instruments, and various frills apparently were of greater importance
than the well-being of the teachers who were actually very significantly
involved in the over-all picture of educational progress. The article
advocated that more money should be spent on teachers' salaries.
New stage curtains, as it happened, had been recently purchased for
this local high school. When questioned, Teacher A stated that he
had not been thinking of the local situation or alluding to a specific
school, but had been speaking generally.

Superintendent X coolly admitted the excellence of the article,
saying it "had some truth to it." But he could not understand *why*
it was written. Was it meant as a note of personal dissatisfaction? A
criticism of the way he was running the school? Or was the writer
embarking on a crusade? Many things needed changing in the world
of education, he granted; "I myself have tried, as have other administrators," he said, but asked, "Why go all out to be a crusader?
What will it get you? What do you know about schools when this is
only your second experience in a school system?"

The writer was shocked at such a reception. He had tried to be
moderate, fair, and realistic. It had been specifically stated in an introductory note to the article that if any parts seemed exaggerated,
such exaggeration was merely for literary effect.

Superintendent X sent the school principal to chat with the writer to find out why the article had been written. The principal was told that there had been no motive other than to express a general opinion that the writer thought obvious to most sincere, hard-working teachers. The writer had been merely calling attention to a prevailing problem. Still the question, "Why did you feel that you must do it?" remained. There was no further publicity about the article. The copy of the magazine disappeared from circulation that month. In spite of the censorship, one or two Board members did read it. The teacher never heard another word about it, and all, apparently, was forgotten.

Discussion

The unenthusiastic reception given to his article had dampened the writer's creative urge. "Crusading" did have a price, and for the moment it was not worth the price. At the end of that school year, he decided to look for a brighter teaching field.

Questions

1. How far should a teacher go—especially in a closely knit, small community in which the administrator is a "big man"—in expressing professional ideas, perhaps taking some "glory" away from his superiors?

2. Why are administrators so sensitive about any criticism of school from within?

3. What can a teacher do when the climate is hostile to self-expression?

*   *   *

This incident is of basic significance, for it illustrates how the lack of psychological sophistication on the part of school administrators can reduce rather than increase the already low self-value teachers have in our society. Unlike other cultures, Americans have traditionally belittled and stereotyped teachers. Nonsensical sayings such as, "Those who can, do; those who can't, teach," are popular. It is certainly a fact that teachers and admininstrators have, due to their low social prestige in our dollar-oriented society, a stronger need for self-assertion and status-seeking than members of the more renowned professions or businesses. The teacher here, for instance, is obviously not significantly satisfied in his ego-strivings by his work with children. Matters that have nothing directly to do with teaching divert his energies and lower his morale. His pupils innocently foot the bill, and are taught by a frustrated person involved in petty feuds with equally petty administrators. Such marginal interactions create pathogenic rather than orthogenic interaction systems in our schools. May I add to the third question a paraphrasing question: "What can a child do about interesting his teachers in teaching and in creating a classroom climate conducive to learning?"

Here, an expressive teacher with an itchy pen and a missionary zeal experiences a lack of enthusiastic response from his superiors as a smashing blow to his emerging identity as a social reformer. Both the crusading style of the teacher's article, and his global unrealistic frame of reference, show strong unconscious identification with the very authority that he criticizes. From his amazement and lack of realistic empathy with the power-consciousness of his superior, his blind spot becomes clear in the depths of his "hurt" after the superintendent's rejection. The authority-orientation is here highly ambivalent. A David who thirsts for Goliath's love should not pick up stones to throw at him. Through psychotherapy, this teacher could easily learn to become realistic either by learning to accept his deep dependency needs, and therefore to cooperate with leadership, or by learning to appreciate his own authority to write any article he pleases without cocking one eye in the direction of Daddy-O's love. A writer should know that publishing is a democratic principle involving every reader's right to question the value and the worth of any author's contribution.

The superintendent and his side-kick principal also look quite unrealistic to me. Their reactions are naïvely content-oriented rather than sensitive to the underlying psychological processes that motivated the teacher. Consequently, they fail to appreciate their own significance in the life of this teacher, who has tried to use them to test and validate his meaningfulness. The realistic job of principals and superintendents includes recognizing such needs of their teachers and using the teacher's motivation to guide his ambitions back into the classroom.

An attempt on the part of the teacher to gain administrative attention is the same as attention-getting devices used by children. At our Institute, several teachers and administrators are working together through the medium of group therapy. Such authority and self-value problems as are illustrated in this incident have been presented and worked through. This clinical experience suggests that school systems would do well to make available to teachers and administrators regular participation in psychotherapeutic groups to prevent the development of destructive interpersonal tensions in the school system. Our schools need teachers and administrators whose personalities are freed from preoccupation with ego-worth problems, so that they can creatively devote themselves to furthering the growth of our children. The question should be, "Are our teachers happy teaching?" not, "Are your teachers happy?"

GEORGE B. BACH

*   *   *

This incident has a high projective quality not unlike the Rorschach used by psychodiagnosticians to reveal conflicts lying under the surface and beyond awareness. It would be interesting to present this incident without including either the superintendent's or the teacher's reactions following the publication of the article, to see if these reactions could not be predicted by psychodynamically oriented observers who are familiar with existing tensions between administrators and teachers.

Repression of feelings inside himself and denial of realities in his environment are quite clearly operating for the "hero" of this drama, the teacher-writer. If this is not an autobiographical account, and we strongly suspect that it is, it certainly was written by someone closely identified with Teacher A. The whole pitch of the story is that of Hero Teacher A, the "good guy," versus Villain Superintendent X, and "bad guy." If only such bad guys would stop mistreating good guys, then education could progress rapidly and brilliantly. Life, alas, even educational life, is not so simple. Let's try to look at some of the underlying factors that have been denied and repressed.

Is it not possible, first of all, that the superintendent's question of *"why"* realistically deserved some response other than shock, injured innocence, and the dampening of creative urge? However true the description we have of the superintendent's personality and administrative methods may be, hostility toward them is revealed in the account. For example, "his was the 'last word' "; his was "an iron-hand"; he "had a tendency to 'put the fear of God' in teachers"; "Superintendent X coolly admitted the excellence of the article." These and other phrases are not simple objective reporting, but carry negative emotional reactions. Descriptions of the teacher-writer, on the other hand, are consistently favorable in their emotional overtones: "very successful teaching experience"; "dynamic . . . brilliant and well-rounded personality, cultured and poised"; "cleverly stated"; "moderate, fair, and realistic." Was the superintendent's quest for the writer's "personal motive" entirely and outrageously out of order? We do not think so.

Further evidence of the probability that Teacher A was not functioning just as a detached educational philosopher are contained in this account. The title of the article—"Are Your Teachers Happy?"—followed by content that must have said quite clearly that they are undoubtedly unhappy, could hardly be viewed by an emotionally concerned and involved observer (in this case, Superintendent X) with the same neutrality as articles "on the teaching of government, direction of debates, plays, research on historical topics." If Teacher A, allegedly so perspicacious, was not denying reality out of his own unconscious needs to do so, how could he fail to understand that this was, indeed, a "hot" topic?

Some uneasy underlying awareness of possible trouble was indicated by the teacher's writing "an introductory note that if any parts seemed exaggerated, it was merely for literary effect." This was like telling his superintendent in advance that in case he felt his nose was being punched, he should realize that it was done merely to sell the article to the national publication. But, then, when the superintendent says that he still does not react enthusiastically to his injured nose, the writer is "shocked at this reception," offended by the question *"why"* and dampened in his creative urge. Was this realistic?

It is clear from the whole account that Teacher A had been deeply influenced by the treatment accorded him and his fellow teachers in this particular school system. His research ("general observation and reading on the topic") did not keep the "new stage curtains," and his attitude toward this "captain of infantry" and his administrative procedures, from appearing in the article. Even the account we have says that the article was written "not *necessarily* from personal experience," that the writer was "imbued with a missionary zeal" (although he is offended when he is accused of "crusading"), and that the article *"cleverly* stated that teachers were the forgotten people." Cleverness is not the tool of the wide-eyed innocent.

Does all of the foregoing indicate that we agree with the superintendent and think that he should be made the "hero" of the drama, "done wrong by" this villainous young whippersnapper out of "a nationally prominent university?" Quite the contrary. We do not doubt at all that Superintendent X is a heavy-handed administrative monarch who does, at times, render his teachers "forgotten people" in favor of impressing his Board of Education and the community with material accomplishments. Our sympathy is all with the teachers, but we do not believe that these and other teachers in comparable situations can be helped basically and permanently in their important jobs of educating children by the polemics of zealous missionaries who fail to recognize their own deep emotional involvements. One most significant aspect of reality, wherever the teacher finds himself, are the emotional blocks and ego-defenses of administrators. Any teacher who ignores these and other reality factors is certainly doing no long-term service of value to the "forgotten people."

Our main point is what we have stressed in our other contributions to this important volume. It is this: "Teacher, know thyself—deeply, not superficially. Until you do, your service is sadly limited."

FRANCES R. HARPER

*   *   *

In Italy, Mussolini made the trains run on time. This accomplishment does not necessitate our admiring him nor agreeing with his philosophy. Superintendent X is described as being efficient but ruling with an "iron hand" and as one who "put the fear of God" into his staff. The analogy is clear and the Messiah-like actions of Superintendent X are far from commendable. While I would in no way advocate "togetherness," by the same token I would not advocate "apartness" in administrative philosophy. In short, one can fall over backward or forward in being too chummy or too clammy, and it appears to me that Superintendent X did fall.

Teacher A had every right to write an article on the topic of "Are Your Teachers Happy?" Those reading the article had every right to agree or disagree, but the superintendent did not have the right to jeopardize the livelihood of the teacher, as he did in effect by censoring the article and censuring its writer. Such an act would also dampen the enthusiasm for the writing of other articles concerning morale in the superintendent's district, a point of which the supervisor was possibly aware. The question of morale is admittedly a touchy one, but nonetheless very important. Such a question is better brought into the open and discussed, as attempted by Teacher A, rather than repressed or buried, as attempted by Superintendent X.

It might be said that the solution to such an impasse would be to bring it up in a parent-teacher group. However, it has been my experience, as president of such a group, that such organizations tend to be interested in every aspect of education except the one most critical to a teacher, namely his economic status. Such groups will without question raise money for stage curtains, lights, games, and communication systems, but will almost zealously stay away from topics that in the long run are important to both the community and the nation, not to mention the child. The very fact that Superintendent X was portrayed as being "aghast" when he read the article indicates that the problem existed. Why, the superintendent asked, did one of his teachers have to "embark on a crusade?" It should be noted that his choice of the word "crusade" is ill-advised; this word, like the word "troublemaker," is loaded and implies, albeit indirectly, that the teacher is probably emotionally unbalanced.

We *do* need some kind of raising of prestige and elevation of economic status of our teachers in order to assure that our children will have the teachers who are best equipped in all ways to teach them. Even assuming at the very worst—that the article was ill-conceived and intemperate in tone—one should also remember that a person who cannot do a foolish thing cannot do a bright one!

The field of education, like any other field, cannot be said to have attained that height of excellence at which all criticism is superfluous. What is needed today is more, not fewer, "gadflies," lest we choke on the cud of complacency.

F. L. MARCUSE

*   *   *

The superintendent was probably more than aghast when he read the article, "Are Your Teachers Happy?"; he was undoubtedly horrified and filled with emotions of fear and insecurity. He probably experienced a very bad night's rest and was demoralized for some time.

Why? Because a favored staff member and trusted employee had unconsciously and unintentionally stomped on a well-calloused toe and opened old wounds, from which poured forth the hidden and festered tensions of frustrations and discouragements from battles of past years. These battles were with school boards, with budget committees, with taxpayers: to get new stage curtains, to get new band instruments, to build a swimming pool, to raise salaries to a level that was still inadequate. These battles and skirmishes had lost friends and support, had required constant recruiting of new supporters, and had left deep emotional scar tissue that was still an irritant. All had been pushed back into the depths of the superintendent's mind. He had been very careful to avoid conversations and control situations that might bring these unpleasant memories to reality.

And here on a printed page were written words that brought forth terrible things from Pandora's box.

The superintendent was submerged by an impulsive wave of disagreeable emotions. He was angry and depressed. He was unhappy and hurt. He just could not understand why one of his teachers could do such a thing to him.

The teacher was caught in a trap of his own making, from which he could not escape. He was identified by the superintendent as the person who had thrust a dagger in his side.

If the superintendent had been a younger man, or had been reasonably new in this school system, still fighting for leadership and approved status, he might not have been so impulsive. He would have considered this published article as a bit of the heckling which is to be expected from all ambitious young men determined to seek leadership in their chosen field.

But the head of the local school system had reached a point of self-satisfaction. He had power. He dominated. He ruled.

As a result of this conflict, a teacher of ability with great enthusiasm for his work and profession was lost to the school system and was forced to think seriously of leaving the profession.

Good school administrators recognize that younger members of their educational group are the individuals who may fill the top administrative posts in future years. They are to be taught, to be reprimanded if need be, to be complimented for achievement, and to be delegated authority and duties as they are able to accept them. Superintendent X could have made good use of the ability of Teacher A to improve the school and educational program. But the superintendent developed "channel vision" and because of his emotion refused to think of anyone but himself.

Teacher A had the drive, the energy, the creativeness to excel and yet was denied the opportunity. He was punished for attempting to live up to his training, his ability, his talents, and his professional obligations. Without question, he was deeply hurt and discouraged when his natural curiosity and enthusiasm were quenched by having praise and encouragement withheld for a task attempted and completed.

A conflict has developed within the staff and line organization of school systems as a result of attempts to upgrade teacher requirements. It is not unusual to have teachers working in school systems who have better training, better judgment, and better capacity for administrative jobs, than those employed in lead positions. This is a problem in every profession. It is the result of progress. It is the battle between the old and the new.

A beginning teacher often has been embarrassed while applying for a position to learn that he has had more training than his prospective employer. But the new teacher must remember that his training does not include the experience of the older teacher. He must realize that he is being employed to teach, not to change the established way of operating a school.

When younger teachers choose to embark on crusades to bring more modern practices to schools with long established patterns of operation, they may get hurt. They should thoroughly evaluate any action other than routine duties and look for possible reactions that could develop. They should calculate their risks against their possible gains. Then, if they lose, they should do so gracefully and cheerfully.

We must remember that every individual is made up of the sum of all his learning and experience. If he chooses to write, he should know that his inner emotions, his feelings, his beliefs, will be reflected to those who read his writings. Such writings will often convey messages to others not intended by the writer. And often false interpretation will be made, since the reading is influenced by the past experience of the reader.

Few principals and superintendents find time for writing. Their duties require their full time and effort. Teachers might do well to devote their time, energy, and creativeness to their assigned job. Their assigned duties, well done, will bring the desired rewards in time.

ROBERT E. PRICE

*   *   *

The written word can often do great damage, and an author must always bear in mind how his writings will be interpreted. It seems to me that although this young teacher was writing with the most honorable of intentions, he did act hastily and in an inconsiderate manner in not discussing this particular article with his superiors before he submitted it for publication. It would appear a foregone conclusion that, even though the teacher wrote the article merely to evoke thinking, it would appear to others to apply to his present teaching situation, especially if the article was of a critical nature. This would cast a reflection on his superiors and their administrative ability.

Although I do not believe in the censorship of articles, I feel that when an individual is writing about his career (work situation) and undoubtedly incorporating some of his present experiences into the writing, he should give his superior the opportunity to pass judgment on the article and to point out any parts that he feels might be interpreted erroneously by the reader. This teacher was carried away by his "missionary zeal," forgetting the criticism that his article might center around his current teaching situation. It is quite possible that the teacher was writing about his present teaching situation even though he did not fully realize it. The illustration of the curtains seems more than mere coincidence. Discussion of the article prior to publication would have led to an understanding by the superior of why the author was writing it, and probably to a better relationship between the two men.

The fact that the superintendent was so upset reveals that there was some truth in the article—we as teachers are well aware of it.

Literary license does not mean that authors can indiscriminately plant seeds of suspicion. Understanding of the superintendent's personality should have given the teacher an "inkling" of how the superintendent would receive his article. The superintendent in the past had supported the teacher's writings and had seen to it that he got publicity. Allowing the administrator to read this article prior to publication would have been a token of respect to him, one which I feel was due him.

The author could then have made it clear that the article was not intended as a reflection on his current teaching situation but as a commentary on the general field of education.

As a corrective or palliative measure, he should have written another article aimed at removing the confusion that this one had created. However, in the eyes of the readers the damage was done, and the reputation of the superintendent had been called into question.

WILLYE B. SHANKS

DISCUSSION QUESTIONS—INCIDENT 15

1. How far can freedom of expression extend and at what point might it be restrained by one who has a responsibility toward his job? What are the general guide lines in public communications for (a) school employees and (b) school administrators?
2. Bach states that in our culture teachers have low prestige. What are the causes (historical, philosophical, economic, psychological) for the present status of teachers in the American culture?
3. Harper states that there are "existing tensions between administrators and teachers." Would you imagine that these "tensions" are greater in schools than in other institutions? If you believe they are greater, what might be the contributing causes? Can you suggest any solutions for these conflicts?
4. Marcuse takes a fairly strong position on the issue of freedom of expression. He suggests that problems such as the one mentioned in this incident should be brought before a parent-teacher group for solution. Do you agree? If not, what methods of settlement seem appropriate?
5. Price remarks that it is not unusual for juniors in a school system to be superior to their seniors in terms of training, judgment, and capacity. Such a situation has potential for tension. Can you suggest ways of handling promotions by properly weighing experience and ability?

16

ETHICS AND CONFORMITY

CRITICAL INCIDENT

Background

The schools in our area are staffed by teachers and administrators with a variety of racial and cultural backgrounds, a variety perhaps unequalled anywhere in the United States. This diversity is reflected in the extreme variations in values, ideals, and ethical standards within and between the several local school staffs.

Ordinarily this does not interfere with harmony within a school, but it is not unusual to find, on occasion, that it creates rather intense and hostile feelings among faculty cliques. This is especially evident when a teacher transfers from one school to another, expecting to find educational values, goals, and ideals to be similar in both places, when in fact such is seldom, if ever, the case.

Incident

At my school twelve of the thirty-five staff members are new this year. Of the twelve, eight are women and four men. A conflict has developed, and is smoldering just below the surface, between two of the new male teachers (I am one) and most of the "old guard" male teachers. The issue is whether or not the male faculty and administrators should be privileged to gamble for money (in poker games) in the male teachers' lounge during the morning and noon recesses. The dominant faction of the "old guard" believes this is a perfectly proper activity and that to prevent it would unduly encroach upon the basic freedoms that the teaching profession affords.

The minority—of which I am a member—maintains on the other hand that such a practice is against school policy, is a violation of city and county laws, and is highly unprofessional. Because I share this view, I have voluntarily denied myself the use of the lounge during recess periods. It is my belief that if I enter the lounge when the games are in progress (they continue every day for the complete duration of both recess periods) I would, even though I do not play, be placed in the same unwholesome light as the participants. This means, of course, that during recesses I have no place to go outside of my classroom to really relax for a few minutes between classes.

Of equal significance is the fact that since I do not enter the faculty lounge when most of the faculty are assembled, I am not able to develop the professional friendships that are one of the rewards of being a teacher. The result is that my life as a teacher is more isolated than before.

Discussion

My problem is to discover what action to take to resolve the conflict. I would like to make use of the lounge to relax and to share my experiences with my fellow faculty members, but I cannot do so for the foregoing reasons. I do not feel that I can bring the matter to the attention of the principal; I am not sure that he knows of the game, and I might be revealing a faculty "secret." I cannot discuss it with the principal's immediate subordinate, the vice-principal; he is one of the key players in the game. To go over the principal's head to the district superintendent would be considered the height of unprofessional conduct. Nor do I feel, as a new teacher in the school, that I can openly express my feelings to the participants in the game.

The situation has reached a stalemate for me. Because of my position, I feel that I have been labelled snobbish, aloof, and hostile by my co-workers. I am not a member of an "in-group," and with nearly half of the current school year gone, most of the male members of the faculty remain complete strangers to me. To maintain such a status quo is, I feel, extremely undesirable from a personal and a professional viewpoint. I would like very much to find a solution without transferring to another scool, but I am at a complete loss.

Questions

1. Should I sacrifice my principles and use the lounge or should I continue to be an outsider simply to maintain an ideal?

2. Should I risk revealing a faculty "secret" and discuss the problem openly with my principal?

3. Should I boldly and vigorously state my case to the "old guard" and rely on their innate but misguided sense of fair play to prevent my total ostracism?

4. Should I strive to maintain the status quo, no matter how unpalatable it may be personally, rather than risk becoming even more of an outsider?

*   *   *

Two facts of significance to the teaching profession are revealed in this incident.

1. School staff members are daily and secretly violating school policy and city and county laws.

2. By their actions, the majority of the staff members are sanctioning the situation to the extent that a climate of difficulty is created for the minority of the more professionally-minded teachers.

In the minds of students and school patrons, the psychological image of teachers includes, consciously or unconsciously, many roles or actual functions in which a teacher will be considerably involved, worthily or unworthily. These roles or functions, broadly defined, include: (1) the images of the teacher projected by the children; (2) the expectations of the profession; (3) the personal intent of the teacher; (4) the demands of the larger community.[1]

In the school situation described, we find the conduct of the gambling faculty members in conflict in some measure with all, and considerable measure with two, of these considerations about role. In the case of the teacher who wishes to maintain his personal and professional code of conduct, his difficulty is clear. He is in opposition to the interests of fellow

[1] Fritz Redl and William Wattenberg, *Mental Hygiene in Teaching* (2nd ed.; New York: Harcourt, Brace & World, Inc., 1959), Chap. 10.

workers, who consider their individual interests synonymous with individual freedom. With the situation unchanged after a few months' time, the irksomeness of it prompts him to evaluate several courses of action designed to improve the social climate for him as a staff member, without compromising his own ethical code.

First, he debates the results of using the lounge or remaining an "outsider." Would he not serve the teaching profession better by adhering to his standards and refraining from becoming a part of what he thinks is clearly wrong? Sometimes the idea of individual liberty becomes distorted and a true sense of values tends to disappear. Breed[2] has stated that freedom is acknowledged as the first principle, but discipline is acknowledged as an indispensable supplement. In the self-discipline that the teacher must exercise in remaining loyal to his own beliefs and standards, he would be reflecting one of the major goals of education, the development of character based on independent thinking and judgment. In the classroom, do we not teach ourselves more than others teach us?

The teacher must decide whether to discuss the situation with the school principal. It seems to be inconceivable that in a well-organized, well-run school, an alert principal would not be aware of this situation. If the principal is as professionally minded as the teacher and is an administrator of competence, proper steps to eliminate flagrant violations of school policy, unprofessional conduct, and violations of city and county laws within the confines of the school establishment would be assured. If the principal is neither so alert nor professionally minded, a talk with him could result in complications most unfavorable to the teacher.

The teacher's third question indicates a desire to bring the situation into the open. This will result in his cause being won or lost—compromise is not likely. In Overstreet's *The Mature Mind*[3] is this statement: "In our organizations there are persons who will not take the trouble, or incur the danger, of raising their voices against a majority when a voice of protest needs to be raised." With this statement few people will disagree, but let us examine the phrase "or incur danger." What danger could the teacher incur from such a course of action as stating "boldly and vigorously" his case to the "old guard?" Total ostracism? Organized pressure by the games' participants to destroy professional standing and/or advancement of the opposing teacher? Loss of prestige or standing with students through the subversive tactics of those opposed? All are possible!

On the other hand, a sense of fair play may work to his advantage, as he hopes, and a feeling of live and let live make the situation tolerable. The

[2] Frederick S. Breed, *Education and the New Realism* (New York: The Macmillan Company, 1939).

[3] H. A. Overstreet, *The Mature Mind* (New York: W. W. Norton & Company, Inc., 1959), p. 279.

personality of the teacher, and the manner in which he approaches the "old guard," will be dominant among the factors determining the results. A sense of humor highlighting the approach could prove a favorable ally.

In the final analysis, the strategy the teacher devises to deal with this situation must be entirely his own. What he decides to do will be determined by his personal character, his ability to weigh values, and the strength of his professional and ethical standards.

Desirable mental health is based on good human relationships with colleagues, among other things; acceptance and recognition by colleagues contribute to self-esteem and emotional strength. Can he maintain good mental health, poise, and professional competence under extended pressure or conflict? Would participation in community activities interests somewhat balance the situation, providing compensatory satisfactions and thus make for less dependence for social acceptance on uncongenial colleagues? Does he wish to become an educator of excellence? A recent definition of a master teacher cites sincerity, knowledge of subject, ability to communicate ideas, and *a distant moral tone* as necessities.[4] Does he desire to become a master teacher?

MARY LOUISE BUTLER

*   *   *

Our attention could be directed first to the question of why the teacher was transferred to this school. Was it at his request, or was it done "for the good of the service"? If he himself requested the transfer because of an inability to find satisfaction in his relationships with professional colleagues, and had experienced similar difficulties in previous work situations, we might suspect that his "principles" or other personality characteristics were making it difficult for him to attain a satisfactory personal and social adjustment, regardless of his assignment. The same thing might be true if a supervisor had initiated the transfer, after noting the teacher's poor relationship with other staff members. The personality of the teacher, as well as the behavior of the poker players, should be a matter of concern and possible action. The teacher could be in need of therapeutic assistance, a problem that might be obscured by his question of how to deal with an instance of unprofessional conduct by other school personnel.

It is unlikely that the principal of the school would be unaware of the poker game, as it had been going on for several weeks or months. If the teacher were to discuss the matter with him in terms of a "personal conflict" as described in the incident, rather than on the basis of "squealing on" the

4 Edwin Gill, "The Master Teacher," *North Carolina Education* 26 (1960), 21-24.

gamblers, both the principal and the teacher might find their positions more comfortable in the conference. The principal would feel less need to be defensive about his failure to have done something about the situation, and would be more able to try to advise and counsel the teacher regarding the course of thinking and/or action he might adopt. There is the possibility, of course, that the principal is the titular head of the school while the real power is held by other individuals or groups. Perhaps he does not have the "authority" to stop the poker playing.

We cannot deny that educators in general, as a professional group concerned about ethical behavior, would be in accord with the teacher in theory if not in practice. If this matter were brought to the attention of an ethics committee of some appropriate teachers' organization (local or state), that group might be impelled to act in accordance with such an ethical code, without the deterrent fear of retaliation that the teacher or even the "vocal minority" of the faculty might experience. But there is little doubt that the identity of the informant would be suspected, if not known positively, and a conflict between some of the poker players and the teacher could well ensue, just as if he had objected directly to them or to an administrator.

When the teacher asks about "maintaining the status quo no matter how unpalatable it may be personally" in order to gain some acceptance by the group, he is posing a philosophical question that confronts each man as his individuality conflicts with the mores of his group. Should he "live and let live," or should he be willing to do battle for a cause he believes to be right and just? The decision must be made by each individual, in the light of his personal philosophy of life, and cannot be reached by the application of cold logic or scientific theory. Nor can it be made for him by another— each of us must face these "moments of truth alone," as surely as must the matador in the bull ring.

WILLIAM J. FIELDER

*   *   *

The teacher in this episode finds himself in a difficult and untenable position. Apparently, he is a rather young teacher who is strongly idealistic and wishes to maintain what he feels are highly professional standards of conduct. On the other hand, he finds himself in a school where many of the older teachers have established patterns of behavior that they find both gratifying and, perhaps, profitable. The reporting teacher pinpoints the issue by stating, "The issue is whether or not the male faculty members and administrators have the right to gamble for money in the male teachers' lounge during the morning and lunchtime recesses." Perhaps this is not the real issue. Perhaps, rather like an iceberg, only the surface portion of the problem is exposed. It would be interesting to have more background information about this problem.

School faculties work best when they pull together as a team. When one person is socially ostracized either because his conduct is regarded as inappropriate by his fellow teachers or because he stands aloof from others due to some type of valued principle, the end result is that the faculty group does not present a unified front. The primary purpose of a teaching faculty in any school situation is the instruction of the students in that school. Dissatisfied and dissident personnel often do not make good teachers. When a person is unhappy in a school situation, the feeling often affects his teaching. There is an old saying, "When in Rome, do as the Romans do." Although this is not a satisfactory answer for an idealist, there are times when one needs to reassess his value structure. There are times when one is faced with situations that call for measures other than those utilized before. In this situation it might be best to enter the lounge, be cognizant of what is taking place, but make no direct comment.

It probably would not be wise in this situation to openly discuss the problem with the school principal. If the vice-principal is a member of the "gambling fraternity," the principal is probably already aware of the situation. A conflict of values is very much in evidence here, and perhaps this is the essence of the matter. The teacher in question is reflecting typical middle-class idealistic standards. He mentions in his description of the school faculty the diversity in their racial and cultural backgrounds. Perhaps this teacher is attempting to apply typical American middle-class standards to a group of people who are not inculated with such values. This may, in part, explain why his sense of morality is outraged. He assumes that everyone else holds the same standards or ideals that he does. I feel that he would only complicate the situation by openly discussing it with his school principal and thereby creating additional problems that need not be brought up.

I do not believe, either, that the teacher should boldly and vigorously state his case to the "old guard." His case would be prejudiced by the attitude he has taken. I am sure that the other faculty members feel that this teacher places them on a step somewhat below the lofty plane that he himself trods. By his very statement, "and rely on their innate but misguided sense of fair play to prevent my total ostracism," he assumes they are wrong and he is right.

The teacher attempts to answer his final question by its very wording. I would feel the answer lies primarily in what is the "status quo." What is the relationship between this teacher, for example, and the other person who, he states, is also with him as a vocal minority? What is his relationship to the women teachers on the faculty? We have no indication whether this teacher is malcontent, whether he is unable to get along with others, or, possibly, whether he is a drifter from school to school. The status quo may very well suit 99 per cent of the teachers. Whether or not we are to condemn the status quo is not the question here, albeit there are many who would not condone this type of behavior.

ALVIN GROSSMAN

*   *   *

This incident as presented reminds me of the question, "What's wrong with this picture?"

In the first place, gambling is illegal in every state except, I believe, Nevada. It is specifically illegal in school buildings and churches. That it should have been going on for half of the school year is beyond belief. The principal of the school would certainly have learned of it by that time. Even if the principal were a woman, she would have known of it within two weeks of the opening of school. Things like that cannot be concealed from the authorities for very long.

Among the many duties of a principal there are three in particular: (1) administration of his school plant and of the program of studies; (2) supervision of the teaching within that plant; and (3) inspection of that plant to see that it is maintained properly. His tour of inspection should include at least a glance into the men's lounge. The fact that the assistant principal is a participant makes the act of gambling all the worse because it shows connivance by the administration.

For the dominant faction of the "old guard" to say that this is a perfectly proper activity and that to prevent it would be an undue encroachment upon the basic freedoms that the teaching profession affords is about as silly a statement as could come from the mouth of any teacher. We know that it is not a "perfectly proper" activity under the laws governing the state, and to say that the prevention of an illegal act constitutes "an undue encroachment of the basic freedom . . ." just does not make sense.

If the principal wanted to inform himself adequately about what was going on—even though he did it solely for his own protection and not as a part of his official duties—he could easily create an excuse to drop into the men's lounge to make a casual inquiry. There are a dozen ways in which a competent principal could acquaint himself with the facts. He could stop the gambling at once and still keep that fact quiet if he wanted to. If by any chance he is as innocent of what is going on as it would appear, then his assistant is certainly due for a raking over the coals for being a participant and for keeping him from knowing what is going on.

The teacher submitting the data asks four questions concerning what his reaction should be, feeling that he does not care to be present where gambling is going on. Certainly he should not sacrifice his principles and enter the lounge, nor should he continue to be an outsider simply to maintain an ideal. Nor should he take a chance on revealing a faculty "secret" by openly discussing the problem with his principal. If he did that, he would certainly be called a "squealer," and his revealing this information is not necessary. If he boldly and vigorously stated his case to the "old guard" and relied on their "innate but misguided sense of fair play" to prevent total ostracism, he would be betting on the wrong horse. They would blame him for any discontinuance in poker playing, and his ostracism would be complete.

His best approach is not to strive to change the status quo in view of the fact that he does not yet "belong" in the school, regardless of how *unpalatable* this may be to him personally. In this way he can continue to spend his free periods in some other part of the building, doubtless under unpleasant circumstances and in generally undesirable surroundings; but at least he is keeping himself from being called a "squealer"; he is not compromising his ideals; and he is not going to be present when the explosion finally comes.

CHESTER W. HOLMES

*   *   *

The tabloid image in the public eye of the school teacher suggests that he or she be a model of perfection and a paragon of virtue. This is especially true of women teachers in elementary schools in small communities. They must be above reproach. Such a person is expected not to smoke, drink, gamble, or be too liberal in his or her ideas. Such a restrictive concept would be bad enough if the salary compensated—but it doesn't. A short time ago I received a letter concerning another incident that is similar to the present one. An excerpt reads as follows:

We have a principal in our district who talked with me about my being too vocal when serving on our district salary committee. He also discussed my shocking habit of smoking in a local coffee shop. He also—well, it is too long to relate here, but I think he lost a good teacher when I refused to work for him any more . . . he probably just can't figure out how I have raised seemingly normal children in such a wicked atmosphere at home.

It should be obvious from the foregoing remarks that I cannot get too excited about the "gambling." Futhermore, it is highly dubious that the stakes were high! It might also be added that in many countries, including the United States, governments are either directly or indirectly aiding and abetting gambling, by state-run lotteries or by horse racing (pari-mutuel). In the latter case, the government collects a per cent of the "take" and indirectly education benefits from the state's obtaining these funds. To ban such gambling might be thought of as an attempt to undermine the government and might even be considered subversive!

The more general question raised here concerns the values held by teachers from different cultural backgrounds, according to the person describing this particular incident. However, probably a majority of teachers come from the middle class and as a result have generally similar values. While it is true that a teacher changing from one type of area to another might encounter a change in values, this is not clearly obvious in the present instance.

It should also be kept in mind that the majority was not trying to force the minority to gamble (although it might be said that the minority was trying to force the majority not to). The nongambler's fear that he will be "placed in the same unwholesome light" seems exaggerated, unless we assume guilt by physical proximity. Admittedly relaxation is, as stated by the complaining teacher, important, and it could quite easily be said that the majority was seeking just this.

If teaching has become an "isolated experience" to the person reporting the incident, then he has no one to blame but himself. Teachers are human, too.

F. L. MARCUSE

DISCUSSION QUESTIONS—INCIDENT 16

1. If you were the principal, and had no knowledge of the gambling situation, how would you respond to this teacher if he came to you to discuss the problem?
2. What should a teacher do when his professional career (at least on an immediate basis) and his sense of values are in opposition?
3. Assume the position of a principal who believes in "live and let live." How would you talk to the teacher in this incident, assuming you find that he is amenable to modification of his standards?
4. Do you see a teacher as an animated teaching machine whose policies, morals, and values are strictly his own business (as long as he does not impose them on others), or as a person whose ethical and moral values should be above those of the average citizen? Should we expect better behavior from teachers than from other people?

17

PROBLEMS OF PROTOCOL

CRITICAL INCIDENT

Background

The following incident, which concerns the dean of our school and myself, focuses on a slow learner in an unusually slow English class. This pupil, whom I shall call Bill, has an IQ of 78, a reading score of 4.3, a past record of failure in academic subjects, and a history of "trouble" with teachers and school officials. From the first day of the term, he displayed an apathetic attitude toward learning and a vicious antipathy toward a few classmates.

The dean was appointed to his position by the principal because other teachers had refused the job.

Incident

I am a floating teacher. The room in which the "slow" class (or what we call "modified" class) met was in an obscure part of the building, necessitating my arriving a few minutes late each day.

When I entered the room one day, I was amazed to see that Bill had just knocked down a smaller, "sissyish" boy and had begun beating and kicking him savagely. The other pupils, apparently stunned by the sudden attack, stood by watching helplessly. I ran over to pull

Bill away, and he attacked me, swinging wildly. In self-defense, I struck him hard, knocking him down. Then I asked a student to escort the small boy, whose eyes and mouth were bleeding, to the Emergency Room for treatment. I took Bill outside, asked a colleague next door to supervise the class, and escorted Bill by the scruff of the neck to the dean's office. On the way I asked him why he had attacked his classmate so violently. "Because he was sittin' in my seat," the boy replied. "Why did you hit me?" I queried. "I guess I just lost my head," Bill answered.

I was even more bewildered when I entered the dean's office. Instead of asking me why I was there, he reprimanded me for leaving my classroom, and for not sending a pink card for Bill before I brought him to the office (a school regulation). After I explained the incident in detail, Bill denied everything. The dean asked me to leave the office. The next day, the boy was sent back to class with a note from the dean requesting me to be more careful about following school regulations in the future and warning me about legal consequences of corporal punishment. The injured "sissyish" youth returned to class within a few days, but despite my requests he was too frightened to tell his side of the incident to the dean.

Discussion

I discussed this incident with my Chairman and with other colleagues. They told me to ignore the episode, saying that other teachers who had tried to oppose the dean had been "called on the carpet" by the principal.

I feel that my actions were justified. If I hadn't intervened, Bill might have seriously injured the boy or me. If I had waited and sent the usual referral card, too much time might have elapsed before administrative action was taken. If I had not escorted Bill to the office immediately, he might have had another violent outbreak. As for my leaving the class, my colleague had made certain that the students behaved well. I discovered later that my quick action had been of therapeutic value to the entire class because it illustrated what I would do to any future offenders and indicated that I was "on the side" of the offended. Furthermore, I do feel that the dean's reactions (which seemed to support the offender and adversely criticize me as a teacher) were unprofessional and unethical.

Questions

1. Would a direct approach to the dean be advisable? He may have had reasons for his actions and may wish to explain them in a private conference.

2. Should I go directly to the principal? This would be "going over the head" of the dean and could possibly cause resentment. It could also involve the risk of being "called on the carpet" by the principal.

3. Should I try to persuade the injured boy's parents to ask their son to tell his side of the story to the dean?

*   *   *

Since the dean may have had good reasons for his actions and may have explained his reasons in a private conference, I believe a direct approach to him by the teacher would be advisable. I feel that the dean's action in this case was neither prudent nor intelligent, as a result, misunderstanding and perhaps friction arose between the two. Every school can and should strive for cooperation and mutual understanding among its faculty; a talk between the two would help clarify the procedures of this case and leave a clear basis of understanding for future cases that may arise.

I would not suggest that the teacher go to the principal in this case, for I believe a "heart-to-heart" talk with the dean could clarify matters. If the talk with the dean produced no satisfying results, the teacher should allow the matter to drop. If similar problems continued to arise with the dean in the future, the teacher should then approach the principal. But first, conflicts should be resolved, if possible, at the primary level.

I would not get in touch with the injured boy's parents concerning this one incident alone, unless, of course, they asked to consult with me. I believe I could accomplish more good by working first with both boys alone. I presume that the parents are fully aware of the boy's basic lack of scholastic ability.

Also, I would not want to be excessively hasty in deciding that just because the teacher caught Bill striking the smaller boy, Bill was therefore completely in the wrong. Sometimes the overt aggressor is actually the victim! A dull-witted boy may sometimes be driven to primitive action by the merciless provocation of another boy. The one who reacts physically and aggressively is then blamed while the one who teases and provokes is considered innocent. Actually, this boy provoked Bill and Bill reacted violently. But so, too, did the teacher.

Everybody in this incident—Bill, the teacher, and the dean—seem to have acted hastily, impulsively, and without due consideration of relevant factors.

The teacher who is in the middle should now strive for clarification, explanation, and agreement with the dean.

DONALD E. BRENNAN

*   *   *

It would be advisable to discuss the matter privately with the dean of discipline, at least to obtain in detail his explanations for the stand that he took. Then, if the teacher were not satisfied, he would be justified in going to the principal to get his reaction. After all, a teacher must ascertain just where the administration stands in regard to him and other teachers as an indication of future courses of action under similar circumstances.

It is normally not a wise course to bypass a subordinate administrator. If the teacher is frank and honest with those in administrative posts, if he follows channels of command, then he will earn the respect of those to whom he is responsible. Not that the teacher should ignore the incident. But he should first try to deal with the dean of discipline.

I would not be concerned about getting Bill to tell the story truthfully, or about getting the other boy to tell "his side." An administration should have enough faith in its teachers to back them, despite the untruth of a pupil; furthermore, a quiet investigation of the class by the dean should establish the accuracy of the teacher's version.

It appears that the teacher in this incident is trying too "hard" to prove himself. His main concern should be changing Bill's attitude and approach, rather than making a life-long enemy of him. The change might be started by having a friendly, but private, chat with Bill, explaining that the incident would be forgotten if the boy would meet the teacher half-way by future cooperation. The teacher should indicate that he is willing to help the lad make progress in his class and be better liked by his classmates. In other words, the teacher must take steps to win the confidence of Bill.

Then, too, the teacher should try to understand Bill and what makes him act the way he does. A check of office records, a talk with a school counselor, and a conference with parents, should shed further light on this young man's behavior. Perhaps the administration of a nonverbal IQ might be in order, along with additional training in reading. The teacher's job is to use the school's facilities (school psychologist, counselor, nurse) to determine just what Bill is capable of learning, and then to enable him to experience some success. The teacher should not waste the time that Bill and the other children need by trying to justify himself to the world.

Finally, the teacher should not have knocked Bill down. There would have been better ways of intervening—even if force had to be applied—than directly striking the boy.

PHILIP HARRIS

*   *   *

There are two important facets to this incident. One, the teacher handled a serious disciplinary problem on the spur of the moment and in such a way that he was probably considerably shaken. He needed help and support. Two, not only was the teacher given no help and no support, he was reprimanded in the presence of the student. In his report, the teacher brings up only the last problem, of which he was acutely aware. The first he does not mention, and he was probably unaware of it, but it must be considered if the incident is to be understood.

The teacher and the dean reacted hastily and in ways they might later regret. The teacher says that his quick action (knocking down the student) was of therapeutic value to the class, because it showed them what he would do to other offenders. This may possibly be true, but only if the students are accustomed to respecting physical violence above everything else. Even in this case, it seems there would be some regret and fear if only because of the school regulation against corporal punishment and the possible legal consequences.

The dean, too, is probably not, or at least should not be, overly proud of the part he played. In reacting to the spectacle of a distraught teacher bringing in a surly and upset student, he reprimanded the teacher for leaving the classroom. Surely the dean must also have acted in haste, in reaction to a situation which unnerved him. Then, probably feeling he had to uphold his action, perhaps to "save face," he wrote the note concerning regulations and legal requirements.

Here, then, we have two men struggling with unadmitted regret and guilt about their actions and probably also feeling that the only way to appear competent is to refuse to admit error. In addition, the teacher has a special grievance—his administration did not help him but made him feel unappreciated, helpless, and isolated.

The teacher, not the dean, is the one who feels acute distress, being the aggrieved party as well as the one in the more vulnerable position. If complaints are made, he will be reprimanded further, and again, there must be the matter of uncerainty about whether he really did help this particular student.

In looking over the three questions, I feel that this teacher's next move is to see the dean directly. He himself points out the danger of going to the principal, and it would be most unwise to go to the injured boy's parents to ask for their support.

Although one understands how crushed and outraged the teacher is and how necessary it is for him to come to terms with his feelings about himself in relation to the dean, it is regrettable that this problem is separated in his mind from that of helping the student. Helping Bill is important not only because he and his peers are the very reason for the existence of schools, but also, in this case, because the teacher has a better chance to solve his own problem if he considers it in relationship to the student's difficulty.

The teacher will only antagonize the dean by asking for an explanation of his behavior. On the other hand, if he can avoid making the dean feel more guilty and defensive, a conference may be productive. The dean will not feel defensive if the teacher can confine his remarks to telling how he felt (not criticizing the dean but simply telling what his own feelings were) and discussing ways to help the student. The dean has too many difficulties of his own (his job is not easy, as indicated by the fact that several teachers had refused it before he accepted) to respond positively to a teacher demanding justice and explanations. But if the teacher can go into the dean's office to discuss his own distress, to point out that he needs help in handling students, and to ask the dean's support in the way he disciplines his students, the two men may begin to develop a good working relationship.

Can this teacher say plainly that he knows he is not perfect, and that he would like a chance to discuss students and their problems? Then he may be able to come to some understanding with the dean that will be productive for both of them. By working together on an important problem, by trying to help Bill, who is struggling in school, who has a past record of failure, and who has personality difficulties as well, they may be able to develop respect for and understanding of each other.

If the teacher is not able to approach the dean on this basis or the dean is unable to respond, then perhaps, as the chairman and other teachers suggested, it may be best to ignore the incident. Only if it is completely impossible to come to an understanding with the dean, and if the teacher feels great personal pressure against discussing his feelings with a superior, would going to the principal serve any good purpose.

ELOISE D. HAYES

*   *   *

Many teachers want to see "blood on the wall." Action takes a higher priority than investigation. The whole incident brings up a number of questions that I should like to have answered.

Why did the teacher parade Bill to the dean's office? Why would he leave a group of subnormal excited children unsupervised even for just a few moments? Would there be a report by the "Emergency Room" about the extent of injuries? Did the parents of the beaten child demand an explanation of their child's condition? What was done by the administration?

And now some opinions.

Retarded children need stability. When excited they easily lose control. The teacher was wrong and foolish to leave the class. They could have, in their excitement, broken out into violent action.

A personal escort is rarely necessary, even with a retarded child. To enter the dean's office in an excited manner, when the dean does not know the facts of the case, is foolish. The teacher demanded action from the dean when he was in no position to make a sound judgment. A matter such as this should go through channels.

Perhaps, however, since I am writing from the bias of an administrator and since my usual advice to beginning teachers is that they learn the policies and procedures of a school, it seems appropriate to me to suggest that the teacher should be satisfied with the way policies and procedures are interpreted by the one who is hired to interpret them. I assume that the dean has had some experience in meeting problems of this sort.

The dean seems to have had a brutal way of enforcing a school rule. Obviously, he lacks finesse. If his methods are consistently unmindful of the feelings of the teachers and if the teachers are genuinely aggrieved to the point that they feel that they cannot work under these circumstances, the professional thing for them to do is to request a meeting with the principal to discuss "professional ethics."

The question about communicating with the parents depends on the policy of the school. In some schools, teachers regularly get in touch with parents to inform them of the progress or the problems of their children. Normally, the dean's office would arrange a conference between parents and children in a case involving a physical attack. If there is a lack of understanding or a feeling of further grievance, the aggrieved party may seek redress from the courts. The school need not be a party to the collection of damages or the payment of doctor or hospital bills. This is a responsibility of parents. The school only wants assurances of proper future conduct.

WARREN W. NIXON

*   *   *

In this incident, both the teacher and the dean were wrong in my opinion, even though the boy was swinging wildly in a fit of anger. Even being hit does not justify a teacher in knocking a student down. In no way could knocking a student down be considered self-defense. The teacher always respects the authority of the school. He must always act so that all others will respect this authority. When the teacher begins to fight with the pupils, he is lowering that authority to a very undignified level.

Escorting Bill by the cuff of the neck is a most unsatisfactory way of taking a pupil to the office. The teacher could not expect the student, who had just been knocked down and brought to the office by the cuff of his neck, to be in any condition to profit from a conversation with the dean.

The teacher could have given Bill a pink card to take to the office; if Bill did not go, then that matter could have been taken up the following day. If Bill has an I.Q. of only 78, he needs to be given opportunities for accepting responsibilities. Being responsible for getting himself to the office is one way of letting him know that one has confidence in him.

William B. Ragan offers a good selection of worthwhile opportunities for children on the elementary level to assume responsibility, as well as suggestions about how to evaluate the progress the pupil is making.[1] Many of these suggestions are suitable on the secondary level.

Gertrude Hildreth[2] lists seven specific ways in which teachers can help children develop an increasing sense of responsibility. Alice Miel and her associates[3] write in some detail of how responsibility can be made effective with groups of children. Any teacher who has not attempted such a process would do well to study this teacher's plan carefully.

William M. Alexander and Paul M. Halverson[4] speak of how the learner develops individual responsibility, and emphasize that the learner is a source of problems and purposes. Teachers must accept the idea that learners have a contribution to make in the establishment of goals for themselves.

Kimball Wiles[5] describes ways of getting pupils from grade one through eleven to assume responsibility for their behavior and lists seven gradations of responsibility. These different degrees of growth, he states, will not become evident to the faculty until the faculty begins to articulate behavior that it considers to qualify as assumption of responsibility at various grade levels.

As will be shown by these and other studies, education is mainly a matter of the environment in which a student lives; that environment furnishes

[1] William B. Ragan, *Modern Elementary Curriculum* (New York: The Dryden Press Inc., 1953), pp. 303-304.

[2] Gertrude Hildreth, *Child Growth Through Education* (New York: The Ronald Press Company, 1948), pp. 290-93.

[3] Alice Miel, *et al., Cooperative Procedures in Learning* (New York: Bureau of Publications, Teachers College, Columbia University, 1952), pp. 379-81.

[4] William M. Alexander and Paul M. Halverson, *Effective Teaching in Secondary Schools* (New York: Holt, Rinehart & Winston, Inc., 1956), pp. 233-35.

[5] Kimball Wiles, *Teaching for Better Schools* (New York: The Dryden Press, Inc., 1953), pp. 210-11.

the experiences by which he grows. One cannot learn by authority, only by experience.

Of course, only part of the blame for this situation is upon the teacher. Evidently the dean had a low I.Q. himself or he would not have reprimanded a teacher who had broken school regulations in the presence of a student. Similarly, the dean should not have sent a note by the student the next day correcting the teacher's action. This should have been done in a private conference.

Principals and/or teachers who still believe that corporal punishment is a desirable way to maintain discipline in school are just ignorant of human nature, or if they are not ignorant, they are afraid to try more wholesome methods. Any really good teacher knows that fear has no place in the educative process.

CLARENCE H. SPAIN

*   *   *

I do not believe that the dean acted unprofessionally or unethically in this incident. On the contrary, I believe his action was extremely professional and unusually kind to the teacher.

The teacher, in striking the boy, no doubt acted in anger more than in self-defense. I have heard and seen too many cases in which a teacher was "forced" to strike a pupil one-third his size "in self-defense," lest he do the teacher bodily harm. The pupil, Bill, was perhaps playing the part of the bully because of his educational inadequacy or emotional problems. But the teacher was the real bully. He was going to show Bill and the class who was the boss. Here he certainly showed little self-restraint, as well as inability to size up the situation. He did about the worst thing he could do— what his teacher-training or his own instincts should have kept him from doing. He brought himself down to the level of the bully, and left himself wide open for criticism by the parents of Bill and by the parents of the boy whom Bill had struck—as well as by the pupils for striking one of their peers. I am sure there must have been grumbling by the class about the teacher having struck someone not his own size.

The administration certainly had grounds for criticism. First, instead of following the proper procedure of filling out a pink card, the teacher struck Bill and then took him to the office. Second, the teacher, during his absence, permitted the class to ponder on his inadequacy. Third, the teacher brought about his own embarrassment by being asked to leave the dean's office and was faced with a reprimand as well as a warning.

The teacher was resentful of the dean, something that helped to make the teacher bitter of the administration as well as suspicious of his own lack of control and inability to enforce class discipline.

The teacher was afraid to wait to send the referral card. There was no urgency in the matter. Had the teacher acted correctly he would not have been on the defensive, would not have placed himself in a position of embarrassment, and would not be subject to counteraction on the part of Bill's parents. The only urgency in the situation was the necessity of the teacher to control his temper.

The one positive step the teacher took was to send the injured boy to the Emergency Room.

The teacher speaks of the therapeutic value of this incident to the class. The only therapeutic value that I can imagine is that the teacher proved to himself that he could strike down a boy smaller than he.

The proper procedure would have been to separate the boys. He might have had Bill sit at his desk and write a description of the entire incident that could be read to the class. When the injured boy returned to the class, he, too, could be asked to write a description of the incident. Since fighting is obviously a gross infraction of the rules, this incident would merit being referred to the dean instead of being treated exclusively by the teacher. The dean, upon receiving the pink card and the statements from the pupils, would of necessity be obliged to take appropriate action.

First, he would be confronted with the lack of administrative arrangements that permitted a class to be unattended because of the apparently unavoidable tardiness of the teacher.

Second, he would be confronted with the possibility of the injured boy's parents issuing a complaint against the school.

Third, with the possibility of serious injuries to the boy, he would be required to report to and confer with the parents, who would probably demand that Bill be punished and perhaps excluded. The dean could not possibly drop the matter because of the injured boy's parents being involved.

Thus, if the teacher had been rational in his approach, he *would* have had some definite therapeutic results in the class. The class would realize how well the teacher had the situation under control. The teacher would have the respect of the class for not dodging the issue. The dean could then only admire the teacher for handling the case so well that he, the dean, would be forced to take action.

Now that the teacher has erred, the only direct approach is to appear before the dean and apologize for his lack of tact, for his infraction of the rules of the school, and for his breaking the fundamental rule of not striking a child. After he has apologized, then he should examine his mistake carefully and conduct a good Socratic examination of himself to improve his attitude toward the malefactors.

I do not believe that I am too harsh in my criticism of the teacher.

Instead of engaging in self-justification, it is wise for the teacher to examine his actions calmly. If there is trouble in the class, perhaps he, the teacher, is at fault at times. Too many teachers blame the administration for their own inadequacies and appeal to their colleagues for sympathy rather than trying to improve themselves, either through education or through self-criticism.

Too many teachers, both young and old, experienced and inexperienced, act as hastily in emergency situations as this teacher did. They try to justify their actions by claiming self-defense or the therapeutic values they hope to obtain. If, on the other hand, a teacher can use a little wisdom, a good deal of love, and superior tact, he will be faced with fewer emergencies and situations in which he has "complaints" against higher authority.

LEO E. TARUTZ

DISCUSSION QUESTIONS—INCIDENT 17

1. It might be illuminating to try to reconstruct this incident from the point of view of the dean, assuming as you do so that he had been appointed to the position "because other teachers had refused the job." What might his attitudes be?
2. In handling conflicts, what are the advantages of dealing directly with the person involved instead of going to a mutual supervisor?
3. Assuming that an administrator is faced with a problem of adjudicating between two versions of a story, one given by a teacher and one by a pupil, do you suggest that teachers' versions be routinely accepted as valid? What may eventuate from this position?
4. It is interesting to note that the consultants, although they do not support the dean's actions, condemn the teacher's behavior. What are the best methods for training teachers to handle such problems adequately?

SUGGESTED READINGS—PART IV

Books

Adams, H. P. and F. G. Dickey, *Basic Principles of Supervision*, New York: American Book Company, 1953.

Cooke, D. H., *Administering the Teaching Personnel*, Syracuse, N.Y.: The L. W. Singer Company, Inc., 1939.

Extra-Classr

Articles

Campbell, _____ Theory and
Research; Sel _____ *rch* 31 (October, 1961),

Chapman, _____," *Clearing
House* 32 (N

Crossan, R. _____" *California
Teachers Asso*

Davies, D., _____ *f Education*
39 (Septembe

Lapman, H. _____ *Iigh School
Journal* 41 (N

Ludeman, V _____ (February,
1958), 337-38.

Lyons, A. F. _____ (October,
1957), 22-24.

Millis, J. S., _____ *of Higher
Education* 28 (

Mills, Queen _____ *onal* Problems of Elemen _____ *search* 48
(December, 195

Nelson, A. G. _____ *lta Kappa*
36 (May, 1955),

Newell, C. A. _____ Key to Good Supervision,"
Education 78 (December, 1957), 221-23.

Rigney, R. P., "Responsibility of the Superintendent to the Classroom
Teacher," *National Catholic Educational Association Bulletin* 55 (August,
1958), 247-49.

Vanderpool, J. A., "And What's Your Concept of Your Profession?" *Journal
of Teacher Education* 10 (March, 1959), 49-55.